BERNHARD SINDBERG

The Schindler of Nanjing

Peter Harmsen

CASEMATE

Pennsylvania & Yorkshire

Published in the United States of America and Great Britain in 2024 by
CASEMATE PUBLISHERS
1950 Lawrence Road, Havertown, PA 19083, USA
and
47 Church Street, Barnsley, S70 2AS, UK

Hardcover Edition: ISBN 978-1-63624-331-3
Digital Edition: ISBN 978-1-63624-332-0

A CIP record for this book is available from the British Library

Printed and bound in the United Kingdom by CPI Group (UK) Ltd, Croydon, CR0 4YY
Typeset in India by DiTech Publishing Services

For a complete list of Casemate titles, please contact:

CASEMATE PUBLISHERS (US)
Telephone (610) 853-9131
Fax (610) 853-9146
Email: casemate@casematepublishers.com
www.casematepublishers.com

CASEMATE PUBLISHERS (UK)
Telephone (0)1226 734350
Email: casemate@casemateuk.com
www.casemateuk.com

Front cover image: Anita Günther

Contents

Preface

On a cloudy November day in 2018, I finally had the opportunity to visit Bernhard Sindberg's cement plant. With me in the taxi from Nanjing's busy city center was Dai Yuanzhi, a retired local journalist who had spent years studying the Danish sailor and adventurer while trying to understand this moving and strange story about an ordinary man who became the savior of thousands of his fellow human beings. We moved from one traffic jam to the next through crowded streets which back in 1937, when Sindberg risked his life defying the Japanese army, had consisted of open rice fields and scattered villages. After a drive of roughly 90 minutes, we reached the factory, Jiangnan Cement. A lone security guard received us at the gate. Dai Yuanzhi told him that there had been a refugee camp here once, managed by a Dane. The guard scratched the back of his neck in a universal sign of bafflement. He had never heard that before. But he did know something about Danish soccer and was much keener to chat about that topic.

Dai Yuanzhi adroitly had us extricated from a sports conversation that obviously was going nowhere, and he became my guide through the factory area. He led me to a part of the compound that was no longer being used, pointing at a yellow building. This was where one of the leading staff members of the cement factory lived, perhaps even Sindberg himself, he said in an enthusiastic voice. Several of the windowpanes were shattered, and paint was coming off the walls in big flakes. Inside, however, it was clear that someone had once called this home. The tiles of the bathroom floor were still visible under decades of dust and dirt. We walked on, among buildings that had long been vacated, wading through ankle-deep piles of withered leaves. There was an atmosphere of decay and neglect, almost indifference.

And then suddenly he was there in front of us—not Sindberg himself, but his likeness in the form of a statue. He was a handsome, somewhat stereotypical-looking Westerner, the way Chinese artists portray foreigners when they want to be nice. Dressed in a suit and holding a Danish flag in one hand, here was the man I had heard about for the first time almost two decades earlier, when I worked in Beijing as a correspondent for the French news agency AFP, covering China's rise to the status of great power. At a time when I was busy writing about China's booming economy, its growing influence in places as far away as Africa, and the upcoming Olympics, there was simply no time left to also occupy myself with Sindberg. Still, the idea of one day writing a book about him stayed with me.

The idea became more concrete years later when I had the chance to do a survey of the extant sources of Sindberg's life. They turned out to be far more plentiful than I expected. At the University of Texas at Austin, I found Sindberg's bequeathed papers and photographs. The Copenhagen headquarters of the company FLSmidth, which employed him during his heroic acts, had letters by him and others describing his service in amazing detail. And in Nanjing, China, there were numerous published documents, about both Sindberg and his contemporaries. In short, spread across three continents was the information I needed to write a biography of Sindberg and hopefully contribute to greater awareness in the West of a man who is already honored in the East. So I started to write.

***

In a book where the sources are in a variety of languages from different historical periods, it is a challenge to ensure some sort of consistency in terms of spelling. Therefore, a few words on the choices made for this book. The Chinese city Nanjing was written "Nanking" by Westerners in 1937, but to avoid confusion, I have opted for the modern spelling. The same goes for Jiangnan Cement, which eight decades ago was spelled "Kiangnan" or "Kiang Nan" and other similar cases.

Modern spelling implies using the pinyin system for transliteration of Chinese names, such as Tianjin instead of Tientsin. The old imperial capital, which was called Beiping or Peiping in the 1930s, is rendered as Beijing here. There are a few important exceptions. The Chinese leader in 1937 is written as Chiang Kai-shek, not Jiang Jieshi or Jiang Zhongzheng, as would be the case if the rules for pinyin were followed. Similarly, the name of China's biggest river is given as Yangtze, not Changjiang.

The Chinese practice is to put a person's family name first, which is also the way Chinese names are most often rendered in Western languages. This practice has been followed here. Likewise, the Japanese place the family name first, and although there is no uniform practice in the West, I have decided to do the same in this book.

The company that Sindberg worked for was spelled "F. L. Smidth" then, and this is the form I use in the text when describing events happening in the 1930s. The modern rendering "FLSmidth" is used when referring to the company today, most importantly in the notes about the corporate archive in Valby, Denmark.

***

Many individuals have contributed to the preparation of this book. First of all, I wish to thank Bernhard Sindberg's niece Mariann Arp Stenvig, who generously shared her time and enthusiastically answered questions about her uncle, while also placing at my disposal important sources, including Sindberg's valuable recollections of the battle of Shanghai in 1937. Karl Günther's niece Anita Günther was also of great assistance, providing unique photos of the refugee camp in 1937 and 1938.

Thanks are furthermore due to the researchers, journalists, and authors who in various ways have contributed to our knowledge about Sindberg and the unfamiliar Chinese world that was his home for years. Dai Yuanzhi, a former journalist for the daily newspaper *Zhongguo Qingnian Bao* and the author of a book in Chinese about Sindberg, has done invaluable work collecting relevant historical documents and, while it was still possible, interviewing old Chinese who knew the Dane. Morten Pedersen, director at the Historical Museum of Northern Jutland, whose pathbreaking book *When China Awakens...* contains important details about the relationship between F. L. Smidth and Sindberg, pointed me towards the essential sources about Sindberg extant in the company's archives. Hans Jørgen Hinrup, a former Asia specialist with the State Library in Aarhus, was the first Danish academic who wrote specifically about Sindberg, providing inspiration for my search for relevant documents at the Danish National Archives. Hinrup also very kindly read the manuscript of this book prior to publication. Peter Abildgaard wrote detailed articles about the subject for the daily *Aarhus Stiftstidende*, after Sindberg had in the year 2000 been definitely identified as the savior from Nanjing. Finally, I wish to thank Julie Brink from the Association Denmark-China for encouraging me to write this book.

In addition, I wish to thank the following individuals, in no particular order, for help, support and advice: Zhang Jianjun, curator of the Nanjing Massacre Memorial Hall as well as his two colleagues Wang Xiaoyang and Zhang Guosong; Sofie Karen Lindberg and Charlotte Degn, FLSmidth, Valby; Søren Bitsch Christensen and Mattias Jonsson Agger, Aarhus Municipal Archive; Gerhard Keiper at the German foreign ministry's political archive in Berlin; Linda Briscoe Myers and Michael L. Gilmore at the Harry Ransom Center, University of Texas at Austin; Caitlin Chegwidden, University of

North Texas Oral History Program; Jamie Carstairs, Historical Photographs of China, University of Bristol and Christopher J. Anderson, Divinity Library, Yale University. Any errors that may appear in this book are of course mine alone. As with my previous publications, the Casemate staff has been a much appreciated source of help and support, and I would like in particular to thank Ruth Sheppard, Tracey Mills, Declan Ingram, Lizzy Hammond, Melanie Marshall, Mette Bundgaard and Adam Jankiewicz.

Lastly, a personal thanks to my wife Hui-tsung and our two daughters Eva and Lisa. Without their patient support this book would never have come to fruition.

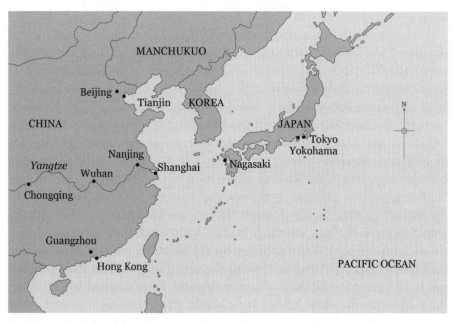

East Asia in 1937.

The Dane

1937

The winter had only just begun when the Japanese arrived. The foreign soldiers did not look like anything the Chinese peasants had ever seen before. "Devils," they whispered. The Japanese were small but strong, and many of them had let their beards grow to considerable lengths. They had been on the road for a long time. Their khaki uniforms were covered with weeks-old dust, and cakes of dry mud stuck to their footwear. The only thing that looked clean was their weapons: rifles that seemed longer than the men who carried them, and bayonets that glittered dangerously in the short moments when the cold sun appeared from behind the gray clouds.

For the people inhabiting the fertile land south of the Yangtze River, the Year of the Ox was about to end. In the West, the same year had the less poetic name 1937. Wang Liyong was 13, and he was old enough to sense the ominous atmosphere all around him.[1] Together with his mother and two younger brothers, he lived in a village just outside Nanjing, China's capital. He had seen how the Chinese army had retreated before the arrival of the Japanese, and then he had heard the sound of fierce fighting as the defenders made a last stand before abandoning the city. Now it was quiet, and people said the war would soon be over. But perhaps the real misery was only about to begin. There were rumors about the Japanese. They were horrible rumors, about looting, murder, and rape.

The violence was intense in the narrow alleys behind Nanjing's ancient walls, but even the countryside outside the city was not safe. The Japanese moved from village to village and left, dragging all livestock with them—ducks, geese, bulls, and pigs. They set fire to buildings along the way, sometimes while the occupants were still inside. A particularly savage episode took place in the village of Chenjiayao, where they had herded together 33 Chinese men. Some of the prisoners were former soldiers, but there were also civilians among them.

Japanese soldiers on the march towards Nanjing. The infantrymen covered the roughly 200 miles from Shanghai in the course of a month. The autumn rains turned most roads into thick mud. (Asahi Shimbun)

Everyone was killed with rifles and bayonets. Next to Xianhemen, one of the enormous gates leading through the wall into Nanjing, the bodies of 80 Chinese soldiers filled a pond along with the bulging cadavers of their horses. And then there was the treatment of the women. There were stories of young girls who were gang-raped by the Japanese, before unspeakable things were done to them with broken bottles.

When the Japanese reign of terror was a week old, Wang Liyong's mother decided that the little family could not stay in the village any longer. They packed a few necessities and started walking east, away from Nanjing. Wang Liyong carried one of his two younger brothers on his back, and his mother carried the other. The first place they stopped was at Qixia Teachers' College. They joined a large group of farmers who had sought shelter in the spacious main hall of the school. It gave them an immediate sense of security, but the feeling was deceptive, and it lasted only briefly. That same evening, a group of Japanese soldiers broke into the hall, looking for women. They dragged away a peasant woman, while her husband, protesting loudly, clung onto her leg in a desperate attempt to save her. One of the Japanese soldiers aimed his gun at the man and killed him with a single shot.

Before the shock of the sudden brutal killing had receded, Wang Liyong's family moved on. His mother had heard from other peasants that protection

Japanese soldier during the war in China in 1937. Many Japanese opted to let their beards grow to considerable lengths while at the front, partly because conditions in the field made shaving impractical, and partly because it contributed to a martial appearance. (Photograph by Malcolm Rosholt. Image courtesy of Me-fei Elrick, Tess Johnston and Historical Photographs of China, University of Bristol)

from the Japanese was to be found at a 1,000-year-old Buddhist temple at the foot of Mount Qixia not far away. Upon arrival, they found a building on a slope behind the temple which did indeed seem safe. They stayed for several weeks, but as time went by, the conditions at the site became almost unbearable. More and more refugees arrived, and the area gradually became overcrowded. Besides, the Japanese disregarded the Buddhist faith, even though it was espoused by many of them, and they often visited the temple in their endless hunt for women. After a month, Wang Liyong and his family departed and found themselves on the road again.

They now came to a place where, for the first time since the beginning of the occupation, they felt the Japanese could not touch them. It was at a cement plant located just a few miles from the temple. Thousands of families had settled here, and they had built small huts wherever there was an empty plot of land. The whole area around the factory was transformed into a town, with narrow streets and smoke from makeshift kitchens. Of course, the Japanese remained a menace. They were waiting just near the factory, and if a young girl ventured outside to gather firewood, they would often attack and rape her. But they did not dare move onto the factory grounds, and what stopped them was the presence of "the Dane."

On the occasions when Japanese soldiers tried to break through the factory gate, the blond foreigner immediately obstructed them. Often he had his flag with him. Wang Liyong had never seen it before. It was red with a white cross. It seemed almost magical in the way it made the Japanese pull back, like demons confronted with a powerful spell. The "Dane" also had a double-barreled rifle. It was nothing against the impressive arsenal that the

Japanese could bring to bear, but there was something about his appearance that intimidated them. No one had dared to treat the Japanese this way before. For the Chinese children, the "Dane" cut a towering figure, and many years later, when Wang Liyong had become an old man, he still remembered the tall foreigner who had saved him from the Japanese.

**

In fact, the "Dane" was 5 feet 8 inches tall. It was the exact average of his compatriots at the time,[2] and in almost all respects he represented the typical rather than the extraordinary. His grades in school had been mediocre, and he had held a number of different jobs where he had been conventionally diligent without really standing out. Apart from a fierce temperament that had repeatedly got him into trouble, there was really nothing remarkable about him. But in the course of 104 days during China's darkest winter of 1937 and 1938, entirely new sides of his character emerged, and he became a savior of thousands of fellow human beings. To use a word that a cynical age often shies away from, he became a hero. He went by several different names in Chinese. Some called him Mr. Xin. Others referred to him as Xinbo or Xindebeige. In Danish he was called Sindberg.

Bernhard Arp Sindberg was only 26 years old when in December 1937 circumstances put him at the center of one of the most remarkable humanitarian actions in recent history. While Japanese soldiers indulged in an orgy of violence in and around Nanjing, committing acts that would later be compared to the Nazi crimes in Europe,[3] he created a safe haven for thousands of persecuted Chinese who otherwise would have had no defenses against a vengeful and ruthless army of occupation. It would be incorrect to say that Sindberg did it all by himself. Others assisted him in making the refugee camp work. But even if he was not alone all the time, he very often was. With a slight rewording of Churchill's famous phrase, one can say that "rarely has one man done so much for so many."

Sindberg had entered into adulthood during the 1930s, a decade of economic crisis when hopes for a more peaceful future were extinguished in one country after another. It was a decade when, compared with today, there were drastically fewer options available for a young man to see the world. For most people, a life at sea was the only way to go abroad—and that was the life chosen by Sindberg. Like many others, he ended up in East Asia, a region which offered unknown opportunities, but also was facing huge difficulties. One of them was a Japanese empire undergoing rapid expansion, led astray by politicians and officers consumed with boundless ambition.

Bernhard Arp Sindberg. The photo was most likely taken in the fall of 1937. (Aarhus Municipal Archives/Mariann Arp Stenvig)

The first time Sindberg personally became acquainted with the Japanese army and its trademark brutality was in the late summer of 1937, when Shanghai became the scene of what was eventually to develop into one of the largest urban battles of the 20th century. Towards the end of the year he went on to Nanjing as the caretaker of a cement factory, built by the Danish company F. L. Smidth on behalf of a local Chinese enterprise. He arrived just as the victorious Japanese army was closing in on the city gates. He was one of a small group of foreigners who voluntarily chose to stay in Nanjing in December, although there was no doubt whatsoever that the city was about to fall, while no one could know for sure how the Japanese soldiers would treat individual Westerners in complete isolation from the outside world.

With almost inexplicable courage, he let Chinese civilians settle down in the area around the factory, ensuring that the Japanese soldiers were not allowed to get anywhere near them. He provided medical care for the wounded and the sick, and food for the hungry. Meanwhile, he traveled the countryside around the factory, photographing the victims of the Japanese, securing a lasting testimony of the atrocities that were happening on a massive scale. Sindberg's efforts in Nanjing enables us to speak of a "Danish Schindler," since in the same fashion as the German businessman, he brought hope where others had created hell on earth.

To be sure, it was not preordained that he would play this role. It is true that he had tried many different trades by the time he wound up in Nanjing in 1937, and that as a man still only in his mid-20s he had probably accumulated a level of experience far beyond his chronological age. Still, it was a matter of coincidence that he became the manager of a refugee camp, in the face of the mighty Japanese army. For Sindberg, the road to war-ravaged east China in 1937 was a twisted one. The story of this unlikely hero began a quarter century before, as far from the banks of the Yangtze as one could get both geographically and mentally, in a city in the middle of peaceful Denmark.

CHAPTER I

Heir of the Vikings

1911–1933

Bernhard Arp Sindberg was born on February 19, 1911, in Aarhus.[1] It was Denmark's second-largest city with a history dating back to the early Viking Age, and it almost seemed more than a coincidence that the appetite for travel that had driven his distant Norse ancestors to the farthest corners of the known world was also evident in Sindberg from an early age. "Right from when I was a small child, I was thirsting for adventure," he said later. "I ran away from home again and again."[2] According to family lore, his first attempt at exploration took place at the age of two, when he left his parents' apartment, clutching his rag doll. He was found a few blocks away, sitting by the side of the street, his tiny feet in the gutter.[3]

Sindberg's father, Johannes Sindberg, was from a rural area near the provincial town of Horsens, south of Aarhus. He was born into a poor peasant family in 1882 in the village of Vinten.[4] The soil was fertile, but the conditions were nevertheless extremely modest, and lives were lived in hardship that is hardly fathomable in our modern age. Death struck often and in all age groups, and fatal accidents were the order of the day. Johannes Sindberg was the second son of the family, but when he was 13, his older brother, nine years his senior, passed away, and suddenly he was saddled with the responsibility to pass on the family line. The options available to him were limited, and in 1906, after completing national service, he decided to train as a dairy worker.[5]

In 1909 Johannes Sindberg was as far away from home as he could possibly get without venturing abroad. He was a coachman on the island of Lolland, at the other end of the Danish kingdom, bringing milk from the farms in Branderslev parish to the dairy at Nakskov Ladegård, one of the biggest local estates. One of the maids employed at the estate was 18-year-old Karen Marie Rasmussen. She hailed from a part of Denmark not far from where Johannes Sindberg had grown up. Perhaps they sensed a connection due to their common background, and a friendship quickly developed. They were married on May 11, 1909, less than two weeks before the bride's 19th birthday. Preparations for the wedding had been sped up, and no family was present.[6] Six months later, a boy was born to the young couple.[7]

Johannes Sindberg advanced quickly, and during the fall of 1909 he went from being a lowly coachman to becoming the chief accountant at Nakskov Ladegård. However, the couple did not want to stay, and shortly afterwards they moved back closer to home, settling down in Aarhus. Here their first-born was baptized in the cathedral on June 5, 1910, and was named Niels Frederik Arp Sindberg.[8] The middle name Arp, which Bernhard and his other siblings were also to receive, was in memory of a male relative who had died 20 years earlier without leaving any descendants.[9] It was a gentle gesture to honor a long-dead family member who would otherwise have left no trace. No one

The building where Sindberg was born, at No. 19, Schleppegrellsgade, Aarhus. (Eva Harmsen)

could have predicted it at the time, but rather than be forgotten, his name was to become known decades later to millions of people on the other side of the world, in China.

After moving to Aarhus, Johannes Sindberg had the title of milk merchant,[10] but life was anything but stable in the big city. Just a few months after Bernhard Sindberg was born, the family moved to a new home, and before he had turned two, they had changed addresses altogether three times. Only in late 1912 things started to settle a little. In November of that year, Johannes Sindberg opened a cheese shop in one of the better parts of the city, and the family moved into an apartment in the same building.[11] He was an ambitious man with great visions on behalf his profession, and six months later he was among the founders of Aarhus Milk Merchants' Association, becoming its first chairman.[12]

The chairmanship was controversial from the outset, and a combative disposition does not seem to have made the situation any better for Johannes Sindberg. The first grand meeting of the new association in June 1913 ended in drama, and a large number of participants walked out in protest. The row continued during the following days in the local newspapers, where critics accused Sindberg of trying to enrich himself by introducing a compulsory membership fee. One of his enemies wrote an angry letter to the main local newspaper, *Aarhus Stiftstidende*, describing the collection of the fee as a type of fraud.[13] Sindberg's sarcastic reply was printed in the same paper a couple of days later, revealing a considerable polemical talent: "It is up to Mr. J. C. to decide for himself if he is the kind of person that fraudsters pick for targets."[14]

The year 1913 had been tempestuous, but 1914 was not to provide Johannes Sindberg or his family with any relief. In the spring of 1913, a third son was born, Verner Arp Sindberg. He became severely ill, and he died, only 11 months old, at an Aarhus hospital in April 1914.[15] Four months later, war broke out in Europe. Denmark was able to stay out of the hostilities, but the Danes were still deeply affected, including Johannes Sindberg. While doing national service he had been assigned to coastal defense, and he was now drafted once more to join a beefed-up military responsible for protecting Danish neutrality. During the lengthy periods while he was serving away from home, the cheese shop was closed.[16]

At the same time, he was embroiled in a new public row. The heightened demand for dairy products caused by the war, not least in Britain, pushed up prices. This also meant that Johannes Sindberg and the other milk and cheese merchants in Arhus had to pay more for the products they purchased from dairies in the surrounding countryside. Never one to miss out on a fight,

The city of Aarhus at the time of Sindberg's birth. (Aarhus Municipal Archives)

he wrote a scathing letter to one of the biggest local newspapers: "It is undeniably difficult to feel any joy at the sudden wealth experienced by the farmers when one lives in a city such as Aarhus and, on a daily basis, is forced to witness the poverty and want that ravages many parts of the community and is to a great extent caused by the enormous increase in prices of all food products," he wrote in December. "How is this all going to end? How are we going to make it through the winter? You hear these questions from every other housewife… and at the same time it is uncomfortable to consider how satisfied the farmers are, every time prices go up—as long as it is the prices of their own products."[17]

The tension grew in the course of the following months, and Johannes Sindberg's vocal style, which especially took aim at a particular large dairy called Vesterbro, was to cost him dearly.[18] The dairies of the Aarhus region were very well organized with Vesterbro as one of the driving forces, collectively deciding to boycott his cheese shop. He did not throw in the towel, but entered into a deal with a dairy outside of Vesterbro's cartel, allowing him to continue selling milk and cheese products from a new shop in the city center. This turned out not to be commercially viable, and to make matters worse, Sindberg was soon called up for military service once more.[19] Shortly after being released back into civilian life in November 1915, he placed an ad in the Aarhus newspaper *Demokraten* looking for a job "in an office, a warehouse, or a shop," adding, with more than a hint of desperation, "failing that, any kind of work."[20]

***

Sindberg and his wife, who now had three sons and a daughter, moved to the city of Vejle, roughly 60 miles south of Aarhus, which was the only place where he could find employment. Here yet another son was born in November 1916. He was named Verner, just like the son who had died as an infant two years before. At the same time, Johannes continued to exploit his rhetorical talent in the press. On October 24, 1916, his opinion piece appeared on the front page of the newspaper *Fredericia Social-Demokrat*, addressing the continuous rise in the prices of basic necessities and displaying lingering anger at the way the dairies in Aarhus had treated him. "Nothing is more unfair than the fact that we have to pay wartime prices for our country's own products because other powers wage war," he wrote, and added his own solution: "Price controls on food that we ourselves produce."[21]

By 1917, the family returned to Aarhus and, for the first time in years, could enjoy somewhat settled conditions. In July 1918, Johannes Sindberg started out in a new line of business as a cheese wholesaler, plying his trade from the same building where he lived with his wife and children. In an advertisement announcing the establishment of his new business, he referred to the scarcity that still affected Denmark due to the ongoing war: "In a time when beef and pork are scarce, one must eat cheese. Cheese is the most natural replacement of meat."[22] He communicated with his customers in a way that comes across as surprisingly modern, ensuring that the ordinary consumer felt empowered: "Is your margarine without flavor?" he wrote in an ad. "Then ask your shopkeeper for Nova Margarine."[23] It appears that times were now getting better. The family could afford a five-room apartment, a maid, a telephone, and an automobile.[24]

After the return to Aarhus, Bernhard started school. Initially he was anything but a remarkable student, perhaps because he was enrolled in the middle of the school year and had to catch up. When the first grades were handed out in the spring of 1918, he was third from the bottom among 31 boys in his class. In the course of the following years, however, he gradually improved, and both in 1920 and 1921 he was in the middle group of students who neither did terribly well nor terribly poorly.[25] After four years, both Bernhard and two of his siblings were moved to a private school, in yet another sign that the family finances were looking up.[26] Yet, in the middle of the general progress, tragedy struck once more, when Johannes and his wife lost a second child.

Dairy merchant Johannes Sindberg with his four sons. Bernhard is at the bottom right. (Mariann Arp Stenvig)

Bernhard's younger sister, Maren Margrethe Sindberg, died in April 1920 at just three months old.[27]

The discipline in the Sindberg household was strict, and no one ever questioned Johannes' authority as the head of the family. He was not, however, exercising his power in random and despotic fashion, but saw to it that he inculcated certain values in his children. Most important of all, he told them, you must be generous to those who are less fortunate than you.[28] Bernhard was also an avid boy scout. As a 13-year-old in August 1924 he rode his bicycle to the 2nd World Scout Jamboree, which was held north of Copenhagen. The event brought the whole world to Denmark—and to Sindberg. There were scouts not just from European countries such as France, Hungary, and Czechoslovakia, but also from much more exotic places: India, Japan, Siam—and China.[29] The experience probably inspired many young Danes to travel, but in contrast to most, Sindberg actually lived out his dream.

A couple of years later, according to an oft-told family anecdote, he repeated the escape he had first attempted as a two-year-old, but this time he managed to get much further. He reached the north German port of Hamburg and was about to embark on a ship bound for New York, before he was stopped by his father, who had rushed all the way in his car from Aarhus.[30] Bernhard had been "saved" at the last moment, and his family now considered it an urgent task to pick a nice, peaceful trade for him to keep him busy and distracted from wilder pursuits. After he graduated from school, he became an apprentice with one of Aarhus's most prominent sign painters, who was even the head of the local industrial association. A solid if unexciting career seemed set for Bernhard, but things were to turn out quite differently.

***

At 16, Sindberg finally had the chance to see the world. The ticket abroad was staring him in the face: the port of Aarhus, which had expanded rapidly and by the 1920s was one of the biggest Danish import harbors outside Copenhagen.[31] The steady stream of vessels from distant shores with their cargoes of exotic products was an invitation to adventure. On December 3, 1927, he was hired as a cabin boy on board the Norwegian ship *Vossa*, which was stopping over in Aarhus, and he now sailed across the Atlantic. The first stop was the Cuban port of Santa Cruz del Sur, moving on to New York, where the ship arrived on March 18, 1928.[32]

Sindberg has not left any testimony about his first impressions of the huge American city. Yet, other accounts from the period reflect the overwhelming impact it had on the senses of young men who had been brought up in much more modest Danish towns, where a building was considered a "high-rise" if it had more than a few floors. Ove Kjeldsen, a young sailor, described his experience: "I immediately realized how much there was to do in New York. There was something for every taste, and we saw things we had never encountered before."[33] Or as the artist Hans Bendix remarked from a visit taking place at about the same time: "New York is the biggest city in the world. But it feels even bigger."[34]

The next 18 months were spent sailing to a number of the most colorful destinations of Latin America. In May, Sindberg and six other Danes were hired for work on board the cargo ship *Kotonia*, owned by the Danish shipping company Hafnia, bound for the port of Cienfuegos on the south coast of Cuba.[35] Later that summer, the ship made a port call at Tampico, Mexico, before once again sailing to New York. Sindberg was still only a slender, not fully grown teenager—measuring 5 feet 5 inches and weighing in at 125 pounds—but he had already advanced and was no longer a cabin boy but a regular sailor.[36]

The year after, in 1929, he was onboard the vessel *East Indian*, where he was employed in the engine room as an oiler, responsible for ensuring that all movable parts in the complex machinery were sufficiently lubricated. In that capacity, he sailed from Buenos Aires and arrived once again in New York in September.[37] It was a fateful time in history. In October, Wall Street was the scene of the Crash, sending shock waves through the world economy. The result was a global crisis which was to last for a decade and was one of the main causes of World War II.

By 1930, Sindberg had returned to Denmark and was now in a position that must have seemed very far removed from his previous life as a sailor. He settled down in the town of Odder, roughly 15 miles south of Aarhus, as his father had moved there in hopes of restarting his career. What followed was Bernhard's second shot at a solid and secure job after his unhappy period as a sign painter. He became apprenticed to dairy owner Niels Sørensen in the village of Bjerager not far from Odder.[38] Perhaps he was thinking about following in his father's footsteps. In any case, it did not work out. He wanted to travel again.

For a thrill-seeking young man around 1930, apart from becoming a sailor, there was one other obvious opportunity in the form of the French Foreign Legion. For generations, the legendary unit had been surrounded by myth and mystery, and at this particular time its pop-cultural impact was culminating. In March 1931, the film *Morocco* premiered in Denmark, featuring Gary Cooper as a foreign legionnaire and Marlene Dietrich as the object of his love.[39] In the real world, the Danish royal family was also doing its part to make the Legion more popular. Prince Aage, the grandchild of King Christian IX, had served under the Tricolor since the early 1920s and had described his exploits in several publications. "The very word Foreign Legion," he wrote, "conjures up images of pride and passion."[40]

Sindberg took the same fateful step as thousands of other young dreamers, and at some point during 1931 he was on board a ship crossing the Mediterranean on his way to Algeria. The end station was the Legion's much-feared boot camp near the city of Sidi Bel Abbès, about 50 miles inland. Here Sindberg and the other recruits were kicked and pushed through basic training, which had as its main purpose to instill military discipline and absolute obedience. Every activity was turned into an exercise in precision and orderliness. Making the bed became a regular ritual: "The blankets are folded into perfect squares and laid at the foot of the bed," wrote the American legionnaire Bennett J. Doty, who served shortly before Sindberg. "The sheets are rolled into two cylinders, one of which is laid across the right extremity of the blanket square, the other across the left. The pillow is placed between them, in the exact center. After the beds had been made, each man swept up the floor under his bed and within his area, and then washed it carefully with a wet rag."[41]

Bernhard Sindberg in the French Foreign Legion. (Mariann Arp Stenvig)

Still, nothing beat the importance of the marches, always under the parching North African sun. The German journalist Erwin Rosen, who spent several years in the legion, described in vivid terms what it meant for the individual soldier: "If the pangs of hunger are gnawing at his stomach or thirst parches his tongue, that is so much the worse for him, but is no sort of a reason for his not marching on! He may be tired, dead tired, completely exhausted—but he must not stop marching. If his feet are bleeding and the soles burn like fire, that is very sad—but the marching pace must not be slackened. The sun may burn till his senses are all awhirl, he must go on. His task in life is to march."[42]

In the cramped quarters, with a total absence of any privacy, loneliness was paradoxically a common problem, especially for recruits from small countries with few compatriots around. In the interwar years, a large part of the Legion's recruitment base was German, just as other big European nations such as Spain and Italy were also represented throughout its ranks. The Danes were in a minority, totaling no more than a couple of hundred, at the most.[43] "It was interesting to see how the various nationalities and races, which the Legion consists of and which you tend to ignore in normal circumstances, seek each other's company for protection or conversation in times of trouble," Prince Aage writes, describing the scene after a strenuous march in the desert. "That evening the Germans assembled around one camp fire to sing their national songs, while from another fire you could hear Italians sing, and from a third fire, Spanish voices."[44]

The Legion did not ask its recruits about their past and therefore it attracted not just innocent adventurers, but also the dregs of Europe, who in many cases had committed crimes so serious that they could never return home and had to start new lives abroad. They were men who did not fear physical punishment, and as a result the Legion was forced to devise particularly rough methods of discipline. Repeated transgressions merited long periods of detention, and in those cases it was paramount to stay on good terms with the brutish wardens, or they would beat you up when no one was looking, the American Doty explains.

He goes on to describe a specific punishment, popular with the wardens, and always taking place indoors: "You were set to marching around and around the room all day, doing as much as forty kilometers between morning and night in that confined space. But there was another trick to it. To do this marching, you took off your wooden sabots and put on *espadrilles*. These were sandals with soles made of twisted rope. The rope soon cut into your feet, and you went on around and around on feet that burned and bled."[45]

This type of punishment, on top of endless beatings and humiliations, was meted out as a matter of course for the worst of all crimes—desertion. Nevertheless, this was precisely the solution that Sindberg chose when after some months in the Foreign Legion he realized he had made a mistake. According to reports, he escaped on a bicycle into the mountains on New Year's Eve.[46] The timing was fortunate, since the legionnaires were following tradition and celebrating the arrival of the year 1932 by drinking themselves senseless. Still, fleeing the camp was the easy part. It was much harder to get out of Algeria, squeezed in between the Mediterranean in the north and the Sahara in the south. At a minimum, it was necessary to have enough money to buy a ticket out of the country and also civilian clothes that would make it easier to pass unnoticed through the border control.[47] Somehow, Sindberg managed to do just that. Most likely he got help from the outside. Perhaps he received money sent to him from his family in Denmark.

Not long after his return to Denmark, Sindberg was back in uniform. He was called up and did national service from March to October 1932 as sailor no. 9089. After the unforgiving conditions in the Foreign Legion, he had no problems adjusting to the more relaxed atmosphere in the Danish military, and in boot camp he performed significantly better than the average. At the end of basic training, he attained the highest assessment possible, and he was considered to have excellent potential.[48] For the last four months, from early June to early October, he was part of the 11-member crew of Navy cutter *Maagen*, which was on its maiden voyage carrying out inspection of fishery activities in waters around Greenland.[49]

Maagen was delivered a few days behind schedule in June, as carpenters were putting the finishing touches to the vessel before it was declared ready for the oceans. As a result, when the ship finally departed from the Copenhagen naval station on June 6, everything on board was brand new. Still, it was to become a physically strenuous mission where a freshwater shower was such an unusual event that it merited mention in the ship's journal.[50] Via the Faroe Islands and Iceland, *Maagen* reached the southern tip of Greenland in early July, and the next three months were spent patrolling the icy waters.

During one of the patrols, *Maagen* surprised a German trawler which was breaching international rules by fishing within three nautical miles of the coastline. This led to a dramatic episode which imprinted itself in Sindberg's memory and was described in detail in his otherwise very short autobiography, written decades later in California: "This little boat sails up to a huge German trawler and puts a cannon shot across her bow. The Germans were caught by surprise. But they were inside the three mile fishing limits. So we put a boarding party on her and headed for port. The trawler was faster than we were. By

The Danish Navy's cutter *Maagen* near the town of Godhavn, today Qeqertarsuaq, on the Greenland west coast. Sindberg took part in the vessel's maiden voyage in 1932. This photo is from 1934. (National Museum of Denmark)

the time we got into the harbor, the boarding party had the trawler tied up and a line of trucks a mile long was unloading the fish for the Eskimos. We confiscated the nets, took the fish and levied a fine."[51]

The main responsibility of *Maagen* and its crew was to control Danish and foreign fishing vessels in Greenland waters, but it also carried mail and was a welcome sight in the isolated communities that it visited. The atmosphere on board was laid-back for the military, and the crew was regularly served rum-laced punch. Still, the months spent in the North Atlantic were long and lonely, and probably not many sailors shed any tears when on October 5, 1932, the towers of Copenhagen emerged out of the distant mist. Three days after the return of *Maagen*, Sindberg was discharged from the military.

His assessment, based on his conduct during the mission to Greenland, was markedly lower than after boot camp.[52] The lengthy period spent in the company of 10 other men, with no possibility of escape, must have got on Sindberg's nerves. He had a violent temper and an uneasy relationship with authority. This was about to get him into serious trouble as he headed to the country that was going to define his life: China.

CHAPTER 2

The Prisoner of the *Falstria*

1934–1937

Before noon on Saturday April 14, 1934, the cargo ship *Falstria* owned by the Danish East Asian Company arrived in the port of Shanghai after a Trans-Pacific journey from Los Angeles carrying a large number of passengers as well as U.S. mail.[1] Immediately the Danish consulate was contacted with a plea for assistance in the arrest of a junior crew member who had disobeyed and even assaulted his officers while at sea. The crew member was Bernhard Arp Sindberg. According to the ship's logbook, on April 10 Sindberg had, without any discernible cause, attacked "Chinese Boy no. 3" in the galley. When the first mate attempted to intervene, Sindberg had flown into a rage, grabbing a carving knife from a table.

The logbook goes on to describe what happened next:

> The captain was summoned, and together with the first mate, he managed to wrest the knife from Sindberg, and subsequently had both his hands and feet chained. Sindberg was left out of sight for a short period of time and managed to extricate his feet from the chains, once again grabbing the knife. When the first mate tried to take back the knife, Sindberg, in a frenzy, threatened to kill him. Only after a violent fight was he disarmed and once against securely chained. He was now locked up inside the office, where he smashed both windowpanes and furniture.

The logbook also noted that Sindberg had lost his job even before this incident because a few days prior he had knocked out several of the boatswain's teeth and been insolent towards the second mate.[2]

The Danish diplomats had no other choice but to issue an arrest order for Sindberg and request that the prison at Shanghai's Amoy Road incarcerate him. That very afternoon, the consulate arranged an initial investigation of what had happened at sea. This was in the form of a so-called consular court, which interrogated all the involved persons, including Sindberg himself, who appeared with a face freshly bruised from the scuffle on the ship.

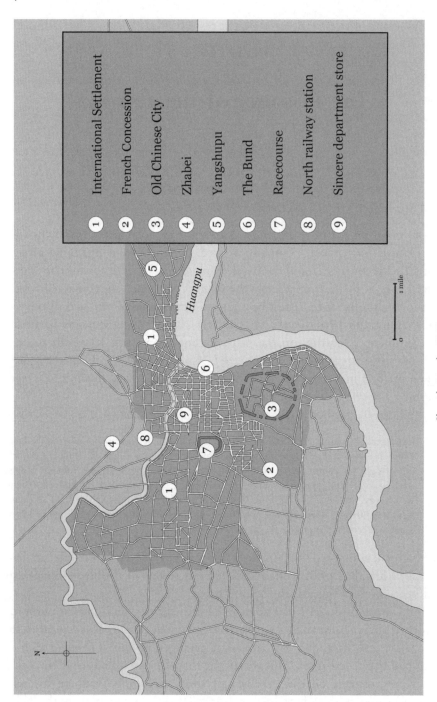

1. International Settlement
2. French Concession
3. Old Chinese City
4. Zhabei
5. Yangshupu
6. The Bund
7. Racecourse
8. North railway station
9. Sincere department store

Huangpu

0 — 1 mile

N

Shanghai in the 1930s.

The interrogation of Sindberg dragged out because he would not admit to any wrongdoing. Even so, Vice Consul Mogens Melchior, who presided over the interrogation, ended up with a positive impression of the detained sailor: "No doubt he has a combative personality with a tendency to complain, but in actual fact, it is probably quite easy to get along with him."[3] At the same time, other testimony suggested that the clash at sea had not necessarily proceeded in quite the fashion described in the ship's logbook, and in the course of the interrogations carried out over the following days, a more complex picture emerged.

The sequence of events which the diplomats now established was the following:[4] Sindberg had joined the *Falstria*'s crew in San Francisco in February, and his relationship with the boatswain had quickly turned hostile. The reason was that the boatswain had repeatedly reproached Sindberg for not being unionized. One day in early April, as the ship was approaching Shanghai, the two had chanced upon one another in the mess, and the argument had been revived immediately. They came to blows, and Sindberg punched the boatswain in the face, knocking out three of his teeth. Some days later there was trouble once again, this time pitting Sindberg against the second mate. The weather was foul, with gales and big waves, and Sindberg shouted from his spot on the foredeck if the ship was sailing at full speed, as it ought to. The second mate replied that "he would be in charge of that." A row ensued violent enough that the day after Sindberg was dismissed for having been impertinent to a superior.

It was against this backdrop that the fierce showdown of April 10 had taken place. That evening, Sindberg, who was now no longer a member of the crew, was sitting with five sailors sharing a bottle of liquor and 12 beers. When they had no more drinks left, Sindberg offered to get another round. In the galley he met a Chinese crew member, named Ching Keong, who agreed to handing out six bottles of beer, but not the exact brand that Sindberg wanted, which was Tuborg Export Pilsner. Sindberg protested loudly, and the first mate appeared on the scene. He ordered Sindberg to leave the galley, but Sindberg refused. This caused the first mate to hit Sindberg in the face, leading to a regular fight. The captain joined the melee, and Sindberg, who was now desperate, grasped the knife. Together the captain and the first mate forced the knife from him, and raining blows on him, they managed to chain his hands and feet.

Meanwhile, the ship's doctor was summoned. He noticed injuries near Sindberg's eyes and mouth, obviously from blows that had been meted out with considerable force. As it was impossible to calm down Sindberg, while he also seemed to be in serious pain, the doctor gave him a shot of morphine.

The *Falstria* during a port call at Vancouver in 1934. (Walter E. Frost)

Only half-conscious, he was carried into a cabin, and the door was locked from the outside. The quiet only lasted for a brief moment, before Sindberg came to and once again panicked. He was scared that the cuffs around his ankles were too tight, preventing his blood circulation. His yells did not produce any reaction from the people outside, and instead he smashed the windows of the cabin, prompting the doctor to enter and remove the chains. However, the cabin remained Sindberg's lodging until the ship's arrival in Shanghai.

The prison in Amoy Road, where Sindberg was locked up in between being interrogated by the consulate, was a building from the mid-19th century with room for about 60 inmates, mostly Russians and other nationalities from the old Tsarist Empire. Several of them were minor celebrities, including Latvian-born red-haired Katherine Hadley, a former cabaret dancer who had been jailed for life after killing an English captain during a row by lodging a knife deep in his neck. The prison was managed by the British authorities according to British rules. New arrivals were issued a uniform in rough gray cotton, with their numbers painted on the back, and they were immediately placed in solitary confinement inside cells measuring 15 by 15 feet and with 12 feet to the ceiling. Work mostly consisted of cleaning duties or tending the prison's small garden. The most common punishment for infractions was to be exposed to a diet of water and bread, or as the prison wardens said with their dry British humor, "wine and cakes." On the face of it, boredom was the worst part of life in the prison. Newspapers were not allowed, and visits from the outside were rare. Still, for privileged Westerners such as Sindberg, it was generally tolerable and definitely a civilized departure from the brutality he had known in the Foreign Legion.[5]

However, there was a darker aspect to Amoy Road. Prisoners who were not lucky enough to come from either English-speaking or Scandinavian countries often talked about treatment verging on sadism. In an open letter complaining about their conditions, they described being beaten, starved, and put in straitjackets at the tiniest excuse, and they quoted the prison chief as calling them "animals in a zoo."[6] In the middle of the building loomed the gallows. It was almost exclusively for use against Indians, who in the words of a former inmate "either were sentenced to very short or suspended sentences or were executed." The same former prisoner described how the mood of the inmates was clearly impacted on days when executions were happening. "You could feel it in a jail when someone's time was up. Something happened to the atmosphere."[7]

The question of how long Sindberg was to remain under these conditions was for the consular court to decide. It met on April 24 to reach its final decision.[8] The court included in its deliberations not just the new, fuller testimony collected during the interrogations, but also a statement issued by the vicar in the Norwegian seaman's church, who had known Sindberg in Buenos Aires and described him as a "cheerful but somewhat stubborn young man, of whom he had formed the best possible impression."[9] By contrast, the consular court was left with a less favorable opinion of conditions on board the *Falstria*—"something of a slave ship," according to one of the Danish diplomats—and noted that the first mate had hit Sindberg in the face without himself having been either hit or even threatened. Given the facts, the court decided to dismiss the case.[10]

As an extra precaution to prevent the conflict from reigniting, Sindberg was to stay in jail until the *Falstria* had left port again.[11] After this, he spent a few months in Shanghai, possibly interrupted by a temporary job on board a ship. In late summer 1934, he left the Chinese metropolis as a sailor on board the American passenger ship *President Grant*, arriving in Seattle in September.[12] In January the following year he was hired for work on the board Danish shipping company A. P. Møller's fast cargo liner *Peter Maersk*, leaving Los Angeles for New York via the Panama Canal. *Peter Maersk* plied routes between North American ports and Far Eastern destinations, and it was likely on board this vessel that Sindberg returned to Shanghai in 1935.[13]

It was no coincidence. All roads, at least at sea, led to Shanghai. It was China's largest city, and the world's fifth largest, with a population of 3.5 million.[14] Its name, in Chinese, meant "the city above the water," and it was exactly that.

Shanghai in the mid-1930s, when Sindberg visited the huge city for the first time. (Photograph by Malcolm Rosholt. Image courtesy of Me-fei Elrick, Tess Johnston and Historical Photographs of China, University of Bristol)

Situated on the brown Huangpu River close to the Yangtze estuary, it had grown faster than probably any other city on earth since the 1840s when the emperor had bowed to pressure from the Western imperialists and opened it for foreign commerce. Now Shanghai was the gateway to China, and half the country's entire trade with the outside world passed by the city's sprawling dock areas.[15] The restless and dynamic atmosphere in the encounter between east and west reminded one of the visitors, the architect Steen Eiler Rasmussen, of medieval Venice: "There is life and trade everywhere," he wrote. "The city changes is appearance every ten or twenty years."[16]

Shanghai's special vibe was a product not least of the many foreigners who resided in the city, but they made up just a small minority even in the two districts under non-Chinese administration, the International Settlement and the French Concession. The Japanese constituted the largest group, numbering altogether 19,000.[17] They represented a young, ambitious empire, and even though their presence in Shanghai was primarily motivated by commercial concerns, it was clear that Japan also perceived a strategic advantage to having established itself near the Yangtze Delta. The Japanese garrison at Shanghai was charged with protecting Japanese citizens in the city, but the soldiers were all but defensive-minded, and their aggressive mentality had manifested itself in early 1932, when they had fought a brief war with the Chinese army in Shanghai's Chinese district.[18]

Besides the Japanese, every nationality was represented in Shanghai. British citizens made up the second-largest group with 8,500 residents, followed by Russian immigrants who had been forced from their homes by the revolution two decades earlier. There were 3,000 Americans and 1,800 persons from British India. These included Sikhs, who often worked as traffic police and added an exotic element to the street scenery with their turbans.[19]

They lived in a city which was in many places shockingly modern. "In few other cities do they built so much, so exuberantly, and so tastelessly," opined Eiler Rasmussen. He was most impressed by the department stores Sincere and Wing-On on Nanjing Road, where giant posters advertising the latest sale covered the seven-story facades. "In the evening, the entire building is inundated in electric light, which turns the long posters into a shining stream of white and red stretching towards the black tropical sky," he wrote.[20] The night clubs were legendary, offering in the words of one traveler "ingratiating jazz bands, French champagne, and entertainment by slim Chinese ladies wearing shining silk and blazing jewelry."[21]

In spite of the Western veneer, Shanghai had none of the basic order that underpinned major European cities. Rather, chaos reigned everywhere. The colors, the smells, and the sounds known from other parts of China were here, too, only in intensified form. "It's like a shaky color movie, accompanied by noise and screaming," a visiting journalist wrote, encouraging other travelers to step out of their cars to take in the full experience: "You must feel the crooked fingers of the beggars grabbing your shoulder, smell the vomit-tinged breath of the coolies."[22]

The Shanghai which the curious tourist could thus experience with a shudder down the spine was a different and more sinister place than the slightly futuristic metropolis advertised by the travel agencies. The misery was especially stark in the city's northwest. Worst of all was the working-class neighborhood of Zhabei, where the bottom of society slaved away in conditions reminiscent of concentration camps. "This is where the most wretched mothers of the world toil from the age of 14 to the age of 40, often while pregnant," an author wrote. "Children aged nine to 14 work the dangerous machinery, many of them actually dying, sickened by beriberi. Still, the machinery cannot stop. If one girl dies while a work, she is immediately replaced with another."[23]

***

The experience of Shanghai depended very much on who you were and on your place in society. The city provided splendid luxury for the elite of Westerners who had already been established as members of the business or diplomatic community before they arrived, and often they were able to maintain living standards that would have been unimaginable for them in their home countries. On the other hand, it was not an easy place for a young man settling down without any preexisting means or connections. It was a daily struggle for survival, and quite a few ended up in the squalor of the slums, or they succumbed completely. Sindberg managed to stay afloat by means of a series

Cathay Hotel, where Sindberg worked for a short period, meeting several illustrious guests, including Charlie Chaplin, who was touring Asia. (Private collection)

THE PRISONER OF THE *FALSTRIA* • 21

of odd jobs, but very often he was unemployed, and sometimes he only had himself to blame for this sad state of affairs.

In 1936 partly due to his knowledge of French acquired in the Foreign Legion, he secured a well-paid job as a receptionist at Cathay Hotel. Located on the Bund, Shanghai's famous riverfront, it was known for its exclusivity and class. For Sindberg, it marked a dramatic and unexpected turn for the better. "From prison to the greatest hotel of the Orient!" he wrote triumphantly in his memoirs, penned many years later in California. "Striped pants and knee-long coat in the daytime; at night, white tie." Among the guests he served were Charlie Chaplin, on a lengthy tour through the Asia Pacific, as well as Doña María de las Mercedes de Borbón Dos-Sicilias y Orleans, princess of Spain. The hotel, Sindberg wrote, "treated royals in a royal manner: flowers and fruits awaited them in the rooms, as well as the best food and wine in the world."[24]

Chiang Kai-shek, China's leader of the 1930s, had also been a guest at the hotel. It made sense for Chiang to stay there, since the Bund was a center of power, both economic and political. It was the seat of the China headquarters of several foreign companies, such as Jardine Matheson and Banque de l'Indochine, and a number of diplomatic representations were located there, too. These included the Danish mission, which moved to Shanghai from the old capital Beijing in 1936. The Bund was also continuously visited by foreign warships which anchored briefly in Shanghai before and after their frequent patrols up the Yangtze River—a routine they had maintained since the previous century, much to the consternation of many patriotic-minded Chinese.

Sindberg could hardly wish for a more central location than Cathay Hotel. Even so, he was fired after just two months' employment. The cause given was his complaints about the food as well as attempts to stir up protests among his colleagues. More importantly, perhaps, Shanghai police had placed him under observation after 5,000 dollars had disappeared from the receptionist's desk.[25] However, the police abandoned the case as they were unable to gather sufficient evidence. Following this unhappy experience, Sindberg signed a contract with the Danish engineering company Bergsøe, accepting a significantly lower pay than what he had enjoyed at the hotel. His new employer recognized him as a skillful worker, but nonetheless the contract was terminated after a few months. "He caused different kinds of trouble and apparently bullied a German worker in the factory," according to a later document from the Danish consulate.[26] Eventually, Sindberg was employed at the Danish-owned Shanghai Milk Supply, where his dairy training came in handy.[27]

News from back home in Denmark was mixed. The family was falling apart, and his parents divorced. While Johannes Sindberg stayed on in the small town of Odder, Karen Marie had now moved back to Aarhus, but kept the surname Sindberg.[28] Ever looking for a new project to keep him busy and successful, Johannes was now active in a political party espousing the theories of the American economist Henry George. He was also editor-in-chief of a weekly newspaper based in Odder, published by a wealthy lawyer and appearing for the first time on August 14, 1936. "Our motto shall be liberty and justice. We will struggle for the idea of liberty and justice in all aspects of life," the first issue stated programmatically.[29]

The weekly newspaper published lengthy articles with a polemical twist, but due to cost concerns it rarely carried any photos. Images from abroad were even rarer. Still, the paper made an exception when it came to China, or rather, Shanghai. Three times in the course of 1937 the front page included photos from that distant city. On August 20, there was a photo of "Chinese soldiers in front of a village near Shanghai."[30] In other words, Johannes Sindberg was keenly aware of the events that played out in front of his son, and very likely he was also worried. If so, it was with good reason. In 1937, Sindberg was to witness some of the bloodiest events in the history of the world.

CHAPTER 3

"A Stupid Nincompoop"

March–August 1937

"A stupid nincompoop." This was how the Danish adventurer Jørgen Juncker-Jensen described his compatriot Bernhard Sindberg. Significantly, he committed this negative characterization to paper not in the heat of the moment, or in reaction to a fresh slight, but nearly half a century after the two saw each other last.[1] Coincidence had brought them together in China in the spring of 1937, and they had hated each other from the outset. It all began at the start of the year when Sindberg was back home in Denmark visiting his family in Odder. He talked about his success with Shanghai Milk Supply, which must have pleased his dairy-educated father. However, at the very moment when he had set out on his trip back to China, a letter from the company arrived with news that there had been a management reshuffle, and Sindberg's job had gone to someone else. Sindberg himself only was informed after he had returned to Shanghai in March. He promptly walked to the local office of Danish Recoil Rifle Syndicate and immediately got a new job.[2]

The company, a major weapons manufacturer, picked Sindberg because of his experience in the Danish navy and the French Foreign Legion. It needed his skills after having sold 75 of its world-famous Madsen machine guns to the Chinese military, leaving it with a requirement to demonstrate their use to army representatives in the capital of Nanjing, roughly 200 miles west of Shanghai.[3] It also contributed to the company's decision to hire Sindberg that he managed to make a favorable impression on its local representative Erik Nyholm—so favorable, in fact, that Nyholm decided to hold onto Sindberg even after he had contacted the Danish consulate hoping to carry out a quick background check, only to be introduced to Sindberg's long, checkered history in Shanghai, beginning with the scuffle aboard the *Falstria*.

It was understood that the consulate had preferred it if Sindberg had not been hired by the Rifle Syndicate. He had built up something of a reputation

Sindberg with a Chinese assistant during a demonstration of the Madsen machine gun, with the metal plate used for target practice. (Bernhard Arp Sindberg Papers and Photography Collection, Harry Ransom Center, University of Texas at Austin)

among the diplomats, and Vice Consul Melchior, who initially had liked the young man, was now considerably less enthusiastic. As a result, when Sindberg was just about to leave Shanghai for Nanjing, Melchior asked him to come to his office for a serious talk. The meeting essentially boiled down to a warning, according to Melchior: "I impressed upon him that from now on he was to behave, and that the Consulate General would no longer accept any complaints about him." Despite actively opposing Sindberg's appointment at the Rifle Syndicate, Melchior decided not to tell Nyholm that he had been investigated by police over the missing 5,000 dollars from Cathay Hotel, "as I understood that the work he had been offered in Nanjing would not involve handling money."[4]

At about the same time Melchior was also instrumental in mediating Jørgen Juncker-Jensen's employment with the Rifle Syndicate, exhibiting no inhibitions about recommending him for the job. As he had served in the Danish Navy, Juncker-Jensen had a skill profile similar to Sindberg, and he also had a motorcycle license. This was necessary as part of the demonstration for the benefit of the Chinese officers involved mounting the Madsen machine gun onto the sidecar of a four-cylinder motorbike made by the company Nimbus—a "big, powerful, impressive monster" in Juncker-Jensen's phrase. After the Rifle Syndicate had approved of Juncker-Jensen, he was sent to Nanjing, where he and Sindberg were put up temporarily at the Yangtze Hotel, featuring the best service of the city, until more permanent lodgings could be found for the duo.[5]

The demonstration of the Madsen machine gun took place on several occasions during May in front of an audience stretching from students of the capital's military academies to ranking officers. Once Madame Chiang Kai-shek, China's English-speaking First Lady, was also present. Everything had been carefully rehearsed: once Nyholm and the Rifle Syndicate's other local representative Kai Suhr had described the various features of the Madsen machine gun, Juncker-Jensen arrived at top speed on the Nimbus motorcycle, with Sindberg sitting in the sidecar. After a screeching halt, Sindberg cocked the machine gun and fired long bursts at wooden sheds erected for target practice. At one point it almost ended fatally. Sindberg shot at the wrong shed, which had nothing to do with the demonstration and was inhabited by a Chinese couple. The two Chinese stumbled out in shock, yelling and waving their arms. "It was their lucky day," Juncker-Jensen wrote in his memoirs. "They didn't get killed, and besides that they ended up with a new and better home and assurance that we would not do it again."[6]

The evenings after the demonstrations were spent having dinner with the Chinese officers, washed down with copious amounts of booze. Even though only a few of the Chinese spoke any English, real friendships were made, and both Sindberg and Juncker-Jensen were invited on picnics in the area around Nanjing. The two Danes had now also moved to a villa on the outskirts of the capital, equipped with both a chef and a servant. It was a kind of luxury that neither of them had experienced before. Everything was perfect except for one thing: they disliked each other intensely. Juncker-Jensen thought Sindberg was overbearing and lacked diplomatic finesse. Perhaps, he speculated, Sindberg suffered from a minority complex.[7] Furious rows became the order of the day, and often they exploded into violent fistfights. "Our situation had deteriorated to the extent that we sometimes reported to work with scratches and black eyes," Juncker-Jensen wrote.[8]

Jørgen Juncker-Jensen rides a motorcycle during a demonstration of the Madsen machine gun in front of representatives of the Chinese military. The Chinese assistant behind him carries the weapon's tripod on his back. Sindberg can be seen behind the two others, half standing in the sidecar while holding the mounted machine gun. (Aarhus Municipal Archives/Mariann Arp Stenvig)

On one occasion the disaster was complete. A general and two colonels had been invited to dine in the villa. The table had been set, and the candles lit. Five minutes before the arrival of the senior officers, Sindberg and Juncker-Jensen wound up in another of their arguments, and before long, they were rolling on the floor in a frenzied embrace. Sindberg was trying with both hands to choke Juncker-Jensen, who was kicking wildly to escape. The chef and the waiter tried desperately to separate the two, while shouting over and over again in sing-song English, "Masters, Masters, please don't." The two combatants managed to stop just before the doorbell rang and the Chinese officers stepped inside in full regalia. "We were still dusting ourselves off and trying to look half-way dignified, and as if nothing had happened," Juncker-Jensen wrote. "I'm sure they detected the wild look in our eyes, this, and our ruffled-up hair, must have been dead give-aways."[9]

Juncker-Jensen admitted in his memoirs that Sindberg was bigger and stronger, adding that "although I was faster and a better fighter I certainly could not help getting my share of bruises."[10] After a couple of months Juncker-Jensen had had enough, and in early May he traveled to Shanghai to be released from his obligations with the Rifle Syndicate, seeking the assistance of the consulate, which had mediated the first contact with the company. In a conversation with Melchior, Juncker-Jensen initially did not want to say why he wished to give up his job, but after being pushed for some time, he provided the actual reason. "It was impossible for him to work with Sindberg, who constantly bullied him and at one point right at the start had even headbutted him repeatedly and subsequently threatened him physically on several occasions," Melchior wrote in a later report.[11]

The Consulate now summoned Sindberg for a meeting with Consul General Poul Scheel on May 15, and when he was confronted with Juncker-Jensen's accusations, he admitted having threatened and hit him. His only explanation

Sindberg, front kneeling down, during a demonstration of the Madsen machine gun. The Chinese behind him shows the machine gun's use as an antiaircraft weapon. Jørgen Juncker-Jensen, without headwear, is seen standing, leaning against the wall. (Bernhard Arp Sindberg Papers and Photography Collection, Harry Ransom Center, University of Texas at Austin)

was that he "felt annoyed" at Juncker-Jensen. The consul general responded with what could only be construed as a last warning. Scheel told him that he had "repeatedly shown a disposition for violence and that in case that he received the slightest information of yet more acts of violence, he should prepare himself for being prosecuted in the consular court."[12] The upshot could very well be that Sindberg would have to leave China, Scheel said.[13]

On the same day, Scheel sent a letter to Nyholm with a request that he and Kai Suhr carefully monitor Sindberg's behavior and take steps to stop his bullying of Juncker-Jensen. "In order to forestall this, I very much advise that the two now longer stay in the same place," Scheel wrote. "Finally, I find it a matter of course that he is not kept in your service beyond the end of this month."[14] He was disappointed in this wish. One week later Nyholm replied that Juncker-Jensen had left the Rifle Syndicate, while Sindberg was to stay on

Sindberg, front row second from right, with a group of Chinese officers who are being trained in the use of the Madsen machine gun. Sindberg describes the situation in comments jotted down on the back of the photo: "After the first successful demonstration we had an equally successful dinner. We drank lots of Chinese rice wine. No man in this photo is sober, least of all me myself." Jørgen Juncker-Jensen is in the front row, second from left. Erik Nyholm sits behind Sindberg. (Bernhard Arp Sindberg Papers and Photography Collection, Harry Ransom Center, University of Texas at Austin)

in his position. "Our demonstrations have been very successful, and we will have even more work to do here during the coming months," Nyholm wrote, and then rubbed it in: "Therefore, we find it necessary to keep Mr. Sindberg, since he has been an excellent employee in every respect."[15]

In conversations with Juncker-Jensen, Nyholm had reportedly said the exact opposite about the prospect of more work in the future: "Well, you wish to leave. As we have less work to do now, I have nothing against your decision."[16] Effectively, Nyholm had directly ignored Scheel's recommendation and dismissed Juncker-Jensen while keeping on Sindberg. Scheel was understandably upset and expressed his "disapproval" in a quick letter to Nyholm.[17] However, the case did not evolve beyond this point, but petered out as for some reason Sindberg decided to quit the Rifle Syndicate in late May. According to Nyholm, who readily admitted that he did not know the details of Sindberg's whereabouts, he had apparently found a job on board a ship in the port of Shanghai and had left China.[18]

***

In fact, Nyholm did not have the correct information. Sindberg stayed on in Nanjing and only left on July 1 with the intention of going on a two-month holiday in California. The passenger ship made a stopover in the Japanese port of Yokohama near Tokyo where he received news about an "incident" just outside Beijing. Chinese and Japanese soldiers had clashed in the vicinity of the centuries-old Marco Polo Bridge. The situation had long been tense, not only in the area around the old imperial capital, but also further afield across large swathes of north Chinese territory. As early as 1931 and 1932, resource-poor Japan had occupied three northeast Chinese provinces with an area corresponding to Germany, France, and Spain combined, aiming to exploit the rich agricultural soil and the copious reserves of coal and steel. It had only been the first step in what amounted to an ambitious plan to control major parts of China, and over the subsequent years, Japanese forces had gradually expanded their zone of influence to ever-larger parts of the vast nation's northern territories. In other words, the fighting at Marco Polo Bridge by no means constituted the first time that Chinese and Japanese forces were confronting each other. Many considered this routine and expected peace to prevail again soon. "I deemed it to be of limited significance and continued my journey," Sindberg wrote later in his memoirs.[19]

While Sindberg traveled across the Pacific headed for the American West Coast, Chinese and Japanese field officers stationed in the Beijing area attempted to roll back the conflict in intermittent negotiations, but in their respective capitals there were strong groups who wanted a showdown. For several weeks the situation in northern China teetered on the brink of war, but at the end of July, the Japanese army kicked off a major offensive against Chinese forces in and around Beijing, and within just a few days it managed to eradicate all resistance. Not only was Beijing now in Japanese hands, but Japanese columns also penetrated fast into the provinces west and south of the city. "When I had arrived in California, the situation had become so serious that I limited myself to a four-day vacation before departing once more on board the first Danish ship sailing for Shanghai," Sindberg wrote.[20] It was not entirely clear why Sindberg considered his presence to be required in Shanghai, but it stands to reason that he figured the outbreak of hostilities would lead to a drastic increase in the Rifle Syndicate's China business.

Meanwhile, the mood among Shanghai's Westerners was cautiously optimistic. Shanghai had managed to escape unscathed from earlier international storms, ran a typical line, and surely it would be able to do so once again. Even so, there were unsettling signs that peace would not last. A paramilitary corps loyal to the Chinese government prepared for battle in Shanghai, and the city's tiny Japanese garrison braced nervously for an attack. The residents of Shanghai's Chinese districts started trickling into the International Settlement, warning that war was approaching. "Japanese man fight Chinese man," they said ominously. Still, only a minority among Shanghai's foreigners really believed that the conflict in distant Beijing would spread all the way south. "What would they want to fight in Shanghai for?" they asked each other, seeking reassurance in their limited knowledge of the politics behind the scenes.[21]

All hopes were soon dashed, and eventually war came to Shanghai after all. The immediate trigger was a clash at a Chinese-controlled airfield just west of the city. On August 9, a Japanese marine officer from the local garrison had his driver take him to the front gate, and a shootout ensued with the Chinese sentries. Both Japanese men were killed, and a Chinese person also lost his life. "It will probably never be known who bears responsibility," the Danish envoy to Shanghai, Oscar O'Neill Oxholm, wrote in a report to the Foreign Ministry in Copenhagen. "Against the backdrop of overall tension, it must, however, be characterized as foolish of the Japanese officer to drive to the airfield… The Chinese claim that he tried to force his entry, causing his car to come under fire, whereas the Japanese maintain that the officer and his driver were actually murdered."[22]

The potentially disastrous consequences of the shootout were obvious, and news of the incident spread around the world. Sindberg heard it on the radio while his ship was still at sea in the middle of the Pacific.[23] Over the next

Soldiers from one of China's elite divisions, equipped and trained by the Germans. They were deployed in large numbers in Shanghai in August in the hope of a quick victory over the small Japanese garrison. (Photograph by Malcolm Rosholt. Image courtesy of Me-fei Elrick, Tess Johnston and Historical Photographs of China, University of Bristol)

few days, Chinese and Japanese negotiators met repeatedly in Shanghai in a frantic bid to seek a peaceful solution, but they got nowhere. Chiang Kai-shek's government wanted war after it had achieved a ceasefire with the communist rebels several months earlier, reaching an agreement to fight the common Japanese enemy instead. A number of highly trained and well-equipped Chinese divisions were stationed in the area near Nanjing and could be dispatched to Shanghai at a few hours' notice. By contrast, the Japanese garrison in the city consisted merely of a few thousand men occupying a slim piece of land along the Huangpu River. From a Chinese point of view, it seemed easy to eliminate the Japanese force and put an end to Japan's presence in Shanghai once and for all. A quick victory over the hated Japanese would rally the Chinese nation and mobilize the population for resistance. "Japan had no wish to fight at Shanghai," Chinese General Zhang Fakui said later. "It should be simple to see that we took the initiative."[24]

***

On August 13, four days after the deadly clash at the airfield, fighting broke out in Shanghai's Chinese district. Chinese troops, who had arrived by train and bus from the Nanjing region over the preceding hours and days, went on the offensive in the afternoon, attacking Japanese positions in various parts of northern Shanghai. The Japanese came under intense pressure, since they were not just outnumbered, but also pitted against the elite of the Chinese army: highly trained, expensively equipped and thirsting for revenge. When the sun set over the city, the crackle of machine guns and the hollow thuds of hand grenades could be heard throughout the narrow streets. The following day, Saturday August 14, Shanghai rose to a new reality. Nothing was as before, for war had arrived. "Large parts of the city are ablaze, and thick, suffocating smoke drifts through the streets, while panic-stricken crowds scramble to flee the ravaged districts," a Western newspaper reporter wrote.[25]

People who had lived in Shanghai for a long period of time were reminded of the situation five and a half years earlier when Chinese and Japanese soldiers had also been fighting it out. Then just as now, the working-class neighborhood of Zhabei provided the stage for most of the combat. It was a conflict marred by great brutality, and as a general rule, prisoners were not taken. "The snipers are treated exactly the same way as in 1932, when caught," a war correspondent reported. "They are executed on the spot… Many are either shot or decapitated. And usually in China decapitations take place in the middle of the street."[26]

The Japanese had fought ferociously in 1932, eventually winning the battle, and once again in 1937 it was clear that they offered firmer resistance than the Chinese had expected. The Japanese had one major advantage, as their Third Fleet was anchored in the Huangpu River just off the Bund, acting as floating artillery in support of the infantry in the streets. The flagship was the cruiser *Izumo*, which had been built at the turn of the century and clearly was aging but still constituted a formidable tactical factor with its twin 20.3-centimeter guns. The Danish dentist Niels Eskelund's clinic was located just abreast of the *Izumo*, and he was able to observe at first hand the Chinese air raids on the ship, and the response of its air-defense systems: "Most of all it reminded me of a little angry terrier barking at a crow."[27]

Already on the second day of the battle the Chinese air force mobilized almost all its available planes for a raid on the *Izumo*. One of the attacks ended in tragedy, when two bombs released from a Chinese aircraft landed near the Bund, exploding at Palace Hotel and Sindberg's old workplace the Cathay Hotel. Eskelund described the apocalyptic situation right after:

> An immense shock wave, but almost no sound. The earth trembles. The buildings shake. The air is no longer air, but an immense pressure, a wall of flame, a hailstorm of sharp shrapnel and stones. And then complete silence, and acute confusion… More than 400 injured people wail, scream and crawl. The big cars are twisted, blown against the kerb, and burn. And living people are burning inside the cars, and blood and blood everywhere![28]

In the early stages of the battle of Shanghai, Japanese troops search a civilian automobile as it crosses Garden Bridge between the international and the Chinese parts of the city. (Photograph by Malcolm Rosholt. Image courtesy of Me-fei Elrick, Tess Johnston and Historical Photographs of China, University of Bristol)

Shortly afterwards yet another bomb from a Chinese aircraft fell in the French Concession and exploded in the middle of large group of people. The three blasts on "Black Saturday," as the day was quickly known, cost the lives of altogether more than 800 people.[29] It was a sinister reminder that anyone in Shanghai could be hit at any time. No one was safe in a battle where little distinction was made between belligerents and civilians.

***

Sindberg had been informed about "Black Saturday" on the radio before the ship he was on had reached East Asia. Several of the other passengers also had to go to Shanghai, and they were concerned that they would be unable to complete the journey because of the increased tension near the city. They were right. When the ship arrived in Yokohama, the captain received orders not to sail on to China. Sindberg was informed that passenger ships still plied a route to Shanghai from the port of Nagasaki in western Japan, but in order to utilize this opportunity he had to obtain a travel permit from the authorities in Yokohama. "I called on the Chief of Police and gave him a sentimental fable about a wife and children [that] I wanted to bring safely back with me from the horrors of Shanghai," Sindberg wrote later in English-language memoirs. "The Chief took pity on me and he presented me with a pass to proceed through."[30]

Sindberg wrote a letter to his parents informing them that he was on his way to Shanghai, and then departed.[31] The train journey from Yokohama to Nagasaki was cumbersome, as the outbreak of war had made the Japanese more suspicious, especially with regards to Westerners, who were seen as potential spies. Sindberg had to produce his papers again and again on the way, and twice, while the train was making a stop, he was ordered to disembark to be frisked, stark naked, inside the station building. At the same time, the journey gave Sindberg an impression of how the war had left a mark everywhere in Japanese society. At every station there were hundreds of young girls, waving the Japanese flag and chanting, "Banzai!" while handing small gifts to soldiers shipping out to China.[32]

In addition, Sindberg had an opportunity to study the Japanese officers, who made up the majority of the other passengers in his class. Several had brought samurai swords, heirlooms that had been passed down from one generation to the next. "The common ailment among the officers was sore feet," he wrote in his memoirs. "This might have been attributed to their new army shoes, or the fact they had had a long march prior to boarding the train. At any rate, as soon as they entered the compartment they removed their boots and aired out their feet over the open window sills. Imagine the variety of sweet aromas filling the coach!" Eventually, Sindberg got tired of the officers' hostile, suspicious glances, and he sought sanctuary in the dining car, where he remained for the rest of the journey.[33]

When Sindberg arrived in Nagasaki, he tried to find an empty hotel room, as his ship was not leaving until late the same evening. It was difficult since Nagasaki was teeming with women and children who had been evacuated from China, but in the end he succeeded. Sindberg now watched the emotional scenes that played out when two ships filled with passengers from Shanghai docked in Nagasaki harbor. "I... witnessed many happy reunions between various relatives. On the same boat were many wounded soldiers returning from the earliest campaign," Sindberg wrote. "These were all removed to a large open-air hospital on the docks, where doctors and nurses were kept busy changing bandages and comforting men before sending them off to various hospitals throughout Japan."[34]

The journey across the East China Sea took place on board a ship which exclusively was handling civilian passengers. The majority consisted of

Westerners who lived in Shanghai and had been on vacation in Japan or northern China when the hostilities broke out. "For the most part they were very worried over their future, the condition of their homes in Shanghai, whether their dear friends were alive and the probable length of hostilities," Sindberg wrote. There were also about 20 Japanese people, who were surprisingly fluent in Chinese and from their outer appearance could easily be mistaken for Chinese. It was easy to get the impression that they were some sort of secret agents and that their mission was to mix with the local population in Shanghai.[35]

The most curious passenger was an old Japanese woman who traveled in third class and slept on the deck on top of a thin mattress that she had brought with her. She also carried several large baskets. One of them contained her food, but the others were filled with small bars of soap, toilet paper, letter paper, envelopes, and a large number of cheap cigarettes. "She was a typical woman peddler, but the steward informed me that she had already made several trips and that what she did with her goods was to distribute them free [of charge] to the Japanese in the trenches," Sindberg explained. "She bought the wares out of her own money and did this just to give the Japanese a little good cheer."[36]

When the ship reached the Yangtze Delta, it was immediately clear how serious the battle had become and how much of the Japanese military had already been sucked in: "There, lying at anchor and moving about were, by actual count, three hundred warships, including submarines, torpedo boats, airplane carriers, hospital convoys and the like," Sindberg wrote. The ship moved up the Yangtze and arrived at the mouth of the Huangpu, the river flowing past Shanghai. After two hours on the Huangpu, the passengers witnessed the first actual combat. They had arrived at Wusong, a Chinese fortress north of Shanghai, and observed an artillery duel between the batteries of the fortress and a group of Japanese warships. Sindberg and the other passengers were ordered to move below deck and be ready to quickly descend into the lifeboats if the ship was to become a target. "We passed within a thousand yards of the fort, but were unmolested. The Chinese apparently had no desire to shell a merchant ship used exclusively to evacuate civilians," Sindberg wrote.[37]

After Sindberg's ship had put the Wusong fortress behind it, it was met by two Japanese torpedo boats and a number of small naval vessels with machine guns mounted on their decks. They formed a cordon around the passenger ship, and now the last, most dangerous part of the journey began. Sindberg described his encounter with modern war in vivid terms:

> Approaching Shanghai we could hear the sickening roar of Japanese planes making power dives, and thundering explosions of bombs. Playing a fanciful accompaniment to these roars was the rat-tat-tat of machine guns and rifle fire. This confusion of noises could be heard from both sides of the river and several times these sounds became more real as bullets hit the side of the ship. When these bullets became too frequent, one of the Japanese motorboats forming our escort would leave the place in the cordon and dart at full speed towards the river embankment and would blast away with machine gun fire in the general direction from where we had last been fired upon.[38]

The nerve-wracking journey was about to end when the ship Sindberg was on slowed down and headed for a section of the docks belonging to the Japanese shipping company N.Y.K. Lines in the district of Yangshupu, located in the northeastern part of Shanghai. They had now arrived in a part of the city where the fighting had been carried out with the greatest intensity over the preceding days. This was where the Chinese generals had deployed their best troops, believing that capture of the part of the port controlled by the enemy would dramatically reduce his ability to send in reinforcements. The passengers were now given permission to walk up onto the deck, but they received strict orders to stay on the side of the ship facing towards the harbor. There was an excellent reason for this precaution. Occasionally the other side of the ship was hit by bullets fired by Chinese snipers lying in hiding on the opposite shore.[39]

Japanese soldiers waiting on the docks were just mooring the ship when a murderous Chinese machine-gun fire swept the entire area. Sindberg quickly found cover: "The bridge of the ship was virtually covered with sandbags for the protection of the captain, mates and helmsman from stray bullets," Sindberg wrote. "I was able to watch the Japanese soldiers through a hole in the sandbags and witnessed how they, after the first surprise, quickly organized and stormed the building occupied by the snipers, blasting away with revolvers as they ran." After this warm welcome, Sindberg and the other passengers could now relax. However, it turned out to be short pause in the tension. Shortly afterwards they were to witness a far more terrifying scene and be faced abruptly with the naked brutality of the new war.[40]

CHAPTER 4

Death in the Streets

August–September 1937

Sindberg and his fellow passengers were still on board the Japanese ship off the Yangshupu docks when they noticed a row of stooped figures who were being led, tied together and in single file, to the water's edge. It was a group of altogether nine Chinese prisoners, guarded by 10 Japanese soldiers, who had been tasked with putting them to death. Nine of the Japanese were privates and had been assigned the dirty work—one for each prisoner—while an officer was in command. The Chinese were ordered to stop and stoically awaited their fate while the Japanese were running around them, brandishing their swords and bayonets, spitting on their prisoners and showering them with abuse. This was the start of a bloody spectacle, which according to Sindberg himself was the most horrific he had seen to date.

Sindberg wrote in his Shanghai memoirs:

> Upon an order from the officer, one Japanese lined up in front of each of the Chinese to be executed. The officer barked out another order, and each Japanese executioner used his own ingenuity in killing his victim. The first victim was brought down on the edge of the dock by the thrust of the bayonet, then the executioner leisurely drew his sword and decapitated the poor Chinese, the head falling into the river. The executioner then pushed the body over the dock, where it hung in mid-air with blood spurting several feet high.
>
> The next Japanese executioner resorted only to his sword and by "gently" pricking his man he got him to kneel down on the dock. The executioner then severed the rope attaching him to the others. Then, with the nonchalance of a butcher, he took hold of one arm by the hand and with one thrust cut it off at the shoulder. The same "operation" was performed on the other arm. Still not satisfied with his mode of execution, the Japanese pushed the captive over the dock and into the water to see if the poor chap could swim without arms. A similar treatment was afforded to all nine men, [who were killed] in the most barbarous manner that each executioner could devise. Those that were still living after they had been pushed into the water furnished the targets for the officer's revolver practice.

Sindberg later heard from a reliable source what had preceded the gory scene. The nine Chinese men were dock workers employed in this part of the port, which was managed by N.Y.K., the Japanese shipping company. When the battle erupted, they had tried to escape to the International Settlement, but they had not been able to slip past the patrols which the Japanese army had dispatched to monitor enemy activity, and instead they had sought shelter in a building near the docks but had been discovered eventually. They had been accused of being snipers, and without any special legal procedures they had been sentenced to death. "Although we remained quiet our indignation was hardly controllable. We did realize the trouble we would get into if we protested such cruelty," Sindberg wrote.[1]

When Sindberg returned to Shanghai in August 1937, the undeclared war between China and Japan had lasted for six weeks, and from day one it had been waged with shocking disregard of all humanitarian laws. Decades of pent-up frustration and animosity exploded with a ferocity that surprised even jaded war correspondents. In the big city of Tianjin east of Beijing, Japanese bombers had spent days raiding some of the poorest districts in an operation which served no discernible military purpose. "The whole tenement district was a mass of smoke and flames," the American journalist Haldore Hanson wrote. "Women and children ran screaming through the streets."[2]

The Japanese behavior was partly triggered by the irate media at home. Jingoistic journalists focused especially on one incident: shortly after the outbreak of hostilities, Chinese soldiers had taken advantage of the fact that the Japanese garrison had left the town of Tongzhou, not far from Beijing. In the course of a day of protracted carnage, they had massacred all remaining Japanese. When recapturing Tongzhou shortly afterwards, Japanese forces found large numbers of bodies, including those of women and children. Over the following weeks, "revenge for Tongzhou" became a rallying cry for many Japanese soldiers, who committed far worse crimes against Chinese civilians. "The gruesome murder of Japanese women and children is being retaliated a thousand time over," the German diplomat Paul Scharffenberg wrote in a report.[3]

***

Sindberg and the other passengers on board the Japanese ship were unable to move on and were stuck in the Yangshupu docks. Fierce fighting prevented them from driving straight through the streets towards the International Settlement, and the only realistic option was to sail the last bit of the way down the Bund. After they had waited for some time, rescue arrived in the shape of a motorboat, with the Danish flag at the stern, passing by Yangshupu after having inspected undersea cables on behalf of the Great Northern Telegraph Company. The crew agreed to transport the passengers to the Settlement, but since their vessel was rather small, three trips were necessary. "Everyone of us felt a certain thankful reverence towards that neutral Danish flag, which saved us from running fire from either side," Sindberg wrote.[4]

Now finally back in downtown Shanghai, Sindberg had hoped to resume work for the Rifle Syndicate, but to his surprise he found out that the company's office had been closed down. Reluctantly he concluded that he would probably have to leave the city again, but then was informed that the Shanghai Volunteer Corps needed new recruits. It was a force of about 2,000 men, trained and equipped to protect the city's two foreign districts in case of war, rebellion, or other kinds of unrest. After applying, Sindberg was immediately accepted, and as a soldier in C Machine Gun Company he was sent to a camp that the corps had set up in the racecourse in the middle of the International Settlement.[5]

To Sindberg, it was a new world, and then again, not entirely. The boots the recruits were issued were a dull grayish color, and they had to spend hours crouched over them, polishing them until they were a shiny black—an activity where his experience from the Foreign Legion came in handy. The corps was steeped in British military traditions. Commands were in English, and the

Members of the Shanghai Volunteer Corps, which Sindberg joined in August 1937. (Photograph by Malcolm Rosholt. Image courtesy of Me-fei Elrick, Tess Johnston and Historical Photographs of China, University of Bristol)

standard weapon was the Lee-Enfield rifle. The helmets were the flat British type which had been produced by the millions during World War I. Even so, the corps was manned by soldiers from a broad range of countries. There was a Russian, a Portuguese, and even a Jewish unit. The mood was cosmopolitan, as in Shanghai more generally.[6]

Besides its military functions, the corps also provided an opportunity for socializing, as its uniformed members not only engaged in drills and weapons training, but also often met in order to play football, chat, or drink whiskey and soda.[7] There was, however, little time for that in August 1937. Immediately after the fighting had erupted in Shanghai, members of the corps were ordered to man positions along the northern perimeter of the International Settlement. The corps was not to engage in the hostilities in any way but simply ensure that the fighting did not spread to parts of Shanghai managed by foreigners. A great number was posted in the vicinity of Shanghai North Railway Station, where the battle was at its most intense and unforgiving, as the railway formed the main supply line for the Chinese.

Sindberg was deployed in this area on August 21 along with other soldiers from C Company with orders to guard a position known as "Windy Corner." At this very spot, a Chinese soldier, nicknamed "Charlie Chan" by the foreign press, had single-handedly held back a far larger Japanese force during the battle of 1932, earning a propaganda victory for China. "Now action was seen again at the same corner," Sindberg wrote. "We were to help the British soldiers, as enough reinforcements had not yet arrived from Hong Kong. By a mere display of might, which included machine guns and armored cars, we prevented the Japanese from entering the Neutral Zone."[8]

***

Sindberg's unit carried out guard duty in the position for 48 hours straight before being pulled out again. It was not one moment too soon, "there being twenty soldiers among us and room for only four to rest at one time."[9] So when the exhausted soldiers marched back onto the racecourse in the morning of August 23, it was in the hope of a couple of days of peace and quiet. That was not to be. At 1 p.m., the soldiers observed an enormous smoke cloud emerge above the roofs a few blocks away. A few seconds later, the air was filled with the sound of a deafening blast. They all knew what it meant: a bomb had been dropped from one of the Japanese or Chinese planes that constantly flew circles in the sky over Shanghai, and it had exploded in one of the city's busiest shopping districts. The trumpets were sounded, and Sindberg's unit was summoned. A few minutes later, they were on their way to the disaster.

It turned out that the bomb had hit the department stores Sincere and Wing-On. The fire brigade was already there, along with boy scouts and members of "Red Swastika," the Chinese equivalent of the Red Cross, using the ancient symbol not of the Nazis, but of Buddhism. Sindberg's unit was put to work searching Sincere for injured people. They started on the top floor and worked their way down. It was soon clear that anyone who had escaped with light injuries had already managed to walk or crawl to safety, and instead they started looking for the dead and severely wounded, some of whom might still be saved. "I saw an arm extending out from under a sofa," Sindberg wrote. "Thinking there was a body there, I removed the sofa and gasped when I saw only the arm lying there."[10]

On all floors of the department store the bomb had killed both employees and customers, the moments of their death frozen in time. Sindberg describes the corpse of an elderly Chinese woman, who had been accompanied by two small children, and had been about to pay for a parcel: "[They] were all killed instantly. The lady still clutched a bank note in her hand, while on the other side of the counter lay the salesgirl with the old lady's parcel grasped in her hand." Many smaller fires had broken out in different parts of the building and had triggered the sprinkler system, so that the water mixed with the blood of the wounded and ran down the stairs in small, red streams.

When there were no more wounded left in the department store, Sindberg and the other soldiers of his unit were faced with a new task. They were to remove the dead, or what was left of them, from the streets outside. "Here a head, there an arm, and hanging from telephone wires were even intestines, in straggling masses," he wrote, describing the "sickening feeling after realizing you have just been walking in warm human blood." Only towards the end of this macabre work did they notice the body of a Sikh police officer who had directed traffic from a crow's nest several feet above street level and had been perforated with shrapnel. All bodies were placed in several layers on the back of trucks and driven to the city dumps where they were hastily cremated.

The entire operation was an exercise in allowing a huge modern city to carry on its normal routines, even while two large armies were fighting each other with all the destructive power that modern military technology put at their disposal. "Our next duty was to clean the streets of all debris," Sindberg wrote. "Following this the fire department came along and washed the streets completely clean again. Meanwhile the public utilities were right on the scene repairing telephone wires, streetcar lines, gas mains, and mending all necessary equipment for the smooth functioning of a large city. After exactly two hours all communications and order was completely restored, and traffic

Soldiers of the Shanghai Volunteer Corps during the cleanup after the explosion at Sincere department store. The man in front carries a Thompson submachine gun, developed at the end of the First World War. A member of the Chinese boy scouts can be seen in the background. (Photograph by Malcolm Rosholt. Image courtesy of Me-fei Elrick, Tess Johnston and Historical Photographs of China, University of Bristol)

once more flowed freely through Shanghai's busiest intersection, the 'Time Square' of China."[11]

***

The same day that Sindberg was involved in the bloody cleanup work at Sincere department store, the first major turning point in the battle of Shanghai took place. Two Japanese divisions, which had sailed up the Yangtze, carried out a landing operation north of Shanghai and opened up a new front, to the surprise of the Chinese forces. While the Chinese generals had until then been able to concentrate on attacking the Japanese troops holed up in the downtown area, they now had to allocate significant reserves to fighting the newly arrived divisions. This meant that the Chinese lost the initiative, and they were now pushed into a mere defensive position, where they primarily reacted to Japanese actions. The chance of a quick Chinese victory in the Shanghai area was gone for good.

Along with the two Japanese divisions disembarking north of Shanghai, General Matsui Iwane also arrived in the area. He was one of the most complex personalities of the entire war. On the one hand, he was an admirer of China and Chinese culture as well as a political activist who thought that Asia led by Japan should rise and fight back against Western imperialism. On the other hand, he was deeply disappointed with Chiang Kai-shek, especially because the Chinese leader had entered into an alliance with the communists, which he considered a deadly threat to entire region. Matsui was determined to place China under Japanese control once and for all. The conquest of Shanghai

Major parts of northern Shanghai are ablaze, as the fighting between Chinese and Japanese forces spreads to ever more districts. (Photograph by Malcolm Rosholt. Image courtesy of Me-fei Elrick, Tess Johnston and Historical Photographs of China, University of Bristol)

was the first step, but it was not sufficient. As early as in August 1937, the Japanese general was eyeing an even more ambitious objective: the occupation of the capital Nanjing.

While the military situation deteriorated for the Chinese, there was a growing risk that partisans in Shanghai would carry out attacks against Japanese citizens and Japanese assets in the city. Therefore, after the deployment at Sincere, Sindberg's unit was ordered to guard a Japanese cotton factory with about 40 employees in the International Settlement. The soldiers had only just arrived when an incident showed that the threat against the enterprise was very real: a hand grenade was lobbed over the wall surrounding the factory area, immediately setting off panic among the Japanese. However, no one was injured.[12]

The following day, there was renewed drama. Two of the civilian Japanese guarded by Sindberg's unit insisted on leaving the factory by themselves. One of the Japanese men had a revolver hidden in his pocket, and when they were stopped by Chinese police outside the factory gate, he pulled out his weapon and started firing furiously. A Chinese police officer was killed on the spot, while another was wounded and collapsed. Still, he was able to return fire, killing the armed Japanese man while injuring his companion. An ambulance arrived, transporting the two injured men, one Japanese and one Chinese, to a Chinese hospital in the neighborhood. The hospital immediately accepted the Chinese police officer but refused to treat the Japanese man. The ambulance now continued in the direction of a Japanese hospital in the north of the city. On the way, it was stopped by a Japanese sentry, who thought the patient was Chinese, and refused to let the vehicle pass. The driver and his assistant stepped out and placed the patient in front of the sentry. "The sentry, seeing the wounded Japanese, pleaded with the driver to carry the victim to the hospital. This the driver refused to do, and thus the inhuman treatment given out by the Japanese boomeranged with disastrous effect," Sindberg wrote.[13]

***

Driving an ambulance was a dangerous job in Shanghai in late summer of 1937, as 30-year-old Dane Einar Nielsen was to find out. He worked for the company Larsen & Trock during the daytime but had volunteered as an ambulance driver in reaction to the carnage on "Black Saturday." One of his early jobs was to join a young Scottish firefighter in an attempt to rescue an American family that had been caught in the crossfire between the two belligerents. When they had almost reached their destination, they came under fire from Chinese soldiers, who thought the ambulance was full of Japanese people. A newspaper reporter described what happened afterwards: "They had to cower in their seats, while Nielsen tried to drive on, steering by the overhead electrical cable of the tramlines, as he could not see the street. Six rifle shots were fired at the ambulance, and the two men even could see one of the shooters, who was firing his weapon at point-blank range." The expedition had to be abandoned, but others eventually succeeded in rescuing the family.[14]

While ambulance drivers were still needed, the soldiers of the Shanghai Volunteer Corps found towards the end of August that their services were no longer required to the same extent, and many of them were able to return to their civilian occupations. "Still, they keep their uniform on and are ready to be mobilized at an hour's notice," a correspondent wrote.[15] In a way, the prewar daily routines were resumed, but it was to the accompaniment of the constant sound of rifle fire and explosions. "As one gradually gets used to the dangers that one cannot avoid on a daily basis, life in Shanghai has returned to some of its usual patterns, and most have plenty to do with their daily work or volunteer activities," the diplomat Oscar O'Neill Oxholm wrote in a dispatch home.[16]

This was also true for Sindberg, even though the job that he got after this was no less risky. After a couple of days without employment he was hired as a

A British officer helps an elderly Chinese woman to safety during combat just outside Shanghai's International Settlement. (Photograph by Malcolm Rosholt. Image courtesy of Me-fei Elrick, Tess Johnston and Historical Photographs of China, University of Bristol)

driver and was to take new, foreign-made trucks along the 200-mile road from Shanghai to Nanjing, where they were to be used by the Chinese army. The trucks were equipped with foreign flags, and they remained foreign property until they had reached their destination. Still, this was no guarantee against raids by Japanese airplanes en route. At about the same time that Sindberg started in his new position, a car belonging to the British ambassador was shot up by a Japanese fighter plane on the road between Nanjing and Shanghai, leaving the top diplomat seriously injured.[17]

Sindberg knew the risk and found a way to avoid air raids: "Whenever I heard or saw a plane I would quickly drive the truck under some trees and run into the open fields, waiting to see if the plane had observed my movements. For the most part the planes would continue on their way, but at times they would power-dive and strafe the truck. However, I came through without an injury." The trip back to Shanghai from Nanjing was done by train and always after dark, since the railways were just as likely as to the roads to be targeted by the Japanese. In this way, traveling back and forth between Shanghai and Nanjing, Sindberg spent several weeks. Soon it was autumn, and the war continued. A kind of monotonous routine set in, right until the luck that occasionally blessed Sindberg favored him once more.[18]

CHAPTER 5

"My Friend Sindbad"

September–November 1937

When the celebrity journalist Philip Pembroke Stephens arrived in Shanghai in early September, the battle had only been waged for three weeks. Still, the amount of destruction that had been wrought within that brief span of time was enough to shock him. It was as bad as the worst he had seen in Spain, where he had just been reporting on the ongoing bloody civil war. Now the 33-year-old Cambridge-educated Englishman was on his way up the Huangpu River on board a French sloop headed for the International Settlement. As his vessel slowly maneuvered past the Japanese warships anchored along the coastline, he got a first impression of the intensity of the fighting inland. Japanese artillery batteries were firing at Chinese positions beyond the horizon, and the Chinese retorted with shells that landed mostly in the river, some of them only a few yards from Stephens. He also saw injured Japanese being carried on stretchers to transport ships waiting to take them home.[1]

Stephens had flown 10,000 miles along a circuitous route from Europe to Hong Kong to cover the battle for the *Daily Telegraph*. It was one of the longest journeys that any plane had ever been chartered for the single purpose of taking a reporter to his destination.[2] Still, it was worth every penny, according to his editors back in London. Shanghai was the top news item worldwide, and Stephens was the one who could convey it satisfactorily to the avid British readers. He was married with children, but this did not prompt him to run fewer risks. With a law degree, he had clear views of right and wrong, and he did not hesitate to express his opinions in his reporting. His critical pen had put him at odds with the Nazi regime in Germany, and he had been deported for his articles about the rearmament taking place under Hitler.[3] Now the Japanese were in for the same treatment.

Immediately upon arrival, Stephens got a room in Hotel Metropole in the middle of the International Settlement and had hardly settled down before he witnessed a Chinese air raid against the Japanese consulate. "It is dark at 7 p.m. as I write this message amid the roar of aeroplanes and the crash of falling bombs," he wrote. "There was a sudden whizz, and shrapnel hissed past my open window."[4] Stephens did not waste his time. The very next morning he went to the fortress-like Japanese headquarters in northern Shanghai and had breakfast with Captain Fujita Risuburo, chief of staff of the Marines. Fujita told him it was only a matter of time before the forces that had landed north of the city would commence a major offensive, but the supply situation remained difficult. "All the food for the army has to be brought from Japan," he told him.[5] Fujita did not say, but soon the Japanese soldiers would be taking what they needed from the local Chinese civilians. Perhaps they had already started doing so.

As an experienced foreign correspondent, Stephens knew he would need a local guide or, as the journalists themselves called it, a "fixer." It had to be a person who knew Shanghai well, and preferably one with a driver's license, to enable him to move quickly from one hotspot to another. Sindberg sent in an application and was hired along with a Chinese translator.[6] With Sindberg at the wheel of an open crème-colored Chrysler Coupe and Stephens in the passenger seat with a pen and a notebook, the duo became a common sight in the war zone over the next two months. They became close, and Stephens nicknamed his new colleague "my friend Sindbad," inspired by the tales of the adventurer of *One Thousand and One Nights*.[7]

Sindberg also acted as a photographer for Stephens, writing home about his exciting new job as an assistant to one of the world's most prominent war correspondents: "It's dangerous work, but I wouldn't want to swap it for anything else. We work, eat and sleep to the sound of airplanes, bomb explosions and artillery thunder. On quiet days we can hear machine guns and rifles far away. After all, the entire northern part of the city, separated from the city center by a small stream, is a battlefield." On the many trips to the front line, it was also possible for Sindberg to pick up souvenirs. One of them was a grenade weighing in at 10 pounds, which Sindberg decided to take home. For lack of any place to store it, he put it in his bathtub, he explained.[8]

On one occasion, Sindberg's cold-blooded demeanor was all that saved him and Stephens from winding up among the battle's numerous casualties. On a tour of the front line north of the city, they had left their car at the side of the road in order to make a shortcut across some rice fields to the trenches. When they passed a cluster of trees, they saw a group of Chinese soldiers on their way to the rear. "They thought we were Japanese and immediately opened fire on us with their rifles. Having no cover to shield ourselves with, I did

ID used by Sindberg during his work as driver and assistant to Philip Pembroke Stephens in the warzone. The document has been signed by the Danish Consul General Poul Scheel. (Mariann Arp Stenvig)

the only thing possible and ran right at them waving a large white [slip of] paper, which was our permit to travel over that particular territory. This action surprised them and they ceased firing and offered us their profound apologies, which we accepted and continued on our way."[9]

***

In the International Settlement there was a mood of slowly growing unease, and most of the foreign powers had sent in reinforcements. In addition to a number of British troops arriving from Hong Kong, fresh contingents had also been dispatched from the United States, France, and Italy. Altogether 16,000 men in uniform, soldiers as well as police, were guarding the foreign districts. Their job was not only to prevent the battle from spreading from the Chinese parts of the town, but also to ensure internal security. "It ought to be possible to keep order among the enormous group of partly starving Chinese who inhabit or have moved into the international area," the diplomat Oscar O'Neill Oxholm wrote in a report. "The evacuation of these Chinese from

Shanghai is now being attempted in order to limit the danger of an outbreak of infectious diseases as well as minimizing the risk of attacks on foreigners and looting of their property."[10]

Oxholm's words reflected the growing concern that the escalating chaos would entail a heavier burden than initially anticipated. By the first days of October, the battle of Shanghai had raged for nearly two months, and there was still no end in sight. As the Japanese chief of staff had announced in his interview with Stephens, the Japanese forces north of Shanghai went on the offensive in an attempt to cut off the Chinese troops inside the city. This meant that the battle's center of gravity moved to the countryside between Shanghai and the Yangtze River, as the frequent downpour turned the roads into mud and slowed down the Japanese advance. In many places, the battle started resembling the immobile war of attrition which the armies on the Western Front had experienced two decades earlier.

"Artillery and machine gun fire never ceases," Stephens wrote home in one of his almost daily reports. "Soldiers with foot wounds are crawling about on their hands and knees. It is like Flanders in 1914–1918."[11] Sindberg later described in his memoirs of the Shanghai battle how the injured moved out into the middle of the road in a desperate attempt to stop one of the cars passing by and get a ride to a hospital in the rear: "It took a great deal of fortitude to turn them down on our way out to the frontline, but in every instance when we [made] the trip back our car would be loaded with the wounded who had awaited our return."[12]

Stephens also described a situation exactly like this in one of his dispatches to his readers in Britain. One day in early October he and Sindberg had visited Chinese positions close to the front line and were returning to Shanghai when the car was surrounded by a large group of injured soldiers who begged to be given a ride. The most seriously injured were let onto the vehicle, but there were many more who needed help: "Those I had been unable to get in stumbled along behind, trying to clutch the side. One man who had lost an eye staggered after me like a blind beggar, his uniform covered with blood. Another wounded in the foot limped along, using a piece of bamboo as a crutch, crying out for help. But their appeals were in vain. I could take no more."[13]

The car reached the border of the International Settlement just as three Japanese airplanes emerged over the horizon, and at the very moment when the vehicle rolled into safety, heavy explosions could be heard behind it. The arrival in the International Settlement was, however, merely the beginning of a protracted odyssey. The Western sentries were initially unwilling to let

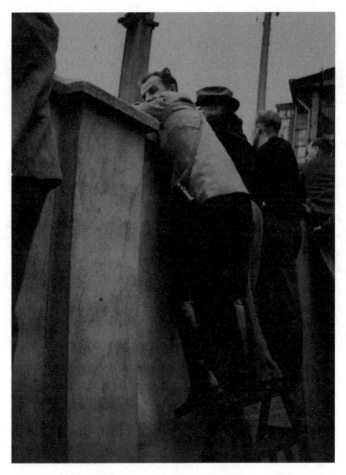

Philip Pembroke Stephens observes the Shanghai battle along with other Westerners. (Bernhard Arp Sindberg Papers and Photography Collection, Harry Ransom Center, University of Texas at Austin)

the car pass with its injured Chinese as it was likely to undermine the image of the Western nations as neutrals in the ongoing war, and only after some persuading was Stephens able to pass. The next challenge was to find a hospital that was not already full. This was impossible, and in the end Stephens was forced to simply drop the soldiers off near the North Railway Station, where they might possibly be able to board a train heading for the rear.[14]

Later in October, Stephens and Sindberg were both on the spot when Japanese artillery had by mistake shot a shell into the International Settlement. It had exploded just outside Honeyland Café, where the 22-year-old British soldier Joseph O'Toole had been enjoying a beer. When the shelling began, the café's Greek owner had tried to persuade his customer to seek shelter.

Philip Pembroke Stephens marches alongside a column of Japanese infantry on the way to the frontline. The large British flag is a safety measure, identifying him as a neutral observer. (Bernhard Arp Sindberg Papers and Photography Collection, Harry Ransom Center, University of Texas at Austin)

"Come on," he said. "This is dangerous. Let's get out." O'Toole had replied: "There's no danger." Those words were to be his last. Immediately afterwards there was a loud blast and smoke filled the room. When the dust settled, the owner saw the British soldier slumped over the table, lifeless, with his intact beer glass still in front of him.[15]

***

Probably the biggest surprise of the entire battle was the tenacity of the Chinese army in and around Shanghai following the initial serious setbacks. China had not won a war in more than a century, but something had happened in the Chinese military in the course of the preceding decade, and the Chinese soldier, previously the object of contempt and ridicule, now suddenly enjoyed unprecedented respect. "The Chinese private soldier," Oxholm wrote in a report, "is honored by all, and the same can be said about the young officers, who have been through the military academies established by Chiang Kai-shek."[16]

Philip Pembroke Stephens' respect for the valiant Chinese soldier also emerged from several of his reports: "Of the many wounded, not one is wounded in the back," he wrote, implying that the Chinese rarely turned around and fled the battlefield.[17] Sindberg was equally impressed by the Chinese soldiers: "The Chinese soldiers were a lot to be greatly admired, as they bravely marched up to the frontlines, signing in cheerful tunes; poorly clothed and carrying heavy loads across their shoulders by means of bamboo poles. All along the way the Chinese reinforcements would see their wounded comrades, yet, rather than being daunted, these pitiful scenes seemed to inspire them to carry on."[18]

The very fact that the Chinese army, apart from a few well-equipped divisions, was shockingly old-fashioned, was a recurrent theme in Stephens' reports. Some of the Chinese soldiers appeared to be "ghosts from the past" with coats of straw and bamboo hats, carrying big old swords. In a report from a nightly operation, he described how they carried "gaily painted Chinese lanterns to guide them over the slippery, muddy tracks."[19] At the end of October, Stephens wrote about a group of Chinese soldiers who wrapped up a desperate fight against the Japanese by withdrawing across the border with

Sindberg visiting Chinese soldiers in their trench near Shanghai. The soldier to the right demonstrates the use of the Czech machine gun ZB vz. 26 against aircraft, while another soldier holds onto the weapon's bipod. (Bernhard Arp Sindberg Papers and Photography Collection, Harry Ransom Center, University of Texas at Austin)

the International Settlement, handing over their weapons to British sentries: "One of the escaping Chinese was a boy of 14, who clutched a sword in his right hand and a hand grenade in his left. He refused to be disarmed, struggling violently with the soldiers. They found that the sword was a toy one of painted wood and returned it to him. In his rage he tried to break it across his knee."[20]

***

Stephens was respected if not feared by his competitors in Shanghai as a correspondent willing to risk everything for a scoop. Similar to Sindberg, he was also notoriously hot-tempered. One evening in early November he returned to his room in Hotel Metropole to find that someone had been through all his belongings. He had a hunch about the culprits, two representatives of a rival Western news organization, and he immediately went looking for them. He found them in the hotel lounge and attacked them physically. A fistfight erupted among the expensive oak panels, attracting a large number of onlookers among the journalists and diplomats at the hotel.[21] One of them described it as a "schoolyard fight" that ended with no serious injury.[22]

At this point in time, Stephens had worked virtually non-stop for two months with only brief breaks in between. He was exhausted both physically and mentally, and the same was true for Sindberg. However, it was clear that their job was approaching an end. The battle of Shanghai would soon be over, and everything pointed towards a decisive Japanese victory. The Japanese had avoided a humiliating defeat with their landing north of Shanghai, and in early November they followed this up with yet another landing, of a bigger scale, south of the city. Tactically, it was a stroke of genius, as it forced the Chinese commanders to divide their resources at a time when they were already stretched thin at the front. There is evidence that Chiang Kai-shek was close to a nervous breakdown when it dawned on him that overnight the Japanese had given themselves a crushing advantage in the battlefield.

Now things started moving fast. In order to avoid being trapped inside Shanghai in a giant pincer movement, the Chinese now had to organize a massive retreat west out of the city. The purpose was to keep as many forces as possible for the defense of Nanjing, which was conceivably the next Japanese target. The retreat started off in an orderly manner, but as the Japanese air raids on the beaten Chinese columns grew in number and intensity, discipline broke down and a wild, disorganized free-for-all erupted, the soldiers scrambling individually and in groups to get to the safety of the rear. Less than a week after the Japanese landing in the south, the Chinese front was dissolving.

The experienced war correspondent Philip Pembroke Stephens shares cigarettes with Japanese soldiers to gain their confidence. (Bernhard Arp Sindberg Papers and Photography Collection, Harry Ransom Center, University of Texas at Austin)

Meanwhile, a small Chinese force stayed on in Shanghai with orders to delay the Japanese advance for as long as possible. The fighting raged through the city's Chinese districts, culminating in the south near the border with the French Concession. Stephens and Sindberg were there, too, on November 11, which also happened to be the 19th anniversary of the end of the Great War. To commemorate the occasion and honor the millions who had died during that global conflict, Stephens wore a red poppy on his left lapel, like many other British citizens on that day.

After having observed fighting near the French Concession, Stephens decided around noon that he would get a better view of the situation from a water tower near the border of the district. Accompanied by Sindberg, he climbed to a concrete platform about halfway up the tower, joining several other spectators who also found it to be an excellent position from which to observe the final moments of the battle. Sindberg later told other journalists what happened next: "All of a sudden, a burst of machine gun fire came from a building around 300 yards south of us. It appeared to be directed at the center of the water tower and lasted about ten seconds. We could not get down because of it."[23]

There was a lull, and the machine gun started firing again. Now Stephens dropped on to his stomach and sought cover behind a concrete pillar, as the machine gun went silent for a second time. "Then came a third attack," Sindberg said. "This was very bad, and I said that it was too dangerous for me. I was sheltering behind a concrete pillar about two feet wide. Bullets were whizzing past me on either side of the pillar... This attack was like hell. Concrete splintered off the structure and bullets clanged in the metal pipes."[24]

Sindberg now noticed a ladder leading to a shaft that ran up inside the tank, and during a pause in the shooting he hurriedly climbed up. At the top of the shaft, he met two French soldiers. "Come up here, Mr. Stephens," Sindberg shouted down the shaft. The British correspondent replied: "I can't. I'm shot in the leg." Seconds later Stephens shouted that he was "Okay." Sindberg wanted to climb down for his colleague and friend, but the two

Chinese soldiers during a lull in the battle with the Japanese at Shanghai, some of them wearing imported German helmets. (Bernhard Arp Sindberg Papers and Photography Collection, Harry Ransom Center, University of Texas at Austin)

Frenchmen restrained him. Forty-five minutes ensued, marked by scattered shooting directed towards the water tower. Then Sindberg heard a French voice from the concrete platform where Stephens was lying. It was a doctor, urging people on the ground to call for an ambulance. Sindberg climbed down and was shocked to see Stephens in the middle of a pool of blood. "He is dead," the French doctor said. The red poppy was still attached neatly to the British journalist's jacket.

Stephens' death on the last day of the Shanghai battle was major news, and Sindberg's testimony, delivered to journalists quickly assembling on the spot, was printed in newspapers all over the world. The Japanese press, too, reported on the incident, also quoting Sindberg. "According to a statement by a Mr. Sindberg, an assistant to Mr. Stephens, made to a member of the Japanese consulate-general, Mr. Stephens and several others were watching the fighting from a platform of a water tower from an elevation of about 50 feet," the English-language newspaper *The Japan Times and Mail* reported two days later, conveniently omitting details about who fired the lethal bullet: "When Japanese troops responded to Chinese shooting from a house about 300 meters to the southwest of the water tower there came a volley of machine gun firing... Mr. Stephens was shot in the leg. A second bullet found his forehead and he died instantly."[25] Another Japanese newspaper, the *Tokyo Nichi-Nichi*, went one step further and reported that Stephens had actually died as a result of injuries sustained during the scuffle with the other journalists some days earlier at Hotel Metropole. *The China Weekly Review* called the Japanese claim "a scandal."[26]

CHAPTER 6

A Capital at War

November 1937

The last day in the battle of Shanghai was also the first day in the battle of Nanjing. On November 11, while Japanese forces weeded out the remaining Chinese pockets of resistance in Shanghai, the Japanese field commander, General Matsui Iwane, issued a fateful order. Instead of much-needed rest, his troops were to begin an advance west, in the direction of Nanjing. In his official remarks, Matsui left the impression that he had not yet made up his mind for or against a new offensive, but the sources indicate that he had actually wanted to expel Chiang Kai-shek from his capital ever since August, when he was sent to the Shanghai front. "This is what I must do," he had said back then.[1]

It would matter greatly both militarily and politically if Nanjing was to fall into Japanese hands. The city, located just south of a dramatic bend in the Yangtze and framed by the Purple Mountain and Lotus Lake to the east, had a population of roughly one million and was the symbol of new China. It had been made the capital of the Chinese Republic in 1927, when Chiang Kai-shek was still in the process of uniting the remnants of the proud, old empire as a modern nation-state under his leadership. The idea of moving the capital from Beijing, which had been the seat of government for centuries, was partly a result of practical considerations. Nanjing was further away from the northern border and therefore less vulnerable to foreign invasion. In addition, it was close to Chiang's power base in his home region. Finally, and perhaps most importantly, it sent off a crucial signal. It marked a new beginning, similar to the Soviet decision to move the capital from St. Petersburg to Moscow, or the Turkish government's move from Istanbul to Ankara.[2]

During the decade that had passed since then, Nanjing had experienced a construction boom, and politicians and officials had moved into new buildings whose size and decoration matched their importance and authority. The Foreign Ministry, to mention just one example, had been built with the advice of New York celebrity architect Henry K. Murphy, making it more

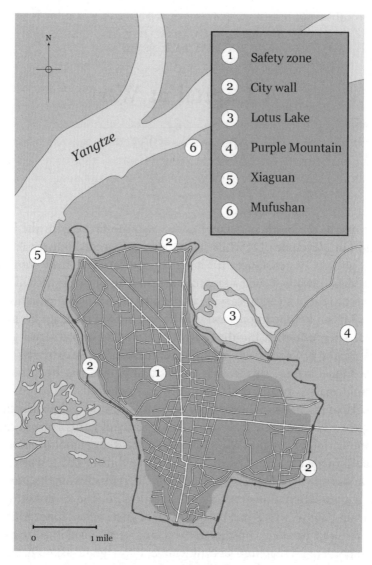

Nanjing in 1937.

modern-looking than Washington's State Department, according to the traveling correspondent of the *National Geographic*.[3] The city also left a deep impression on Jørgen Juncker-Jensen, Sindberg's rival and colleague. "Nanjing was a beautiful city, I thought," he wrote in his memoirs. "The government buildings were impressive, colorful and richly ornamented. The city gate I never got tired of seeing. The avenues were wide and the buildings were far apart. There was something ancient and yet something real modern about it."[4]

While construction of new Nanjing was happening at a brisk pace, large parts of the old city were being demolished. Existing housing, much of it in a decrepit state, was being torn down mercilessly to create more space, with the open Parisian cityscape as the most-cited model. Those who had seen Nanjing just five years earlier would hardly be able to recognize the city now, declared the newspaper *The China Press*. Where before there were narrow streets and alleys there were now broad tree-lined boulevards. More and more large buildings were added, equipped with all modern conveniences, but still retaining the beautiful features of traditional Chinese architecture. Instead of rickshaws and sedan chairs, now it was possible to avail oneself of an efficient bus and taxi service.[5]

In Chinese, Nanjing means "the Southern Capital," reflecting the fact that the city had previously been at the center of the vast Chinese empire. The first emperors of the Ming dynasty almost 600 years earlier had ruled from palaces here and had laid the foundation of a flourishing culture. Now Nanjing was to recover some of its past splendor. The city was not just to be an administrative center, but also to assemble all China's intellectual and creative potential, becoming a "source of energy for the whole nation and a role model for the whole world."[6] Around the mid-1930s, the hard work was coming to fruition. Some of China's foremost scholars, authors, artists, and poets had been attracted to the city, bringing back some of its old status as the nation's "cultural center," *The China Press* said.[7]

Not everything was new and modern in Nanjing in the mid-1930s. The most archaic element in the city's architecture was its medieval wall. It was 20 miles long, 50 feet high, and measured almost 50 feet across. The young German student Erwin Wickert spent long hours walking along the top of this impressive structure during a visit in the summer of 1936, wondering about both what he saw, and what he did not see. Despite years of ceaseless construction, Nanjing still felt somewhat unfinished. In some places it appeared to have an almost rustic character. "Where is the city?" Wickert asked himself. "Here among the foliage, a few office buildings pop up, followed by a few fields, then a street where farmers pull their carts, rickshaws, then the Lotus Lake with a little teahouse on an islet in the middle, gardens, villas, peasant dwellings, hut, and once again fields. No palaces, no old temples, no pagoda."[8]

Those with an intimate knowledge of Chinese history, including Wickert himself, were well aware that the wall was the most visible testimony to Nanjing's violent past. Sometimes the city's defenders had been able to keep attacking armies at bay, and on other occasions they had failed. The most recent siege of Nanjing had taken place as late as 1864. The city had been at

Street scene from Nanjing shortly before the outbreak of the war in 1937. The city on the banks of the Yangtze had been made China's capital a decade earlier, and the government had spent large amounts of money to modernize it in the meantime. (Zhao Lishi)

the center of a successful rebellion, which had spread to several provinces and led to the foundation of a new dynasty, based on a peculiar interpretation of the Christian faith. The Taiping rebellion, as it had been called, had constituted an existential threat to the reigning Qing dynasty, and when the emperor's soldiers had penetrated past the defending rebel armies into the city, they had gone on a killing spree, massacring every man, woman, and child they could find. About 100,000 had lost their lives, Wickert had been told by his host, John Rabe, who was the head of the local branch of the Siemens company. Among Nanjing's oldest residents, quite a few remained in the 1930s with a recollection of these brutal events.

Nanjing remained an unforgiving place. Just as in Shanghai, there was another more sinister reality behind the picturesque facade. It was a shadow world of poverty and misery, which revealed a small part of itself to Wickert. During a walk on the city wall, he passed through a patch of knee-length grass, when he caught sight of a child's bright red cap hidden in the vegetation.

He picked it up and threw it away again immediately in disgust. The cap still contained the half-decomposed head of the child, crawling with fat white maggots. The rest of the body was flattened against the masonry of the wall. Perhaps the child had starved to death, or had succumbed to some treatable disease. No one knew, and no one cared to find out. Nanjing was home to a faceless army of the desperately poor, living in misery as old the Chinese empire itself.[9]

***

The foreign community in Nanjing was significantly smaller than in Shanghai, and according to some estimates, it did not exceed 800 individuals.[10] As the national capital, it was primarily a center of political and diplomatic activity, and it did not entail the same economic possibilities as Shanghai. Only a handful of Danes were present in the fall of 1937. They included Kai Suhr from the Recoil Rifle Syndicate, whom Sindberg had already met, as well as engineer Harald Badstue from the machine manufacturer F. L. Smidth & Co. accompanied by his wife.[11] Most prominent of them all was Johannes Mørch-Hansen, who had lived in China the past 16 years and was employed by Texas Oil Company, or Texaco, as the leader of its Nanjing branch.[12] He had a villa in Luojia Road in central Nanjing, right next to a high-ranking officer by the name of Tang Shengzhi.[13]

While there were not as many businesspeople in Nanjing as in Shanghai, a few stood out. One of them was the Siemens representative John Rabe, a German national. He was old school in his management style, with everything that this entailed. He expected to be obeyed unquestioningly by those below him in the corporate hierarchy, but then at the same time also felt a genuine responsibility towards his staff and their families. Likewise, he wanted to give back to society. On the compound housing his company, called "Siemens City" by the local Germans, he had been one of the most ardent supporters behind the establishment of a small German school.[14]

Generally, it was as if Nanjing attracted a different type of people than Shanghai. While Shanghai was a place you would go to make money, Nanjing was your destination if you had some kind of calling. One example was the American teacher Minnie Vautrin, who had turned Ginling College, a school for women, into her main purpose in life. There were also many missionaries, almost all of them American, motivated by a fervent wish to combine the teaching of the Christian faith with the dissemination of general knowledge. Finally, there was a large number of diplomats. A number of foreign powers, including the United States, Great Britain, and Germany, had moved their embassies to the new capital from the old one, Beijing.

One group of foreigners stood apart from all the others. There was a corps of German officers, most of them on short-term contracts with Chiang Kai-shek's regime to train his army according to modern European principles. The Germans kept to themselves in a special residential area reserved for them by Chiang. It was a kind of miniature Germany, where they mostly socialized among themselves, exchanging gossip about who had been promoted and who had got stuck on the career ladder back home, or entertaining each other with wartime exploits.[15] Many of them were veterans of the Great War and educated their Chinese counterparts in tactical principles that had proved useful on the Western Front from 1914 to 1918. They knew how to make a position virtually impregnable with the copious use of barbed wire and land mines, and it was partly because of their presence that the battle in Shanghai had been so protracted and bloody.

Most of the Germans intended to return home after their contract was up, and therefore they engaged very little with the Chinese society surrounding them. To most other expatriates, however, the relationship with China was more complex. Many had lived in the country for decades. Some had even arrived when there was still an emperor on the throne in Beijing. Still, while China had almost become a second home to them, only a minority had mastered the language. Mørch-Hansen from Texaco spoke fluent Chinese, but he was a rare exception.[16] In this respect, John Rabe was far more typical, according to his compatriot Erwin Wickert: "He was one of the legendary Old China Hands, who were able to speak perfect English without an accent, but not Chinese, and therefore communicated with the Chinese in Pidgin English. Even so, they could think in Chinese. They understood the Chinese. They appreciated and loved them."[17]

***

One evening towards the end of August 1937, the Danish nurse Marie Knudsen sat on a train which was passing by Nanjing just as the city was subjected to a Japanese air raid. "Exploding bombs and anti-aircraft shrapnel formed the most splendid and at the same time most horrifying fireworks imaginable in the night sky," she said.[18] What she witnessed had become part of daily life for Nanjing's citizens. Since the beginning of the battle of Shanghai, the Chinese capital had also been bombed by Japanese aircraft. China's entire military and political leadership was concentrated in Nanjing, which was also a logistical center, so from a strategic point of view it made sense to make the city a primary target. However, several raids were directed squarely at civilian districts.

Japanese bomber en route to Nanjing passes over the mausoleum of Sun Yat-sen, the founder of the Chinese republic. (Japanese press photo)

The first air raid against Nanjing took place on August 15. Japanese planes flew in over the capital in three waves, focusing their efforts on an airfield in the middle of the city as well as a barracks south of the city wall. "The planes flew in formation and very low apparently indifferent to numerous anti-aircraft attacks," U.S. Ambassador Nelson T. Johnson wrote in a report to Washington after having observed all three attack waves from the embassy compound. "No Chinese planes appeared until after the Japanese planes had finally disappeared."[19]

Minnie Vautrin described in her diary on August 27 a night spent sheltering from a Japanese air raid, an experience that was gradually becoming routine.

> Just about midnight and the warning siren sounded and we got up and dressed and went to our trench. Before long we heard the slow, dull thud of the Japanese planes. During the course of the next four hours, it seemed to me that they came over the city six different times. Occasionally we could hear the heavy thud of a dropping bomb. The aircraft guns sounded out at times, but for most of the time there was silence as we listened to the dull sound of the slowly moving, heavy bombing planes.[20]

Spokespeople in Tokyo said afterwards that the attack had been directed at a weapons factory and other military targets, but eyewitnesses reported that many bombs had fallen among civilian homes. "They found many charred bodies in crouching positions in the ruins of what had been miserable mud huts," an American correspondent wrote.[21]

The air raids carried out during the first days of the conflict triggered concern in Nanjing's population about Japan's long-term objectives. In particular, there was a nagging fear that the Japanese would attempt a chemical attack from the air, and sales of primitive gas masks were brisk.[22] Many had done as Mørch-Hansen, the Texaco executive, and sent their families to secure locations before the outbreak of the war, and now others followed suit. As early as on August 16, almost all American women and children were evacuated from Nanjing to safer cities further up the Yangtze,[23] and by the end of the month, most foreigners had left the capital.[24] Many Chinese residents, especially the ones with money, also fled Nanjing, if they had the opportunity to do so, and in the course of the first couple of weeks of war, the city lost about one fourth of its population.[25] The mood was one of near-panic, an expatriate told a journalist: "All rickshaws and all taxis were taken. All day long there was a steady stream of people leaving the city. Furniture, beds, mattresses and birdcages were piled upon rickshaws, and then they would depart for family in the countryside."[26]

No one could survive a direct hit when the Japanese bombs started falling, and therefore most focused on the risk of being injured by the shrapnel of Chinese grenades fired at the incoming aircraft. "The first thing was if you were downtown," explained Badstue, the engineer. "Then you had to run into doorways to protect yourself from shrapnel from the anti-aircraft guns."[27] The same worry prompted the Siemens representative Rabe to dig a shelter in his own garden. "It doesn't protect us against bombs, but at least against shrapnel," he wrote in his diary. He had also got an idea, which he hoped would protect his home against deliberate Japanese attack, as it played on the Japanese fear of damaging foreign property: "In the garden, I have suspended a large piece of canvas, measuring ten times twenty feet, on which we have painted the swastika flag."[28]

After the first days of fierce air raids, the Japanese suddenly stopped, and for a protracted period of time, the air raid shelters of Nanjing were empty.[29] "In Nanjing, everything is peaceful now," Mørch-Hansen wrote in a letter to his mother. "For several weeks we have been spared visits by the Japanese." This did not, however, mean the end of Mørch-Hansen's worries. Due to the crisis situation, the Shanghai-based diplomat Oscar O'Neill Oxholm asked him to be the consulate's unofficial representative in Nanjing, looking after Danish citizens who had not yet left. Mørch-Hansen had allowed engineer Badstue and his wife as well as Suhr from the rifle company to move into his villa, and there was plenty to do, but he ended the letter to his mother on a reassuring note: "I know you can't stop worrying, but I can assure you that have experienced no danger and will not either."[30]

Just a few days later, his words were disproven. On September 19, Admiral Hasegawa Kiyoshi, the commander of the Japanese navy in the Shanghai area, issued a warning that beginning from noon on September 21, Japanese aircraft might attack Nanjing at any time. Therefore, he felt compelled to encourage all foreign officials and citizens in Nanjing and its vicinity to voluntarily move to safer areas.[31] The announcement triggered profound dread among the foreigners who were still in the city. As rumors circulated that this time the Japanese might use gas, a big part of the U.S., French, and Italian embassy staff was moved onto gunboats in the middle of the Yangtze, while other citizens of the three nations were put on steamers and sent upriver.[32]

No Japanese planes appeared in the sky over Nanjing on September 21, allegedly because of poor weather conditions,[33] but on September 22 at 10:10 a.m., less than 24 hours after the end of admiral Hasegawa's deadline, one of history's hitherto largest air raids commenced.[34] Almost 40 Japanese bombers attacked Nanjing and were received by a Chinese defense consisting of both fighter planes and antiaircraft batteries. A Japanese bomb landed near the city wall, almost on top of a shelter. Eight people were killed. Among them was a woman who had been peeping out the entrance of the shelter exactly when the bomb hit. Her head was never found.[35] Mørch-Hansen watched the attack from a hillock near the U.S. embassy and later told the British news agency Reuters that the fire from the Chinese batteries could hardly be any more accurate. "The eyewitness saw two bombers explode high up in the air and fall to the ground engulfed in flames," Reuters wrote. "It was a terrible but also beautiful sight."[36]

***

The Japanese air raid on Nanjing triggered a vehement protest from the U.S. State Department, which described the bombing of civilians as "contrary to principles of law and of humanity."[37] However, this did not move the Japanese to halt their offensive against the city. In the course of the next many weeks, air-raid alarms once again became routine, and a clear sky was no longer welcomed by the inhabitants of Nanjing, as it was also excellent flying weather. In the middle of October, an American professor employed at one of the city's universities remarked that since the Japanese deadline had run out on September 21, every hour with bright weather had spelled an air raid.[38]

Mørch-Hansen still did his best to continue work as the local representative of Texaco, but the war made it more and more difficult. "Our company remains in business, but as we cannot receive new products due to the blockade on the river, it will only be a few months before we have nothing left to sell and must close down the office," he wrote to his mother. "Still, we maintain the hope that the war will be over by then, at least as far as Shanghai is concerned, but of course it is impossible to say anything definite about this."[39] The fighting in Shanghai did indeed come to an end in the middle of November, but any hope that would mean an end to all hostilities in this part of China was soon dashed. By the second half of November, it was clear that the Japanese intended to follow up their victory in Shanghai with a quick campaign aiming for Nanjing.

Japanese war correspondents followed close behind the advancing columns and reported home about one splendid triumph after the other. Neutral foreign journalists, by contrast, had less direct exposure to events on the battlefield after the war moved from Shanghai to the areas west of the city. This was exploited by the Japanese propaganda apparatus, which tried hard to leave the impression of a "clean" war. Japanese are told from childhood not to attack civilians, a military spokesman in Shanghai said.[40] The real situation was entirely different. The Yangtze city of Zhenjiang, which had boasted a population of half a million before the war, was taken by the Japanese in early December, and immediately became the scene of an orgy of destruction and violence. "A river that flowed unceasingly," the factory owner Zhang Yibo wrote about the Japanese, who paraded through the houses again and again in search of objects of the smallest value that they could loot. "Within just a few days of the enemy army entering the city, every house was ransacked, with things strewn about everywhere. Homes no longer resembled homes: they were just trash heaps where there was no place even to step." Soon afterwards, the rapes and the killings began. In the poor districts of the city, the Japanese set the houses on fire to smoke out the women. Men and boys were called up for work duty, and many never returned. Injured Chinese soldiers discovered by the Japanese during their rampage were doused with gasoline and burnt alive.[41]

At the same time, the Japanese military carried out a comprehensive bombing offensive not just against Nanjing itself, but everywhere where it encountered resistance during its march towards the capital. Following suspicions by the intelligence service that a Chinese headquarters had been established in the city of Lishui, a little outside Nanjing, the Japanese commanders assembled a force of 36 bombers and fighters. The air raid was kicked off at noon, while the residents of Lishui were about to prepare lunch. When the bombs started falling, reducing the old city to an inferno, the horror-stricken residents poured out into the streets in the hope of reaching safety outside the city border, but many fell victim to strafing by low-flying aircraft. Altogether 1,200 people were killed.[42]

Rumors of the Japanese atrocities spread quickly, and the inhabitants of areas that had not yet been occupied fled by the hundreds of thousands, if not by the millions. The German correspondent Wolf Schenke was sitting in a Nanjing-bound train, which stopped at a major city en route, and was literally flooded with desperate people: "Like a wave, which finds its way everywhere and fills every space, the crowd of people spread down the entire train. I counted seven people, all carrying a heavy load of luggage, clambering through my train window."[43] Other locals packed their most essential belongings and hit the road in a wretched bid to escape the war. Only a tiny minority had any idea where they were going, the aimless wandering of the faceless masses adding to the nightmarish chaos all along the lower Yangtze.

By now, the Chinese army had largely given up defending the entire area between Shanghai and Nanjing. In early fall, the Chinese generals had still commanded well-educated and expensively equipped divisions and could often count on tactical support from artillery, tanks and airplanes. Now their entire elite had been essentially wiped out in the grueling battle in and around Shanghai, and what was left of Chiang Kai-shek's once-proud army was more in line with foreign prejudices about Chinese military prowess. Typically, they were now units of questionable quality from remote provinces, manned with poorly trained and poorly clothed young men with little idea of what they were fighting for.

In the preceding years, the Chinese military had constructed two defensive lines between Shanghai and Nanjing. One of them had been impressively named "China's Hindenburg Line," referring to a group of defensive positions which the German army had built on the Western Front during the Great War. The two lines never got to constitute any kind of real threat against the advancing Japanese, partly because of plunging morale among the Chinese defenders, Oxholm said in a report home: "These troops have further lost their spirit due to incessant Japanese air raids, and when the good troops withdrew, they did not find reserves that could offer genuine support, but rather looting mobs without any real command. As a result, all the prepared positions had to be abandoned."[44]

Soon the beaten Chinese columns began drifting through Nanjing, withdrawing further west. The German police officer Horst Bärensprung, who worked as an advisor for the Chinese military, described in his diary standing for seven long hours just outside the capital, watching one company after the

A Chinese infantryman prepares to throw his German-designed hand grenade. After months of fighting in the Shanghai area, many of the Chinese army's elite units were a shadow of their former selves. (Photograph by Malcolm Rosholt. Image courtesy of Me-fei Elrick, Tess Johnston and Historical Photographs of China, University of Bristol)

other march past along muddy roads, fleeing the Japanese army: "On their feet they had only straw shoes. No rucksack, no coat, only thin summer uniforms in spite of the chilly wind. Every man had only a piece of canvas or a carpet rolled up and slung across the shoulder. That was all. Our own soldiers are sheer kings by comparison, each with his own rucksack!"[45]

***

As the front moved closer to Nanjing, it became painfully clear that it was mainly the poor part of the city's population that had been left behind. They had no protection against the horrors of war, trapped as the defenseless victims of the soon-to-arrive Japanese army of occupation. A number of foreigners who had still not been evacuated began considering what they could do to help. They were inspired by one of the few bright spots in the stream of bad news arriving from Shanghai. Here the French Jesuit priest Robert Jacquinot de Besange had succeeded during the last days of the battle in setting up a safety zone for the city's civilians. Within a brief period of time, 100,000 men, women, and children had moved into the zone, which had largely been respected by all belligerents.[46] A similar arrangement might work for Nanjing as well.

A group consisting of American, British, and German citizens, as well as a single Dane, Mørch-Hansen, met on November 22 in Nanjing to establish a committee with the purpose of preparing a safety zone as soon as possible.[47] Mørch-Hansen was deeply involved from the outset. "Together with a few other foreigners I have been working on a plan to get the agreement from both the Chinese and the Japanese government to set aside one of the city's districts as a neutral zone," he wrote in one of his letters to his mother. With some pride he explained that he had been offered to head the committee but had turned it down: "The committee absolutely wanted me to serve as chairman, but I declined, as I didn't want to feel compelled to stay if my duties required me to go elsewhere."[48] Instead, the job went to John Rabe.

At this early stage, the committee members were not primarily worried about the Japanese army, which still had a reputation for its strict, Prussian-type discipline. Rather, they were concerned about the Chinese military, which tended to become unpredictable once the officers lost control of their troops. "Attacks by Japanese airplanes and artillery were not the primary fear. That danger was nothing compared with what was to be expected from the deluge of retreating Chinese troops," the German correspondent Schenke wrote. He described the bad impression some of these troops had left on the foreign residents of Nanjing earlier that fall when they passed by on their way to the battle of Shanghai. "They looked like half-bandits, and that's what they were. During earlier civil wars it had been the order of the day that Chinese soldiers, especially beaten armies withdrawing from the battlefield, would extort, rob and loot the civilian population," Schenke wrote, imagining what could be expected now: "Would their anger and their hatred not be channeled towards white people? The old xenophobia would probably emerge again."[49]

Under Rabe's energetic leadership work on the zone progressed at a brisk pace, and during the first week of December it gradually took form. It covered roughly one eighth of the entire area inside the city wall, and like the rest of Nanjing it was a mixture of districts with dense urban habitation interrupted by spots left vacant for future construction, which still came across as being almost rural.[50] Neither the Japanese nor the Chinese authorities were enthusiastic about the whole concept. The Japanese, who now had come down decisively in favor of occupying Nanjing, announced that they would respect the zone, but they would not recognize it officially. Probably they predicted that they would soon take over Nanjing, and the existence of an area outside their control would undermine their authority as the occupying power in all of east China. It was a bigger surprise that the Chinese officers, too, were lukewarm towards the idea of the zone. They predicted that a large part of Nanjing's civilian population would escape into the zone after the arrival of the Japanese. Instead, the officers thought, they should stay put and assist the army in its bitter fight against the enemy.[51]

In contrast to the resistance from the Chinese officer corps, the inauguration of the zone was welcome news for Nanjing's civilians. When the local press published the plans in early December, the Japanese troops were closing in on Nanjing's city wall, and a large number of civilians decided to move into the zone. "All the roads leading here are dotted with groups moving whatever possessions they can and with whatever they can," the American missionary Ernest H. Forster wrote to his wife. "Tireless rickshaws, some even drawn by students, wheelbarrows, trucks, baby carriages, anything with wheels on it."[52] Some Chinese soldiers also moved in and started digging trenches inside the zone area. This was potentially disastrous as it undermined the entire raison d'être of the zone as a demilitarized area and could give the Japanese an excuse to enter following their occupation of the city. And if that happened, the last defense the Chinese civilians had against abuse would be gone.[53]

CHAPTER 7

A Very Dangerous Job

November 30–December 1, 1937

In the evening of December 1, 1937, the Danish Consul General Poul Scheel was the host of a dinner party in his apartment in Grosvenor House, a palatial structure across from Shanghai's Canidrome, the city's special tracks for dog racing.[1] Among those invited were Niels Jensen, the top representative of Danish engineering company F. L. Smidth in China, as well as Okazaki Katsuo, a Japanese diplomat who had participated in the 1924 Paris Olympics as a middle-distance runner.[2] When it was time to eat, the two guests were seated next to each other. The conversation flowed in a pleasant manner and did not just revolve around the war. It turned out that Okazaki's father was friends with one of F. L. Smidth's most important Japanese customers, a cement manufacturer, and that the Japanese diplomat himself had been close to entering the cement business, but in the end had opted for the foreign service instead. As was often the case in Asia, it was important to find a personal connection in order to break the ice.

In fact, the purpose of the dinner party was anything but just social, and it was no coincidence that Niels Jensen had been seated next to Okazaki. Scheel was a close friend of Jensen's and he had orchestrated this so that his compatriot would get an opportunity to talk to the important Japanese. For as a matter of fact, Jensen had an agenda. It was about one of F. L. Smidth's most ambitious projects in China to date—a brand-new cement factory near Nanjing, which had now ended up in jeopardy because of the war. As one of the diplomats that had been picked to travel to Nanjing in the immediate aftermath of the impending fall of the city, Okazaki was potentially of great importance in this respect.[3] In the course of the evening, Niels Jensen managed to explain the broad outlines of the case—or at least aspects of the case that he wished to acquaint his Japanese counterpart with.

The factory, Jiangnan Cement, was located 14 miles east of Nanjing, Jensen told the Japanese diplomat. It was directly in the path of a Japanese

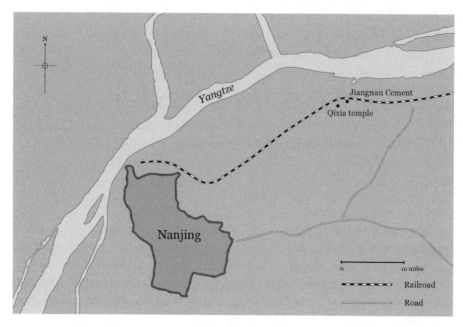

The Nanjing region in 1937.

column which had been moving along the southern bank of the Yangtze since mid-November, heading for Nanjing. It would only be a few days before the first Japanese troops would arrive in the area, and everything suggested that the Chinese forces, with their backs to the wall, would put up a desperate fight to delay the Japanese advance. Construction of the cement factory had lasted for the preceding two years, with F. L. Smidth in charge of delivering the machinery, Jensen said. Since the plant was not yet operative, the Danish company had still not received the full payment from its Chinese customer. If the factory was to be destroyed in the upcoming battles, it might very well be that it would never see the money.[4]

The day after the dinner party, Consul General Scheel followed up on the case. He was the right person to approach the Japanese, having acted as a senior diplomat in Tokyo from 1928 to 1930 and receiving the Order of the Rising Sun Third Class,[5] and in a letter to the Japanese consul in Shanghai, Okamoto Suemasa, he described the status of the factory. "I ask for your kind intermediary, in order that the appropriate Imperial Japanese military authorities may be advised of the great Danish interest in the Jiangnan Cement Works," he wrote. "As you will be aware, Messrs. F. L. Smidth & Co. are well known all over the world, and have also for many years supplied cement making machinery to Japan, and it is therefore my earnest hope that the Imperial Japanese military authorities may do the utmost to take all necessary measures, so that damage to the factory may be avoided."[6]

***

Jiangnan Cement was designed to become an emblem of industry in the Yangtze valley, with a capital of 4.5 million dollars, an area of 380 acres, and a projected output of 5,000 barrels of cement a day.[7] The project was so large that it contributed to a decision by Nanjing's power company to triple its capacity.[8] Jiangnan Cement was located just south of the railroad linking Shanghai and Nanjing, close to Qixia Train Station,[9] and an ancillary line was built all the way up to the factory gate to facilitate the transport of the cement.[10] The factory was a central element in China's endeavor to become a modern nation, giving it both economic and political significance—and F. L. Smidth had positioned itself as a central actor due to its involvement in the construction.

A special shareholding company had been established for Jiangnan Cement in May 1935, featuring as its major shareholder Chee Hsin Cement, China's biggest cement manufacturer headquartered in the city of Tianjin near Beijing. The factory was a national priority due to the fact that cement was considered a strategic resource, essential for the construction of not just bunkers, fortresses, and other military installations, but also critical infrastructure such as bridges, harbors, dams, and tunnels. It was no surprise, then, that Jiangnan Cement had close connections to the nation's political elite and did nothing to hide it. The post as chairman of the board was handed to the politician Yan Huiqing, who had been prime minister for a brief period and also, in 1913 right after the collapse of the empire, had been the newly founded Chinese Republic's first ambassador to Germany, Sweden, and Denmark.[11]

"This factory is, in my opinion, essential for F. L. Smidth's future in China," argued Erik Nyholm, who had a job as a local representative for the Danish company at the same time as he was busy selling the Madsen machine gun to the Chinese army.[12] Nyholm was known throughout F. L. Smidth for his extensive network of contacts in China, and they had been put to good use in 1935, when Chee Hsin Cement was still in the process of planning the Jiangnan project and had not yet made up its mind if it wanted to use machinery built by F. L. Smidth, or rival products from the German company Polysius. In his correspondence with the F. L. Smidth management, Nyholm described how his efforts to create the necessary level of confidentiality with his Chinese counterparts had required "endless whiskeys and sodas at Chinese dancing halls and at less respectable Chinese houses with virgins."

Chee Hsin Cement's management, accompanied by engineers, during an inspection tour in the mid-1930s of the area near Nanjing where Jiangnan Cement is to be built later. (FLSmidth Archives, Valby)

He also pointed out that during meetings with the Chinese, he made sure to sit next to Niels Jensen so he could step on his foot when he was about to make a faux pas. "Unfortunately," Nyholm added, "I had to use this signal very often."[13]

Niels Jensen was newly arrived from Denmark in 1935, and according to Nyholm, he tended to decline every proposal, causing negotiations to end in gridlock. Nyholm may, however, have exaggerated Jensen's flaws as a negotiator, as would soon emerge. His most important counterpart on the Chinese side was Chee Hsin Cement's chief engineer Wang Tao, described by Nyholm as "exceedingly clever and straight [with] all the virtues of the Chinese and apparently none of their faults."[14] The problem was that Wang Tao had received his education in Germany, which could make it hard to persuade him to select a Danish product rather than a German one. Jensen understood that completely, and he decided to take Wang Tao on a tour of factories in Japan that had bought F. L. Smidth's machines. "It is undeniable that you get closer when you travel together for several days," Jensen wrote to his boss. "It is my hope that Wang Tao will have so much influence that our personal acquaintance can become useful."[15]

Chinese workers during construction of Jiangnan Cement, circa 1936. (FLSmidth Archives, Valby)

He may have been right. In the spring of 1935 Chee Hsin Cement opted for F. L. Smidth over Polysius. It may also have helped that the Danish company had spent 300 British pounds on presents to its Chinese partners. These were not bribes, Nyholm emphasized, but "our expression of appreciative friendship for those who gave us help." Even though Polysius had lost its bid, the project maintained a certain German element, since Siemssen & Co., a German trading firm with almost a century of experience in the Far East, delivered engines and other electrical equipment produced by the Berlin-based manufacturer Allgemeine Elektricitäts-Gesellschaft.[16] When the partners completed the contract, the conditions of F. L. Smidth's participation were fixed in a way that no one paid much attention to at the time. The Danish company was to receive 80 percent of its pay on the handover of the factory, with the balance to be paid over a five-year period. Both the German participation and the 20 percent credit were to prove fateful.[17]

**

It was in order to work on construction of the cement factory that the engineer Harald Badstue was present in Nanjing in 1937. He had arrived with his wife in May 1936, and by the time war broke out one year later, he had almost completed his stint for F. L. Smidth, just as a representative of Allgemeine Elektricitäts-Gesellschaft was also wrapping up the installation of the German-produced apparatuses.[18] When the first air raids against Nanjing began in August, it was a nerve-wracking experience for Badstue to drive to the construction site outside the city every morning and watch the downtown explosions from a distance. "As my wife and several acquaintances remained in Nanjing, it was with a certain trepidation that I saw the Japanese pass by overhead heading for Nanjing, and after each air raid I made a phone call to hear what had happened," he said.[19]

When after the long interruption in the air raids the Japanese warning of a resumption of the attacks was disseminated on September 20, Badstue only heard the news after he had returned home from the factory late the same evening. As a result, during the night between September 20 and 21, he called F. L. Smidth's office in Shanghai informing his colleagues there that the Japanese had urged all foreigners in Nanjing to leave the city. He added that he had not had the opportunity to discuss the situation with his Chinese colleagues, who all stayed in the factory compound. The representative of F. L. Smidth responded by giving him full discretion to use his own judgment about how to act, and shortly after daybreak on September 21, he departed Nanjing along with his wife and other foreigners, sailing up the Yangtze on board a steamship owned by the trading firm Butterfield & Swire, headed for the big city of Wuhan.[20]

The steamer that Badstue was on had only got about 10 miles up the Yangtze when the crew and passengers listened to radio reports about the Japanese air raid, which had taken place as announced. Even though it had been serious, it had apparently been less destructive than feared initially, and the ship turned around, returning to Nanjing on September 24. However, Badstue remained worried that the war would engulf the Chinese capital, and after having obtained permission from F. L. Smidth in Shanghai he decided once more to leave Nanjing. This time he also succeeded in reaching one of his colleagues at Jiangnan Cement, Thomas K. Yu, who reluctantly gave his green light for the Dane's departure, and on September 25, he sailed with his wife from Nanjing to Wuhan.[21]

Thomas K. Yu was relatively far down the hierarchy, but further up the corporate ladder at Chee Hsin Cement's headquarter in Tianjin, there was intense dissatisfaction with Badstue's decision to desert his post. While F. L. Smidth favored delaying the opening of the cement factory until a time in the future when the situation had settled down and the war might even be over, Chee Hsin Cement demanded that Badstue return immediately to Jiangnan Cement, so that the factory could become operational as soon as possible. The Chinese government desperately needed cement in the Nanjing region, and if Chee Hsin Cement was not able to deliver, the orders would go to its competitors instead. The Chinese executives' frustration with Badstue was only intensified by the fact that the German representative of Allgemeine Elektricitäts-Gesellschaft had stayed at Jiangnan Cement and had finished his work before permitting himself to be evacuated. The old Danish–German rivalry put extra pressure on F. L. Smidth. "As we have always used every opportunity to impress upon the Jiangnan people the service we give them, we were very anxious to avoid that our good relations should be jeopardized," Niels Jensen wrote in a report to Copenhagen.[22]

While Badstue waited in Wuhan, protracted negotiations between F. L. Smidth and Chee Hsin Cement took up most of October, revolving around the conditions for the Danish engineer's continued work on the factory near Nanjing. A special bone of contention was the amount of money Chee Hsin Cement would have to pay to Badstue or his family if he was hurt. Only at the end of the month did they reach an agreement. Chee Hsin Cement promised to set aside a sum of 6,000 pounds which would be paid out if Badstue was either killed or injured so seriously that he would never again be able to work. On October 31, Niels Jensen sent a telegram to Badstue, inquiring if he was willing to return to Jiangnan Cement, "as I emphasize," Jensen added, "that F. L. Smidth does not put pressure on you in any way if you have the slightest concern, and that it will not impact your position in our company if you feel that you cannot go."[23] Badstue replied after a few hours: "Ready to go. Stop. Depart immediately."[24] That evening he and his wife were on their way down the Yangtze towards Nanjing.[25]

***

Amid the ongoing war, all travel was difficult, and it was five days before Badstue returned to the factory.[26] The plan was for him to meet up with Chee Hsin Cement's chief engineer Wang Tao, who was to arrive from the headquarters in Tianjin via Shanghai to carry out the last trial run of the machinery in cooperation with the Dane. However, Wang Tao did not get further than Shanghai before the Japanese had won the battle of the city, and the entire plan for the cement factory was overtaken by events on the ground. "The general opinion was that when the Japanese had driven the Chinese forces away from Shanghai, the Japanese would make a halt and probably start negotiations with the Chinese," Niels Jensen wrote in a report to F. L. Smidth in Copenhagen. "Contrary to expectations, the Japanese, however, pushed violently towards the capital, and it is now generally held that the Japanese will not stop before they have seized Nanjing. If that is the case it will be practically impossible to start the works."[27]

Large resources went into building the Jiangnan Cement factory, which was seen as having national importance. In this photo taken during construction, the Yangtze river can be seen in the distance. (FLSmidth Archives, Valby)

Chee Hsin Cement's management agreed and abruptly abandoned the idea of starting up production at Jiangnan Cement. During the days that had passed, Badstue had completed his work at the factory, and there was nothing left for him to do. On November 17, Niels Jensen wired a permission for him to leave Nanjing,[28] and the very next day, Badstue was on his way to Shanghai.[29] Here F. L. Smidth arranged for his onwards journey via northern China and the Trans-Siberian Railroad to Europe. "It is of course to be regretted that Jiangnan could not at an earlier stage be induced to give up the start of the factory, but we must admit that at the time when the arrangement as to protection and compensation to our man was made, Jiangnan might with some right maintain that it looked as if the start could actually be carried out," Niels Jensen wrote.[30]

Wang Tao hurried back to Tianjin to consult with the other members of Chee Hsin Cement's management and then returned to Shanghai on November 30. Now it was no longer a question of whether to initiate production or not. The top priority was to salvage as much as possible. It was important to protect the plant against acts of war, and at the same time prevent a Japanese takeover. In Chee Hsin Cement's opinion, this might be achievable if the Japanese were led to believe that the factory was partly foreign-owned. It was now only a matter of a few days before the Japanese vanguard reached Nanjing, and time was of the essence. Wang Tao immediately met with representatives of the German partner Siemssen & Co., which agreed to a measure of creative accounting to make its role seem bigger than it actually was. Even though the Germans had largely received all the payments that were due because of their work on the cement factory, they were willing to collude with Wang Tao to retroactively change the original contract to make it appear as if they were still owed money, and that part of the plant had been provided as security for eventual payment.

Shortly afterwards, Wang Tao met with Niels Jensen to suggest a similar arrangement. More specifically, the Chinese engineer wanted to get around the part of the original contract from 1935 which guaranteed that F. L. Smidth would receive 80 percent of the payment upon completion of the project, with the other 20 percent to be paid out after five years, or 1941. Wang Tao intended to do this by tearing up the old contract and replacing it with a forged document which allegedly committed Chee Hsin Cement to paying the remaining 20 percent as early as in the summer of 1937. This was to support a fictitious narrative in which Chee Hsin Cement had failed to pay the 20 percent and instead given F. L. Smidth shares in the factory, which consequently became partly Danish-owned.

It is possible that Niels Jensen, as claimed by Erik Nyholm, was in the habit of saying no to everything, but at least this one time it was an advantage. He declined participation in Wang Tao's imaginative scheme, thus in all likelihood averting a major scandal, which could have cost F. L. Smidth dearly. Forgery was not an activity that F. L. Smidth engaged in and would have severely harmed its cooperation with the Danish consulate in Shanghai. Oscar O'Neill Oxholm, who was very well familiar with the details of the contract, including the late payment of the last 20 percent, would have noticed it immediately if the agreement had been changed. The Danish diplomats could not be counted on to offer their support for F. L. Smidth's activities in China unless it kept a completely clean record of conduct, Niels Jensen argued. "Furthermore," he wrote, "we felt sure that as Mr. Wang Tao had told us openly about the readiness with which the Germans were willing to assist Jiangnan by signing a made-up agreement, he would likewise inform the Germans if our firm agreed to his suggestion, and as we never know if the Germans might some time later on use this against us, we wanted very much to find a solution whereby we did not commit ourselves in any way."[31]

Besides, it was almost a given that the Japanese would see through the fraud, in which case F. L. Smidth's business not just in China, but also in Japan might be at risk. F. L. Smidth's Japanese interests were not a subject that Niels Jensen wished to broach with Wang Tao at a time when China was involved in a life-and-death struggle with Japan, and therefore he merely told him he thought it was necessary to adopt a different approach. The Danish businessman agreed to formulate a counterproposal to be delivered the following day at the latest. It was a race against time, as he was painfully aware of the dilemma he had been placed in. Saying no to Wang Tao might mean that F. L. Smidth would have to leave China for good. Siemssen was also an agent for F. L. Smidth's German rival Polysius, which might conceivably be given privileged access to the Chinese market if the Danes failed to provide sufficient backing. Or, as Niels Jensen phrased it, the Chinese "would not look upon us as straightforward people who refused to enter into any [dubious] agreement, but would remember us as those who let them down when they were in trouble."[32]

Niels Jensen met with Oxholm the same evening and provided him with all the details, including the Sino-German plan to commit forgery. Oxholm agreed that the scheme was unlikely to succeed and pointed out that other similar attempts to transfer Chinese property to foreign ownership were already taking place in a major way, especially with German or American participation, and that consequently, the Japanese had stopped altogether wasting any time on that type of transaction. "We were already convinced that the only feasible arrangement would be to stick to the facts as they were, and then try to make the best of it," Niels Jensen wrote in a subsequent report. "And the facts are that we have an outstanding amount of 20% of the order sum which amount is not due until 1941, and which it is in our interest to try to secure and protect in every possible way." F. L. Smidth shared the same top priority as Chee Hsin Cement, which was to safeguard the factory, and "the only way in which we could do anything to this end, would be to notify the Japanese military, naval and consular authorities about our interests in the plant."[33]

***

Oxholm promised to use all available diplomatic channels to inform the Japanese authorities about the status of the factory. He also suggested emphasizing to the Japanese that the factory had not yet started producing cement so that they might get the impression that F. L. Smidth had not yet handed it over to the Chinese owners. In addition, Oxholm had one last suggestion: "He furthermore considered it advisable that there be a Dane stationed at the factory as a kind of supervisor, and so that the Danish flag might be hoisted near to his house at the works," Niels Jensen wrote in his report. "It would of course be a very dangerous and exposed job to stay up at the works during the advance of the Japanese troops, especially as the works is situated very near to the fortified zones."[34]

Fortunately, a suitable candidate for the assignment was readily available, most likely brought up by Oxholm himself: Bernhard Sindberg. After his previous employer Philip Pembroke Stephens had been killed by a Japanese bullet, he had been out of a job, and besides he had exactly the qualities that were needed. Niels Jensen described the new employee in his report to headquarters in Copenhagen: "Mr. Sindberg has previously been in the Foreign Legion, and he has been working as a chauffeur for Mr. Pembroke Stephens, the English journalist who was recently killed in the French Concession... He is a young chap at about 30, and is somewhat of a rough-neck and a die-hard."[35] Even though Sindberg's violent proclivities caused some hesitation among F. L. Smidth's management, Oxholm explained that there was not really a choice: no other Dane would be prepared to go to Jiangnan Cement in the current conditions.[36]

Niels Jensen met with Wang Tao the day after, on December 1. Earlier in the morning, Wang Tao had spoken with the Germans' lawyer, collaborating on a first draft of the falsified contract. Niels Jensen saw the document and was surprised at how amateurish it looked. "We perused this draft, but it was made in such a way that it was in our opinion only too obvious that the whole arrangement had been cooked up so as to protect the Chinese interests," he wrote. "It is evident that no Chinese would in these days sign such a document whereby they transfer part of their plant to a foreign firm unless it were actually to protect the Chinese interests."[37]

Wang Tao immediately gave in and acknowledged that it made more sense to be upfront about the entire issue, but at the same time emphasize as strongly as possible that foreign interests were at stake at Jiangnan Cement. The German-educated engineer was in no doubt that it was particularly important to signal that German business was involved with the factory. The relationship between Berlin and Tokyo was improving fast, and while Japanese soldiers might not be held back by the sight of a Danish flag over Jiangnan Cement, a German swastika would certainly make them pause. It was also on Wang Tao's insistence that Sindberg was to be joined by a German representative. His choice was the engineer Karl Günther, who already was closely connected with Chee Hsin Cement through a cousin, G. Schultz, who had excellent personal ties with the management of the Chinese company.[38] Günther, born in 1903, was the son of a German factory manager who had built up a tense relationship with F. L. Smidth over the years. Given this history, it is unlikely that the Danish enterprise thought he was a suitable candidate, and it did not get any better after Günther, in his first meeting with the Danes, made the impression of being "a rather quarrelsome type."[39] However, he was born in China and understood the culture better than most while also speaking the language fluently. And most important of all: Chee Hsin Cement wanted him.[40]

Later on the same day, before the dinner party in Poul Scheel's apartment, Niels Jensen met with Sindberg for the first time and introduced him to the new job, stressing that he had to commit himself for as long as the war lasted. He "was more than anxious to take the job," Niels Jensen reported. The salary was 100 British pounds a month for at least two months, paid for by Jiangnan Cement. "We furthermore made it very clear to him that in consideration of the very big salary he was to receive, he would have no claims either on the Chinese or on us in case he was killed or disabled, and Mr. Sindberg was perfectly willing to take the job on those conditions."[41] Immediately afterwards he signed a contract which explicitly stated that his stay at Jiangnan Cement would be "entirely at my own risk."[42]

For Sindberg, who had been forced to make do with no steady income for the preceding three weeks and was staring at the prospect of returning to Europe empty-handed, this was excellent news. The salary—about 50 times the current value of 100 pounds—was huge for someone like him with no real education.[43] Besides, the money was sorely needed. The evidence suggests that Sindberg was toying with the idea of getting an education in the United States and had started considering how this could be financed. The money was to remain in Shanghai until he returned. If he was killed, the Danish consulate in the city was to see to it that the money was transferred, in two equal amounts, to each of his divorced parents.[44] Even though he was not offered a life insurance, Sindberg was enthusiastic. He wrote a letter home just after he had got the new job and mentioned "the handsome pay": "It's very dangerous, but if it goes well, it will have been worth the risk."[45]

CHAPTER 8

Journey to the Heart of Darkness

December 2–5, 1937

Sindberg and Günther left Shanghai at dawn on December 2, while both the Danish consulate and F. L. Smidth did their utmost to minimize the risk that the buildings and machines at Jiangnan Cement were damaged. On the same day, Scheel wrote to the Japanese consul, Okamoto: "There is a Danish supervisor, Mr. B. A. Sindberg, in charge of the factory, and no Chinese military are at present there or will be admitted to same."[1] At the same time, Niels Jensen did what he could to prepare Sindberg for the delicate task ahead, as he explained in a report to his superiors: "Before his departure we gave Mr. Sindberg strict instructions not to interfere with the Japanese if they take possession of the factory, but only to inform them that he is staying there in charge of our interests. We had to make this clear to Mr. Sindberg as he is somewhat of a roughneck, who might be likely to take to force and thereby get himself into serious trouble. We have furthermore told Mr. Sindberg that if the Japanese order him to leave the factory, he will have to comply with their orders, and if they should haul the Danish flag down, he will simply have to let them do it."[2]

Sindberg and his new German colleague had a risky journey ahead of them, and to overcome some of the hazards, they were accompanied by two Chinese men. One of them, Yan Liufeng, spoke Japanese and had been offered up by Chee Hsin Cement. The other, Li Yulin, acted as a translator between English and Chinese and was also very familiar with the route to Nanjing.[3] Knowledge of facts on the ground was not just necessary, but could save lives. Due to the Japanese advance and the fighting in the area east of Nanjing it was no longer possible to take the fastest route by either train or car from Shanghai. It was also no longer a viable alternative to sail straight up the Yangtze, partly because of hostilities taking place on the river, partly because the Chinese navy had sunk a large number of vessels across the river in one of its narrowest spots in order to prevent Japanese warships from sailing west towards Nanjing.

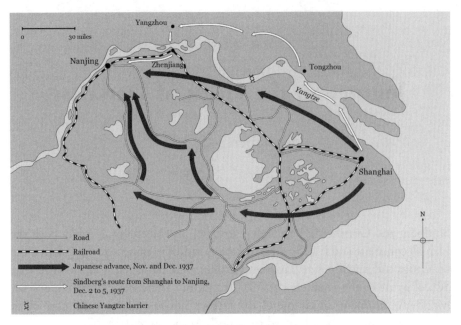

Nanjing and the lower Yangtze area in 1937.

Instead Sindberg, Günther, and their two Chinese companions were forced on a difficult detour, prolonging the journey by several days. Like everyone else attempting to reach Nanjing in the period after the fall of Shanghai, they had to cross the Yangtze and disembark on the northern shore, moving west until they had reached a point where they had overtaken the Japanese forces marching towards Nanjing south of the river.[4] The inhabitants north of the river were not used to the sight of foreigners, other than the odd Christian missionary, but this had changed because of their location along the emergency route between Shanghai and Nanjing that had now appeared. When new boats with foreign travelers arrived in the harbor of Tongzhou[5] on the river's northern shore, the residents were greeting them with complacent smiles "convinced that their city, and by extension they themselves, had gained in reputation and importance," wrote a German correspondent, who was passing through at about the same time.[6]

For Sindberg and the three others, the journey went anything but according to plan, and if it had not been for the Chinese translator Li Yulin, it is highly unlikely that they would have ever reached their destination. Hardly had they arrived in Tongzhou when they realized that no tickets were available for vessels undertaking the onwards journey west. Only with great effort and all his powers of persuasion was Li Yulin able to get four seats on a boat that plied a complicated route through a network of small streams and canals, taking them

Sindberg with his Chinese translator Li Yulin. (Bernhard Arp Sindberg Papers and Photography Collection, Harry Ransom Center, University of Texas at Austin)

to the city of Yangzhou, also on the Yangtze's northern shore. In Yangzhou he borrowed a car from an acquaintance and was able in this way to transport Sindberg and the others the last bit of way to a Yangtze ferry readying for departure. They now traveled back across the river to the southern shore and arrived in the city of Zhenjiang, which was in a state of upheaval. The Japanese forces were only a few miles away, approaching at a rapid speed, and a large part of the population was fleeing. Once again Li Yulin proved irreplaceable, as he managed, in time-honored Chinese style, to use the services of friends

Major parts of northern Shanghai had been reduced to rubble when Sindberg left the city in early December 1937. (Photograph by Malcolm Rosholt. Image courtesy of Me-fei Elrick, Tess Johnston and Historical Photographs of China, University of Bristol)

and acquaintances to get a hold of tickets on the last train out of Zhenjiang bound for Nanjing.[7]

Yan Liufeng, the Japanese interpreter, later wrote in a report to his employers at Chee Hsin Cement about the pervasive chaos that accompanied the four travelers during their long and exhausting trek. Following the defeat in Shanghai, he explained, thousands upon thousands of Chinese tried desperately to flee to the west, creating bottlenecks everywhere: "There were large concentrations of Chinese troops, and the civilian refugees created serious traffic jams. The canals were jammed with boats, and the roads with vehicles. The panic was only made worse by Japanese air raids. There were control posts and constant obstacles," he wrote, and then continued, evidently wishing to please his bosses: "We had to face numerous difficulties, and on more than one occasion we were left with severe scares. Still, duty called. We braved all hardship, prepared to sacrifice everything, and without shrinking back from any danger we eventually reached the factory."[8]

Nearly four days had passed since the departure from Shanghai, and by the time Sindberg and his three companions finally arrived at Jiangnan Cement, it was December 5. The following day Sindberg undertook the first of what was to become many trips to downtown Nanjing. He bought food wherever he could find any still for sale and he visited the German embassy, where he sent a telegram back to the F. L. Smidth office in Shanghai.[9] Due to the ongoing war, the telegram had to follow a circuitous route via the company's representative in the south Chinese city of Guangzhou and was underway for three days: "Arrived December fifth. Stop. Factory alright. Stop. Management money gone. Stop. Factory location therefore dangerously exposed. Stop. Need money urgent. Stop. Inform all. Gunther. Sindberg."[10]

***

Clearly, the war was moving closer. The location of Jiangnan Cement near the railroad from Shanghai to Nanjing automatically placed it in the danger zone, as the railway line marked the main route of advance of several units of the 16th Japanese Infantry Division as it approached the Chinese capital. The fighting was brutal and bloody. The same day that Sindberg and Günther arrived at the factory, a war correspondent who followed the division for the newspaper *Tokyo Nichi-Nichi Shimbun* described a sinister competition between two of the unit's officers. They raced to be the first to kill 100 Chinese with their swords. "It will be hard to find a winner in the Hundred-Killing-Contest!" the journalist wrote in a headline. "The score is 89 to 78."[11]

It is entirely possible that the journalist exaggerated the numbers, but even so his account reflected the casual attitude towards human lives which had evolved on the battlefield. Still, not everyone was indifferent to the suffering of the civilian Chinese. Kitayama Atou, a 32-year-old reservist who had been called up that summer to serve as a private in the campaign in China and now was also fighting with the 16th Division, happened to strike up a conversation with three Chinese children.

"Do you have a mom and dad?" he asked.

"Yes," the children answered. "Or rather, we don't at the moment. They have both been led away by the Japanese army as forced labor."

"Do you have place to live?"

"Our home has been bombed by the Japanese."[12]

On the Chinese side the area where Jiangnan Cement was situated was the responsibility of the 2nd Army Group consisting of the 41st and 48th Infantry Divisions.[13] The two divisions were primarily manned with soldiers who had not taken part in the long drawn-out battle of Shanghai. They were rested, but they were also bitter that they had not had the opportunity to participate in the vast showdown over China's largest city. Some had deserted—not in order to get home, but in order to get to the front. They had stepped onto civilian buses in the vain hope of reaching Shanghai but had usually been caught and

The population in the area near Jiangnan Cement, where Sindberg arrived in early December, consisted mostly of peasants, but there were also villages and towns in the vicinity. (FLSmidth Archives, Valby)

returned to their units. "We are also soldiers for the motherland," they had protested. "Why can't we go to Shanghai to fight the Japanese?"

Now they had the chance, not in Shanghai but in Nanjing. On December 2, the two divisions of the army group both departed from Wuhan on board troop transports that took them east along the Yangtze towards Nanjing. "We were under-strength, and we hadn't had enough time to train, but everyone was wild with joy that we could now go to the frontline and have the opportunity to kill some enemies," wrote Guo Jun, a brigadier in the 48th Infantry Division, in his postwar memoirs. Several of the troops were completely untrained and untested, and some were even wearing their civilian clothes when they embarked on the ships. They were immediately issued uniforms and weapons, and their officers used the days spent on the Yangtze to familiarize them with the most rudimentary military skills—practicing with their rifles and throwing hand grenades—so they did not end up as mere cannon fodder.

Parts of the 41st Infantry Division had arrived in Nanjing on December 4 as foreseen in the plan, and it had been soldiers from that unit who had been consolidating their positions near Jiangnan Cement, when Sindberg and Günther moved into the factory the following day. The bulk of the army group, however, took longer to arrive, which was due to the Japanese air superiority, which also covered Nanjing. Some of the troops were surprised by Japanese aircraft while they were still sailing on the Yangtze, while others were exposed to air raids after they had disembarked and found themselves in open countryside. The battle for Nanjing had not even really started, but casualties in the 2nd Army Group were already alarmingly high. The Japanese were favored by a crushing superiority in materiel terms, which did not bode well for the defenders of Nanjing.[14]

***

By December 1, the prospect of severe fighting had prompted most of the workforce at Jiangnan Cement to flee to the other side of the Yangtze, and when Sindberg and Günther turned up, they found almost no one inside the fenced-in factory compound. All they were met by was a single junior manager, Shen Jihua, and a handful of workers. At the same time, the facilities struck them as better than expected, even including a clubhouse where privileged personnel could stay during their time off. There was also a brand-new American car of the brand Dodge, but it was useless as the driver had left, taking with him the keys.[15] In a way, the absence of staff was an advantage as it was essential to convince the Japanese that the factory had not yet started producing cement, and that the foreign partners were still busy installing the machinery. As one of their first acts, therefore, Sindberg and Günther placed a sign at the entrance of the factory written with Chinese characters, which could also be understood by the Japanese: "Jiangnan Cement, German–Danish Joint Venture." The fact that the plant was overwhelmingly Chinese-owned was not mentioned at all.[16]

From the outset it was clear that the German rather than the Danish presence would leave the bigger impression on the Japanese, and a large swastika flag, brought by Günther, was immediately hoisted over the buildings. It was joined shortly afterwards by a Danish flag, which F. L. Smidth's Shanghai office had purchased at the last moment from the Great Northern Telegraph Company, allowing Sindberg to bring it with him on the journey.[17] Sindberg also saw to it that a Danish flag, measuring 1,350 square feet, was painted on the roof of one of the factory buildings.[18] "It ought to be visible from the air, as I believe it is the biggest Danish flag in existence," he wrote to a friend.[19] On one of the first days after his arrival he bought yet another Danish flag. It had belonged to Rifle Syndicate executive Kai Suhr, who had used it at his private home in Luojia Road until he left the capital in November, leaving his villa to the committee in charge of the safety zone.[20]

Since Denmark had no official representation in Nanjing, the German embassy in the Chinese capital had been picked as the main communications channel between F. L. Smidth in Shanghai and Jiangnan Cement. The very same day that Sindberg's and Günther's telegram arrived with news that there was no money left, F. L. Smidth's office in Shanghai approached the German

Sindberg's Chinese translator Li Yulin, left, with Karl Günther, right, at the main gate of Jiangnan Cement. The sign at the entrance claims that the compound houses a German–Danish joint venture. (Nanjing Municipal Government)

consulate with a request to ask Germany's embassy in Nanjing for financial aid. The embassy was asked to pay up to 1,000 British pounds to Günther and Sindberg, against a promise that it would receive a refund at a later date.[21]

The request from F. L. Smidth came at a busy time for the German diplomats in Nanjing. Following the evacuations of the preceding days, the embassy's staff had shrunk to just three, who all had their hands full helping German citizens to safety. "Most found it difficult to leave Nanjing," wrote the German war correspondent Wolf Schenke, who passed through the city at this time. "Almost all Germans had houses or at least an apartment in Nanjing, and they had to leave behind most of their property."[22]

The evacuations had continued while news from the front became more and more sinister, and consequently the foreign community in Nanjing now only totaled about 50 people, including journalists who had arrived to cover the war.[23] The Danish community had also almost gone. The only Dane left inside the city wall was Texaco's Johannes Mørch-Hansen. As he wrote with more than a touch of pride to his mother: "I have arranged for all Danes in Nanjing to reach Shanghai safely."[24]

Of the original Chinese population of one million, only 200,000 were left,[25] and the capital was now a shadow of its former self, Mørch-Hansen wrote in a letter:

I am writing from a city that is more dead than alive, from a nearly empty office, from a nation that cannot possibly escape united from this conflict, which has been forced upon it. Poor China, which, despite its large population, is not yet so modernized that it can wage a modern war with any hope of winning. All trains and all cars, indeed all roads are filled with panic-stricken people who scramble to avoid an almost unavoidable fate.[26]

It was generally anticipated that the Japanese would be in Nanjing within a matter of just days, and the question that attracted the most attention was what the Chinese defenders would do. Would they withdraw at the last moment and avoid a battle that they were bound to lose, thus saving the city from massive destruction? Or would they make a stand in a symbolic act of defiance to show the world that China would not abandon its capital to the enemy without a fight? Everything pointed in the direction of the latter, according to Mørch-Hansen, who knew what was talking about as the neighbor of General Tang Shengzhi, who had now been promoted to Nanjing's commandant. "It is probably no use trying to persuade him to give up. We had hoped that the Chinese would realize how pointless it would be to defend a city with no strategic significance," he wrote to his mother.[27]

There were two reasons why General Tang Shengzhi had been put in charge of the defense of the capital. First, he was intensely loyal to Chiang Kai-shek, and second, even if he ended up among the casualties it would not be a major loss to the Chinese war effort. Tang Shengzhi failed to impress virtually every person he met. "He appeared to be dazed if not doped," wrote W. A. Lovat-Fraser, the British military attaché in Nanjing. "It was obvious that any call upon his intellect was a strain and he gave one the impression of being the most unsuitable man for a very difficult task."[28]

Access to insider information about General Tang made Mørch-Hansen valuable for the committee in charge of the safety zone, but it was perhaps not even the main reason why the committee's chairman, John Rabe, was pleased that he had chosen to stay, while most other foreigners had left. Simply put, it caused Rabe to feel less lonely: "So I am not the only one taking a risk!" the Siemens manager wrote in his diary.[29] In fact, by early December, Mørch-Hansen was fully occupied preparing his own departure. "I have packed most of our valuable possessions. They have now been placed on the ship owned by Standard Oil. If the situation here becomes so bad that I am no longer safe, I am supposed to board the same ship," he told his mother in a letter. "In that case, we will sail out into the river alongside an American warship, so that nothing can happen to us. You don't have to worry about my safety."[30]

CHAPTER 9

The Fall of Nanjing

December 6–12, 1937

From the very first moments after their arrival at Jiangnan Cement, Sindberg and Günther could hear the thunder of artillery. With each day that passed, it grew louder. The Chinese 2nd Army Group, which had moved into the area around the factory and was gradually achieving full strength, had received intelligence that the Japanese vanguard had been observed only a few miles to the east. The army group's main force reacted by advancing to a ridgeline stretching along the horizon roughly three miles southeast of the factory. Here they dug in and waited for the enemy. The Chinese officers knew that they were up against the 16th Japanese Division. It had a history stretching back more than 30 years to the Russo-Japanese War of 1904 and 1905, and it had participated in a series of battles since the outbreak of war that summer in northern China. Time would tell how the untested Chinese troops would measure up against a battle-hardened adversary.

The Japanese storm of the Chinese positions began on December 6. Guo Jun, the Chinese brigadier, witnessed the panic that struck many young soldiers under his command when they tasted battle for the first time, and shots fired in anger whistled by them.

> Some buried their faces in the ground while they raised their rifles in front of them and fired completely at random without even looking. Others forgot to ignite the fuse of their hand grenades before they threw them. Yet others remembered to do so, but threw them over such a short distance that they did not hurt the Japanese in the least, but sometimes caused death and injury among our own soldiers.[1]

Japanese aircraft appeared over the horizon again and again to deliver their deadly load, while the Japanese artillery shelled the Chinese positions with such ferocity that it took many men in the front line, the ones who survived, days to regain their normal hearing. It was exclusively due to a cadre of experienced officers and NCOs that the Chinese front did not collapse immediately, and the 2nd Army Group was able to put up an organized defense against the Japanese attack. Still, some of the old soldiers had given up hope even before the shooting started. Guo Jun described another brigadier in his army group with a long career behind him who now seemed to have completely resigned himself to inevitable defeat. Rather than staying at the front with his men, he spent most of his time in a little grove far in the hinterland where he played the traditional game of mahjong with his bodyguards. "Every hour his chief of staff called the frontline just to get a quick update," Guo Jun recalled.[2]

It was only a question of time before the Chinese were forced to withdraw, and on December 9, the fighting moved closer to the village of Qixia and the cement factory nearby. Yan Liufeng, Sindberg's translator, described in a report to Chee Hsin Cement the tough measures that the Chinese army undertook in order to ensure that nothing useful was left for the Japanese: "Along the main road, scorched earth tactics were adopted. The peasants were forced from their farms, and no one was allowed to return home." Shortly afterwards, the Japanese attacked Qixia, and Japanese planes dropped numerous bombs. One of the bombs exploded just outside the factory compound, the shockwave smashing the windowpanes in several of Jiangnan Cement's buildings.[3] No one was hurt inside the compound, but in Qixia proper there were both military and civilian casualties, according to Yan Liufeng: "The fighting cost a significant number of deaths, but it is impossible to arrive at a precise number of local inhabitants that were either injured during the combat or infected by diseases which had broken out as a result of the war."[4]

The battles near the cement factory just formed a small part of an all-encompassing Japanese offensive. The Japanese army had approached Nanjing from both east and south and was now advancing rapidly along the entire front line. The 2nd Army Group's section was not the only area where Japanese troops with months of combat experience were met by sparsely trained Chinese units that had been sent to the war zone at the last moment without the necessary preparation, and the result was, predictably, carnage. The correspondent F. Tillman Durdin from The New York Times observed a Japanese unit surround 300 soldiers from the two newly arrived Chinese divisions and then seal off any escape route. "The Japanese set a ring of fire around the peak," he wrote. "The fire, feeding on trees and grass, gradually crept nearer and nearer to the top, forcing the Chinese upward until, huddled together, they were mercilessly machinegunned to death."[5]

The Japanese vanguard could now see Nanjing's medieval city wall with the naked eye, and large parts of the suburbs outside the wall had come under

Japanese field artillery shells the Nanjing city wall in preparation for the final attack. Soldiers in the foreground are waiting with fixed bayonets. (Asahi Shimbun)

Japanese control. A mausoleum for the founder of the Chinese republic, Sun Yat-sen, located in hilly terrain east of Nanjing not far from Purple Mountain, had already fallen into Japanese hands, and the same was true for Chiang Kai-shek's villa. Chiang himself, who had stayed on in Nanjing until the very last moment in order to strengthen morale, had now also flown out of the city. Meanwhile, the Japanese commander-in-chief, General Matsui Iwane, had traveled from Shanghai to the front at Nanjing in order to personally witness the last triumphant assault on the Chinese capital. After all, this had been his objective ever since the start of the campaign in August.

Nanjing had effectively already been lost. The only question, now as before, was whether there would be any fighting. The Chinese defenders seemed to have decided to make a stand. They ignored Japanese leaflets thrown from low-flying airplanes with dubious offers of merciful treatment if they capitulated, instead embarking on work to fortify their positions on top the city wall. The Japanese responded by shelling the capital with artillery assisted by observers able to get an overview of the entire city from Purple Mountain. Meanwhile, the Japanese main force had now reached Nanjing and was preparing to storm the wall. There was only one way to do this, and it had not changed since the Middle Ages: the Japanese soldiers started constructing makeshift ladders, which they planned to use to scale the vertical wall and reach the defenders at the top. No one entertained any illusions that this would be anything but a bloody affair.

The Japanese army had been informed about the coordinates of the safety zone, and most artillery shells fell outside the area. This contributed to a significant increase in the stream of civilian fugitives entering the zone, pushing its population to close to 200,000. In other words, almost all of the remaining residents of Nanjing were now squeezed together inside the zone, while the districts outside had been transformed into a ghost town. The problem was that Chinese military units were also tempted to seek admission to the zone, which was clearly marked with small flags along the entire perimeter, and the members of the zone committee still had serious difficulties ensuring that only civilians were to be found inside the area. "The soldiers and artillery are not yet out of [the] Safety Zone," Vautrin wrote in her diary. "In fact this morning I discovered that trenches were still being dug within college boundaries."[6]

John Rabe, the chairman of the committee, was also concerned about the uncertainty surrounding his ability to protect the zone and its inhabitants from atrocities. The zone committee did not have access to any means of self-defense, making it entirely plausible that he himself would not survive. Still, he decided to stay on until the bitter end. More than anything he was driven by a sense of duty towards his second homeland. "Since one has worked here for more than 30 years and spent almost one's entire life here, one should also be prepared to risk a little," he told the German war correspondent Wolf Schenke, who visited Rabe's office briefly before leaving Nanjing. Schenke could not liberate himself from a nagging sense of guilt when he turned his back on the Siemens manager and got onto a steamship that took him up the Yangtze: "One way or the other, I feel like someone who flees to safety while others approach almost certain death."[7]

Nearly all escape routes out of Nanjing were now closed off. Johannes Mørch-Hansen left on Friday December 10 on board one of three ships which formed a small fleet owned by the American company Standard Oil, which were departing Nanjing as the last vessels. "I had received instructions from Shanghai to leave Nanjing for Wuhan in order to take over management of the district there," he wrote in a letter. "The instructions had arrived on December 3, but there was no opportunity to leave Nanjing until December 10, when one of our ships sailed off... All of our positions had been stowed securely on one of Standard Oil's ships."[8] Mørch-Hansen and the other foreigners on board could breathe a sigh of relief, or so they thought. In reality, they were sailing towards an even worse death trap than the one they had just left.

***

The Standard Oil fleet, with Mørch-Hansen on board, had a comparatively smooth journey up the Yangtze River for the first two days. The fact that the three civilian vessels were escorted by the gunboat USS *Panay* contributed to the feeling of safety. This all changed early in the afternoon on Sunday, December 12, when the convoy was about 30 miles west of Nanjing and three twin-engine aircraft appeared in the sky. Despite the distance, the red circles on their wings were clearly visible. The planes were Japanese. Without warning the airplanes dropped a number of bombs on the American ships. A violent explosion sent a geyser into the air near the *Panay* and one of the civilian ships. Shortly afterwards, six Japanese fighters flew in over the river at a low altitude and dropped their bombs while also strafing the American gunboat with their machine guns.[9]

The American gunboat USS *Panay* is sinking on December 12, 1937, after having been attacked by Japanese aircraft in the middle of the Yangtze. The photo is taken from a smaller boat ferrying survivors to the riverbank. (Naval History and Heritage Command)

The attack resulted in death and injury on board both the *Panay* and the civilian vessels. The *Panay*'s captain was wounded in the leg and unable to perform his duties, and one of his officers took over the command. He continued in that role even after shrapnel hit him in the neck, temporarily rendering him unable to speak, which led him to issue his orders in writing on small slips of paper instead. The *Panay* started sinking, and it was clear that the order to abandon ship had to be issued. Two lifeboats were lowered into the river and transported passengers and crew safely ashore. At the same time, two of the civilian ships were so severely damaged that their crews also had to abandon them. One of the ships, which was transporting oil, was burning, and the blasts from the exploding oil barrels was carried across the surface of the Yangtze for hours.

Mørch-Hansen was on board the only Standard Oil ship that made it through the attacks without serious damage. However, all his belongings, souvenirs of half a life spent in China, were on board one of the ships that sank to the bottom of the river. "It's all gone, but I myself am all right," he wrote to his mother.[10] One of the passengers traveling with Mørch-Hansen, a tobacco merchant, could not believe that they had been attacked. "There were American flags everywhere," he said.[11] Similar bewilderment was expressed again and again during the subsequent days and weeks, even after the Japanese had issued a formal apology. Did the Japanese know that they were attacking an American warship? Was it a deliberate act, perhaps carried out on the initiative of a field officer to show that Westerners should not expect any special treatment in the Nanjing region? Even if it was not on purpose, it served as an efficient warning to all foreigners that the Chinese were not the only ones risking their lives.

After Mørch-Hansen's departure, only one Dane was left in the entire Nanjing area: Sindberg. Jiangnan Cement was now in the middle of occupied territory, but so far, no Japanese soldiers had ventured past the factory compound's fence out of respect of the German and Danish flags and the sign at the entrance describing it as foreign property. The soldiers of the 2nd Chinese Army Group had abandoned their positions and marched north in the direction of the Yangtze, quietly preparing to withdraw across the river. They were losing the battle of Nanjing, and the officers of the various units were considering ways that they could save their men from a sinister fate at the hands of the Japanese.

Throughout the day on December 12, there was heavy fighting along the city wall. The Japanese infantrymen had completed their ladders, and after the Chinese positions had been exposed to intense artillery shelling, they now tried, with courage bordering on the suicidal, to scale the wall in sections where the Chinese defenses were deemed to be weak. In hopes of motivating the

Crew members of the USS *Panay* jump into the Yangtze after receiving orders to abandon ship. (Naval History and Heritage Command)

soldiers, the Japanese officers had arranged a contest among the various units to become the first to place the banner of the Rising Sun on top of the city wall. Close combat erupted on every spot where the Japanese made it to the top. The short distances made it impractical to use firearms, and the frequent use of bayonets and swords imbued the scenes with an archaic flavor.[12]

It was a form of war in which the technological superiority of the Japanese was not always useful, but in the middle of the afternoon it was clear who had the upper hand. Throughout the day, Nanjing's commandant Tang Shengzhi shifted back and forth between resolve and resignation. He was not helped by his boss, Chiang Kai-shek, who sent him confusing signals from his command post hundreds of miles in the rear. "If you do not shrink away from making sacrifices," Chiang wrote to Tang in a telegram early in the day, "we will be able to hold high the banner of the nation and the army and perhaps even turn defeat into victory."[13] It was in this spirit that Tang ordered his troop to continue fighting for most of the day, right up until 3 p.m., when he received a telegram from Chiang Kai-shek which could not be misunderstood: Evacuate Nanjing immediately.[14]

***

Shortly afterwards, Tang Shengzhi and his staff boarded a boat in Nanjing harbor, hastily sailing up the Yangtze. Orders were issued to the Chinese troops to pull out of the capital, but the communications network was in tatters, and many units were told nothing. Therefore, as rumors started to spread that the commandant had already left the city, discipline among the Chinese defenders collapsed completely. A paradoxical aspect of the Chinese character, mentioned by a foreign resident before the battle, was now in evidence: "Either they are completely fearless, even in the face of death, or they run around in daze, men and woman in one big crowd. The Chinese are extreme, whether they show no fear at all, or they are overpowered by confused panic."[15] In Nanjing, on Sunday evening, December 12, it was all panic and confusion.

The total breakdown of the defense of the city led to immediate anarchy. In several areas the officers lost control over their men, who walked through the streets in small groups, looting abandoned shops.[16] Fighting broke out between Chinese units from different parts of the country, speaking different dialects and therefore unable to understand each other. "Heavy casualties resulted from this internal slaughter," a leading Chinese general said afterwards.[17] A large number of Chinese soldiers had got rid of their uniforms and other equipment and put on civilian clothes before escaping into the safety zone.[18] "The road for miles was strewn with the equipment they cast away—rifles, ammunition, belts, uniforms, cars, trucks—everything in the way of army impediments," an American witness wrote.[19]

Most soldiers understood that their best chance of survival was not to disappear in the zone, but to reach Yangtze's northern shore, which by and large had remained under Chinese control. Many tried to get to a part of Nanjing harbor not yet seized by the Japanese, an area known as Xiaguan just outside the city wall. Throughout the day and the evening, there was a constant human stream in the direction of the docks, but when they reached the wall, they realized it had been blocked off. "In desperation many Chinese troops attempted to lower themselves over the wall with the aid of improvised ladders and articles of clothing tied together, but a large number remained trapped within the city," the British military attaché said in a report.[20] The American missionary George Ashmore Fitch also witnessed the violent chaos and described it in his diary: "Trucks and cars jammed, were overturned, caught fire; at the gate more cars jammed and were burned—a terrible holocaust—and the dead lay feet deep."[21]

The ones who made it past the wall joined a growing and increasingly unruly mob that filled the port in a desperate attempt to get access to any vessel that could get them across the Yangtze. There were also civilians. Once more fighting broke out among the Chinese soldiers vying for the hopelessly few spots available on the boats and ships. "It is not known how many succeeded in crossing the river to comparative safety but it is suspected, owing to the Chinese predilection for overcrowding boats, that many must have been drowned," the British military attaché wrote.[22]

Nanjing had fallen. It could hardly have ended any differently given the uneven strengths of the Chinese and Japanese armies, and from a military point of view it was an advantage that it had happened without a bloody, lengthy, and ultimately futile defense. "The only question," Oscar O'Neill Oxholm wrote in a report to Copenhagen, "was if Chiang Kai-shek was to waste his core troops in a real defense of the capital, or if he wanted to keep them in reserve. He opted for the latter, and that way he avoided making the conquest of Nanjing the military disaster that some had expected."[23] Still, an era was over. Fitch, who was born in China and had lived his entire life in the country, described in his diary the melancholy mood that overwhelmed him: "So ended the happy, peaceful, well-ordered, progressive regime which we had been enjoying here in Nanjing and on which we had built our hopes for still better days."[24]

CHAPTER 10

The Massacre Begins

December 13–15, 1937

On Monday December 13 a young Chinese couple turned up with their children at the gate of Jiangnan Cement. They had walked three miles from their village, escaping from the Japanese soldiers, who had started killing and looting randomly among peasants in the area. Rumors had spread about the factory that the Japanese did not dare to enter, and the terrified family could think of no other solution than to seek refuge there. The cement factory only had limited resources. There was a sparsely equipped clinic as well as a vegetable garden meant for the factory's own staff, but even so, Sindberg and Günther allowed the family to settle down outside the factory fence, where a refugee camp was already beginning to form.[1]

Shortly afterwards a Chinese soldier staggered through the factory gate. He was from the 88th Division, one of Chiang Kai-shek's original elite units which had been almost annihilated in the grueling battles of Shanghai and Nanjing. When the order to withdraw from the capital was issued to the division, only 1,000 men out of a force that had totaled 15,000 in August managed to get across the Yangtze.[2] The rest had either been killed or wandered around aimlessly in the vicinity of Nanjing, hoping to avoid Japanese patrols. The soldier who had now reached the cement factory had walked the entire distance from 88th Division's area of operation south of the city wall, and he was in an extremely weakened state. "He had been injured by a bullet in the left arm. It was very serious," Sindberg wrote in an official report after the man had received what little treatment was possible at the factory clinic.[3]

In this way, Chinese civilians and soldiers, moving alone or in groups, started arriving at the factory around the time of the fall of Nanjing. Some were from villages in the area near Qixia, and others had been displaced from their homes further east.[4] They had fled ahead of the Japanese, who had now

During the very first hours after the Japanese occupation of the area near Jiangnan Cement, locals started converging on the plant. Rumors had spread that the foreign flags helped keep the Japanese at bay. Karl Günther can be seen in the middle. To the left, holding a Danish flag, is Sindberg's Chinese translator Li Yulin. There is a deep irony in the fact that the German swastika, which symbolized a regime that would soon cause the deaths of millions, was used to save lives in Nanjing. (Anita Günther)

caught up with them anyway. Many had heard stories of how the Japanese artillery had carefully avoided shelling the factory, except for the one shell that had exploded just outside the gate and smashed several windows. They understood that it was the foreign presence, underlined by the German and Danish flags, which caused the Japanese to behave in such an uncharacteristically cautious manner. Even though Sindberg and Günther had to make do with little, they let them stay. The camp grew fast and after a short period it had reached a size that made it impossible for the staff at Jiangnan Cement to close it down, even if they had wanted to. "There are about 4,000 refugees outside the factory," Günther wrote in a letter to his cousin G. Schultz at the time of Nanjing's fall.[5]

Ge Jiansen, the 16-year-old son of a farmer forced to flee his home along with his family by the fighting between Chinese and Japanese troops, was among the many refugees who made their way to the new camp just about the time when the last resistance in Nanjing ended. What made the biggest impression on him, as well as on others, was Sindberg's personality. Decades later, when he was interviewed about his wartime experiences, he still recalled it clearly: "The foreigner at Jiangnan Cement had an impressive physique. He had a huge foreigner nose, and his face was long and almost white. When he hoisted the Danish flag, the Japanese didn't dare come anywhere near."[6]

***

On December 13, while the camp at Jiangnan Cement was being formed, the first Japanese troops marched into Nanjing. After the often bitter fighting at the city wall, they did not encounter any real opposition any longer, and they immediately went about occupying the most important buildings—the ministries, the telegraph offices, the hospitals.[7] The same evening they were in control of most of the urban area, and the Japanese flag was hoisted everywhere.[8] Maybe the worst was over now, many believed. They assumed that the riskiest time has been in the interregnum, full of potential for violence and anarchy, when the Chinese troops were moving out, and the Japanese were moving in, and there was no real authority to maintain order. The Japanese would bring stability, or so they hoped.

Obviously only a tiny minority were so naïve as to think that a military operation of this magnitude could be carried out without some abuse taking place. Young men, full of adrenaline and armed to the teeth in a conquered city were a dangerous combination. Still, the Japanese army had a reputation for draconian discipline, founded at the end of the previous century, and it was generally expected that in Nanjing, too, its soldiers would behave in a correct manner. "We all breathed a sigh of relief, thinking new order would be restored after the panic and stampede caused by the retreating Chinese army," the American missionary and hospital administrator James H. McCallum wrote in his diary.[9]

The first contacts with Japanese troops actually gave rise to tenuous hopes that Nanjing would now, after four months of war, experience more peaceful times. George Ashmore Fitch, a member of the zone committee, was told at 11 a.m. that a group of Japanese soldiers had appeared at the entry of the safety zone. He quickly drove up to meet them and gauge their mood, and he was initially pleasantly surprised. "They showed no hostility," he wrote in his diary.[10] Some hours later, Minnie Vautrin was informed that a Japanese soldier had turned up inside a coop run by Ginling College. He was polite but hungry and wanted to buy geese and chickens. With the help of sign language, the American teacher made him understand that this was not possible. He accepted this with a reverent nod.[11]

Already on the same day, however, several of Nanjing's foreigners experienced glimpses of another and more sinister side of the Japanese army. John Rabe drove through Nanjing and saw corpses lying in the streets every 100 or 200 yards. There were civilians among the dead, and they had all been shot in the back. They must have been killed when they tried to run away, Rabe reasoned.[12] Japanese soldiers in groups of 10 or 20 began systematically looting the city. It was a behavior many had expected from undisciplined units of the Chinese army, but not the Japanese. "If I hadn't seen it with my own eyes, I wouldn't have believed it," Rabe wrote.[13]

On December 13 there were far worse things going on that Rabe just did not know about yet. After the defense of the city had collapsed, Chinese soldiers started surrendering to the Japanese in great numbers. They were, with very few exceptions, all killed. That was the way the two sides had treated their prisoners since the summer, and there is no indication that the Japanese ever seriously considered any other way to approach a defeated enemy. The 16th Japanese Infantry Division, which had passed by Jiangnan Cement earlier that month, was killing prisoners by the thousands while the battle of Nanjing was still in its last stages.

The division's officers were surprisingly frank in the diaries they had brought with them in the field. The divisional commander, General Nakajima Kesago, wrote in his entry for December 13 that the 30th Brigade had "disposed of" 15,000 Chinese prisoners, and that in other sections of the front, 7,000 to 8,000 Chinese were awaiting their fate. "There are constantly more who surrender," he wrote. "We need a very big hole for them, and it's not easy to find. I think we will end up dividing them into groups of 100 to 200 men and take them to suitable places where we can handle them."[14] On the same day, the commander of the 30th Brigade, Major General Sasaki Toichi, described the situation in his diary: "The number of killed enemies in our area alone is between 10,000 and 20,000 today. On top of that are soldiers whose boats were shot up by our armored cars while they tried to cross the Yangtze, as well as prisoners of war taken by our troops. Altogether our brigade has gotten rid of over 20,000 enemy soldiers."[15]

The foreigners of Nanjing were initially not aware of the enormous scale of the massacres. However, during the night between December 13 and 14, shots could be heard continuously in the streets. "We put that down as caused by the fact the Japanese soldiers were 'jittery' their first night in town," wrote Lewis S. C. Smythe, a lecturer at Nanjing University.[16] Before Minnie Vautrin went to sleep that evening, she committed her thoughts to her diary: "Three dangers are past—that of looting soldiers, bombing from aeroplanes and shelling from big guns, but the fourth is still before us—our fate at the hands of a victorious army. People are very anxious tonight and do not know what to expect."[17]

***

A new reality had descended in and around Nanjing, and the cautious hopes that Minnie Vautrin and the other foreigners had entertained about the behavior of the triumphant Japanese were quickly dashed. Many noticed that the attitude of the Japanese forces towards the city's civilians changed markedly on the second day of the occupation. "On December 14 morning, Japanese soldiers did not adopt a hostile attitude towards the Chinese civilian population," said a journalist from the British news agency Reuters, who later was able to be evacuated. "By noon, however, smaller Japanese groups of 6 to 10 men had formed in many places who had removed their regimental badges and were plundering from house to house."[18] The German national Christian Kröger, who was treasurer for the zone committee, also described a "precipitous worsening of the situation" on the same day: "The Japanese combat troops... were released on the city and especially towards the most destitute and innocent they behaved in a manner that no one could have imagined."[19]

The first sure sign that discipline had collapsed in the Japanese army was the widespread looting that happened throughout the city. Shortly after the Japanese troops had marched into Nanjing and determined that there was no real military resistance, they went plundering, often in small gangs. "They smash windows and doors and steal what they take a liking to, allegedly because they are out of food," Rabe wrote.[20] A group broke into the missionary Grace Bauer's home, stole a couple of fur-lined gloves and then focused their attention on the dining table. "[They] drank up all the milk on the table, and scooped up sugar with their hands," she declared.[21] During a visit to a hospital managed by the American doctor Robert O. Wilson, the Japanese lined up all the Chinese nurses in a row. The young women trembled with fear over what was now going to happen, but they were "only" robbed. "They... took away their pens, flashlights and wristwatches. They did a pretty good job of looting the nurses' dormitory, taking all kinds of petty things," Wilson wrote.[22]

Others were not so lucky. It was a cause of special concern that many of the cases of looting taking place on December 14 were accompanied by violence meted out by the Japanese. "Not just resistance, but also a reluctant or slow handover [of personal effects] was answered with the bayonet," the German ambassador Oskar Trautmann wrote in a confidential report to Berlin.

"Many became victims in this way, simply because they did not understand the language."[23] Similar incidents happened outside Nanjing's city wall, and they were perhaps even more frequent there. In the village of Xinhe, not far from Jiangnan Cement, the Japanese had noticed a fishpond close to the fields, and they demanded fish. When one of the inhabitants told them he did not have any, they dragged him to one of the biggest ponds on the outskirts of the village, ordering him to jump into the chilly water and catch fish with his bare hands. The man, standing in chest-deep water, tried to explain to the soldiers that it was an impossible task, begging them to let him go, but every time he tried to move near the side of the pond, they pushed him back with their rifles. The man froze to death, and when the Japanese had disappeared, his neighbors pulled his body out of the pond and buried it.[24]

The violence spread fast. Civilians were at particular risk of attracting Japanese attention if they showed any signs of nervousness.[25] "It seems to be the rule here," wrote Fitch, "that any who run must be shot or bayoneted."[26] Even a brief loss of self-control could have fatal consequences. The American clergyman John Magee witnessed an episode when a Chinese man was walking down a street in Nanjing and happened to pass by two Japanese soldiers. It was evident that he was a civilian since he was wearing a long silk gown. The soldiers shouted at him to stop, and he panicked and started running. He tried to get around a corner in a bamboo fence and disappear, but with no luck. "The soldiers walked in front of him and couldn't have stood more than five yards in front of him," Magee said. "Both of them shot him in the face. They were both laughing and talking as though nothing had happened; never stopped smoking their cigarettes or talking... They killed him with no more feeling than one taking a shot at a wild duck, and then walked on."[27]

***

Alongside the individual acts of violence, the Japanese army also began, during the first hours after the conquest of Nanjing, the systematic elimination of all members of the beaten Chinese army who had not succeeded in escaping. It was a continuation of a practice both sides had adopted in Shanghai, where virtually no prisoners had been taken. The difference now was that the prisoners could no longer be counted in the dozens or the hundreds, but in the thousands or tens of thousands. Another difference was that the mass killing soon developed a momentum of its own, while the border between POWs and civilians was rapidly blurred. In the course of very few days Nanjing developed into a slaughterhouse. In the area near Mufushan,

Chinese soldiers who have changed into civilian clothes in order to hide among peasants at Jiangnan Cement. (Bernhard Arp Sindberg Papers and Photography Collection, Harry Ransom Center, University of Texas at Austin)

a series of hills northeast of Nanjing, thousands were murdered, and their bodies pushed into the Yangtze.

Since the war had broken out in the summer of that year, the Japanese soldiers had observed again and again how the Chinese enemy sometimes almost vanished before their eyes and seemed to melt into the surrounding terrain. In Nanjing, too, the Japanese were aware that until a couple of days earlier, they had been facing a numerically strong adversary, and now that adversary had simply disappeared. Some of the Chinese soldiers had withdrawn north across the Yangtze, but the Japanese officers also assumed that a significant number were still present in and around Nanjing and could strike at any given moment. These suspicions were further strengthened when they saw large heaps of Chinese uniforms in the streets. It was obvious that the men who had worn these uniforms had changed into civilian clothes and were hiding among the populace. Therefore, the Japanese made it one of their first priorities to find the escaped soldiers and kill them.

Nakajima Kesago, the commander of the 16th Division, wrote about this in his diary with a candidness that suggested he did not expect anyone else would ever read it:

> Everywhere there are POWs. There are so many it is almost impossible to handle them all. Generally speaking, it has been decided not to take any prisoners. It's up to us to solve the problem in a thorough manner. But they turn up in hordes of 1,000 men, 5,000 men, even 10,000 men. There are so many we don't even have the capacity to disarm them all.

According to Nakajima, the Chinese soldiers had now completely lost the will to fight and no longer constituted any threat. "Still," he continued, "even if it seems safe at the moment, they could very well become a risk if the situation suddenly became less stable."[28]

The consequences of this way of thinking became evident the next day, December 14, when a large number of men from Nakajima's division were sent into the safety zone to hunt for Chinese soldiers hiding among the civilians. Among those ordered to take part in the operation was Corporal Masuda Rokusuke, who was determined to do his best. After all, this was about enemies who the day before had been heavily armed and highly dangerous. "Not a single one would escape now," he wrote in an account shortly afterwards. "We were determined to go on, search every nook and cranny, flush them all out, and exact revenge for our fallen buddies."

They went from house to house. In one of them they found a group of about 100 Chinese soldiers. Masuda described their fate in shocking detail:

> What a sight! Next to them were tons of rifles, revolvers, swords, and other weapons. Some of those men were still in uniform. Some were hastily changing into ordinary [Chinese] clothes. Others wore civvie shirts with army-uniform trousers. All of the clothes were either unsuited to winter or mismatched as to shirts and pants, so the men obviously had grabbed and donned these in a big rush. We led all of them off, stripped them down, checked them out, and tied them up with downed telephone wires... With dusk approaching, we marched close to 600 of these defeated stragglers over towards [a gate in the city wall] and shot them dead.[29]

Nanjing's foreign community slowly understood what was happening. They heard it from the few who survived the massacres. John Magee later talked about his chef's 15-year-old son, who along with 100 men had been driven outside the city wall near a railway line. Here they were divided into two roughly equal groups. Their hands were tied in front of them, and the Japanese started killing those in the front row. "He was in the back, and... was gnawing frantically at the ropes around his fists and finally got them released and slipped into a culvert or a dugout or a drain underneath the railroad track," Magee said. "He escaped back about thirty-eight hours or more later, telling us the story. That was the first proof we had of what was happening to these groups of men that first were being taken off."[30]

CHAPTER 11

"Blood, Blood, and More Blood"

December 16–19, 1937

On Thursday December 16, Sindberg was summoned to a village three miles from Jiangnan Cement. Something terrible had happened. A young Chinese man, who had arrived with his wife and children at the cement factory three days earlier, had returned home with some of his neighbors to fetch rice. They had been surprised by a Japanese patrol looking for enemies trying to escape. They had accused the young man of being a soldier and had decided to execute him on the spot. They forced him to kneel down, and one of the Japanese raised his sword to decapitate him. The Chinese man was wearing a coat with a thick collar, preventing the blade from hitting him with full force. Rather than severing the head from the body, the cut left a deep gash in the main's neck. The patrol left him to die. This was where Sindberg and his companions found him. Carefully they carried the injured man back to the clinic at Jiangnan Cement.[1]

It was a busy day for Sindberg. Also on that Thursday, a Chinese soldier turned up at the factory. He was from the 41st Infantry Division, part of the 2nd Army Group, which had been deployed in the area earlier that month. His shoulder had been injured 10 days prior, during the first battles between the army group and the attacking Japanese, but in the intervening period he had received no medical treatment whatsoever. Sindberg cleaned and dressed the wound to the best of his ability and conscientiously wrote down details about the state of his patient.[2] The following day, on December 17, yet another Chinese soldier arrived. He was from the telegraph troops and had received a gunshot to his left arm.[3]

What both soldiers had in common was that even though they were badly injured, their wounds were of a kind that one could expect in a war where two armies meet each other in the battlefield. They were perhaps in a somewhat more desperate situation than soldiers in many other modern wars, since the

Chinese army had, in a fatal oversight, omitted developing a proper medical branch, meaning injured soldiers often had to look after themselves. At the same time, however, a new type of patients was starting to turn up at the factory gate. They were soldiers who had not received their injuries in battle but had been subjected to violence after surrendering to the Japanese. For example, this was the case with a soldier from the 18th Infantry Division who was suddenly standing at the factory gate in the middle of the month. "He had been in a group of three who had laid down their weapons," Sindberg wrote. "Even so, the Japanese decided to kill them. While his two friends had been put to death, he got away with minor injury to the head because he pretended to be dead."[4]

On December 18, Sindberg treated a soldier whose story indicated that the killings were not just isolated episodes of violence but happened in a systematic fashion. The soldier was from the Training Division, an elite unit that had suffered huge casualties as a result of the severe fighting in Shanghai that fall. Sindberg reproduced the man's testimony in his English-language report:

> On December 13, he with 8 others had surrendered to the Japanese, they were kept prisoners for 3 days without food and water, then they, together with other soldiers and civilians, about 200 in all, were made to walk to a place near the Purple Hill outside Nanjing, there they were lined up in 3 long rows for executions by machine guns, this soldier let himself fall down [as if he had] been shot and acted dead when the firing stopped, then the Japanese poured some sort of acid all over the dead bodies and set fire to them, some of this acid was poured on the soldier's legs, as this outrage was done late in the afternoon, it was already dark when the Japanese had finished this, so [under the] cover of darkness this soldier crawled away and came here. As this is written, his wounds are not yet healed, this acid inflicting a very painful and difficult wound.[5]

***

In a letter to a friend back home in Denmark, Sindberg described the sinister landscape that surrounded him at Jiangnan Cement: "You have no idea of the amount of bloodshed everywhere. Since August I have had any opportunity to study the horrors of war. Blood, blood, and more blood. The Chinese have really shed a lot of blood this time around. But then again, they have a population of 450 million, and it takes a lot really to make a difference to them."[6] Gradually it became clear to Sindberg that he was faced with an almost uniquely horrible crime, and it did something to him. During the first days after the Japanese occupation, perhaps even during the very first hours, he transformed from merely watching the refugee camp grow bigger and bigger, to deciding to act. He saw it as his job to save as many as possible with the resources at his disposal.

Chinese soldiers executed by the Japanese outside Nanjing's city wall. Several have their hands tied behind their backs. Sindberg, who took the photo, attached a note saying they "surrendered to the Japanese when promised safety and good treatment." (Bernhard Arp Sindberg Papers and Photography Collection, Harry Ransom Center, University of Texas at Austin)

Sindberg was in a unique situation in the Nanjing area because of his access to a radio. While the remaining foreigners in the city were cut off from the outside world, he was able to listen to Western broadcasts from Shanghai on a regular basis. Specifically he tuned in every evening to a popular news program on the Shanghai station XMHA provided by the U.S.-owned paper *Shanghai Evening Post & Mercury News.*[7] It left Sindberg with the impression that the violent chaos that prevailed in the area around Jiangnan Cement did no repeat itself in downtown Nanjing, leading him to conclude, erroneously, that the best chance for the many injured who had gradually assembled at the factory was to be transported to the capital. Therefore, he began preparing an expedition to the city.

Sindberg could not have known this, but the conditions inside Nanjing's city wall were actually getting worse by the day. The Japanese forces still made their way repeatedly into the safety zone hunting for Chinese soldiers, since they feared, unrealistically, that they could emerge and attack them at any moment. "The Japanese are rounding them up by the hundreds and shooting them, putting their bodies in the conveniently handy dugouts built for air-raid protection," wrote the doctor Robert O. Wilson.[8] Despite their frantic efforts, the Japanese were convinced they had only succeeded in finding a small part of the soldiers that had escaped, and that more remained to be done.[9]

On December 16, a comprehensive sweep of the safety zone was undertaken with the Japanese army's 16th Division playing a key role. The soldiers led young men away in big groups, whether they had ever carried a rifle or not, the American missionary Ernest H. Forster wrote. "They murdered most of them in cold blood. We heard that they took a group of two to three hundred to a pond, shot them one by one and let them fall into the water. Another big group was forced into a mat shed, surrounded with machineguns and burned alive."[10] Sun Yuanzheng, a Chinese man, was forced by the Japanese to work in a kitchen near the place where many of the executions took place. "The sound of the machinegun fire so close to me deafened somewhat the left ear, which is still affected," he said almost 10 years later.[11]

Several of the Japanese soldiers described their actions in frank detail. Mizutani So, a private of the 7th Regiment, wrote in his diary about an operation in the afternoon of December 16, when the safety zone was searched:

> We placed sentries with bayonets at the intersections, blocked these off, and went about our work rounding up virtually all young men we came across. We roped them off, surrounded them with armed guards, tied them up in rows, and led them away so they looked like children playing choo-choo train. Our First Company clearly took less than other units, but we still got a hundred and several dozen. Lots of women, no doubt their mothers or wives, soon caught up with us to cry and beg for their release. Right away, we released those who clearly looked like civilians.

However, 36 others remained in the custody of the company and were shot shortly afterwards, Mizutani wrote. His description of the execution indicates that the Japanese soldiers in Nanjing considered it legitimate to kill prisoners of war, and that they mainly saw it as problematic insofar as civilians lost their lives due to mistakes. "All of them wailed desperately to be spared, but there was nothing we could do. Even if some unfortunate innocent victims were mixed in (we couldn't tell for sure), it just couldn't be helped. Killing some innocent victims was unavoidable," he wrote.[12]

Corporal Inouie Mataichi, also from the 7th Regiment, was in a company which by the end of the day had captured 335 prisoners, all young men among the refugees who just happened to look like soldiers. It was obvious that many of them were indeed civilians, but this made no impression on the Japanese: "Man! Some had family members there, and did they ever wail when we tried to take their men folk away! They'd latch onto our arms and bodies, pleading with us… We took these 335 down to the Yangtze where other troops shot them dead."[13]

***

The water supply in Nanjing had been interrupted since December 9, and by December 12 there had also been no power.[14] This made the hours after sunset even more dread-filled. It was completely dark on the evening of December 18, when the missionary Forster was sitting in his villa, which had been turned into a temporary home for over 100 Chinese refugees. Among them were a group of Buddhist nuns, who went across the street that night to eat dinner with some acquaintances. They did not return until much later. They had been stopped by a group of Japanese soldiers and raped.[15]

This was just one instance among countless others. Miner Searle Bates, a professor at Nanjing University, described a series of rape incidents committed on the same evening throughout his campus: in lecture halls, workshops, and the teachers' private homes. The university was part of the safety zone, and it ought therefore to have been protected against attacks, but instead many Japanese soldiers saw the campus as an area where helpless women were conveniently concentrated. At a high school attached to the university they raped eight and spread terror among the others. "One frightened child killed by a bayonet; another critically wounded and about to die," Bates reported in brief telegram fashion.[16]

A rape epidemic spread in Nanjing from the first days of the Japanese occupation, potentially targeting anyone, regardless of age. On the Nanjing university campus alone, the youngest victim was nine, while the oldest was 76.[17] On December 17, the hospital administrator James H. McCallum wrote in his diary: "Rape! Rape! Rape! We estimate at least 1,000 cases a night, and many by day. In case of resistance or anything that seems like disapproval there is a bayonet stab or a bullet. We could write up hundreds of cases a day. People are hysterical… Women are being carried off every morning, afternoon, and evening."[18]

A dangerous atmosphere of lawlessness had descended over Nanjing. "The most horrible thing is the raping of the women, which has been going on in the most shameless way that I have ever known. The streets are full of men searching for women," wrote the clergyman John Magee.[19] McCallum described the same mood of anarchy: "The whole Japanese army seems to be free to go and come anywhere it pleases, and to do what it pleases."[20] As had often been the case, the rapes served several purposes. They were also a way to humiliate the subdued enemy by demonstrating that the men were unable

Japanese officers complained repeatedly about lacking discipline among the units under their command. Many of the Japanese soldiers in the Nanjing area were reservists who had recently been called up from their civilian lives to participate in the war in China. (Photograph by Malcolm Rosholt. Image courtesy of Me-fei Elrick, Tess Johnston and Historical Photographs of China, University of Bristol)

to defend their wives, daughters, and mothers. "There are documented cases where the perpetrators have forced husbands and fathers to watch the outrage that happened to their families," wrote the German diplomat Georg Rosen.[21]

It was not a case of a suddenly emerging aggressive attitude among the Japanese soldiers. Rather, as was the instance with the systematic killing of prisoners, it was a practice that had been in evidence since the beginning of the campaign. The Japanese 10th Army, which was responsible for storming the southern part of the city wall, acknowledged in a letter issued to its officers shortly after the fall of the city that its soldiers had committed widespread rape even while the fighting was still ongoing: "We have told troops numerous times that looting, rape and arson are forbidden, but judging from the shameful fact that over 100 incidents of rape came to light during the current assault on Nanjing, we bring this matter to your attention yet again despite the repetition."[22]

***

The few foreigners left in Nanjing, who were forced to watch the horrific atrocities, had difficulties understanding how this could even happen. Forster vented his feelings in a letter home to his wife: "It is impossible to write all that has happened, but I never dreamed that such human beasts existed as we have had to deal with."[23] At the same time, Forster was careful not to generalize about all Japanese, referring to conversations he had had with Japanese diplomats who were just as shocked as he was and at the same time powerless against soldiers who destroyed their nation's reputation and undermined the possibility of a peaceful accommodation with the subdued Chinese population. "The [Japanese] Embassy people have been decent, but have lost face over their inability to accomplish anything with the military," Forster wrote.[24]

The Japanese conduct was all the more incomprehensible because the Japanese army had over the years established a reputation for its uncompromising discipline, and now its soldiers were behaving like a gang of naughty schoolboys unexpectedly finding themselves without supervision and able to do as they pleased. Even while the atrocities were still taking place, some of the foreign eyewitnesses tried to think of explanations for the brutal anarchy that unfolded. Some emphasized the fact that the Japanese army traveled light. It was expected of the soldiers that they themselves carried most of the food they were to consume, and that they would somehow requisition what else they needed along the way. At times, this implied purchasing provisions from civilians, but often it resulted in simple looting. It was a method of survival adopted by armies around the world since the dawn of time, but the Japanese army had carried that tradition into the 20th century.

The situation further deteriorated during the Nanjing campaign because the infantry was advancing so fast that the supply columns, which mostly relied on horse-drawn transport, could not keep up. The Yangtze was also just being cleared for navigation after months of fighting, and it was not possible for the Japanese to supply their troops by ship. Forster referred in one of his letters to a conversation he had had with a Japanese soldier who as a civilian had been a merchant in the port city of Yokohama and had a good grasp of logistical matters: "He said their soldiers were very short of food upon their arrival, since their service of supplies could not get things to them as they neared Nanjing."[25] While the initial impetus of the Japanese might have been to obtain essential supplies, it quickly deteriorated into a situation where the soldiers stole everything they could get near. Often the victims were the most destitute among the Chinese. The Japanese soldiers took away everything, "their last coin, their last bit of bedding, and it is freezing weather," Fitch wrote.[26]

The atmosphere of recklessness which many described in the period after the fall of Nanjing was also noticed by the Japanese officers themselves, and many found it a cause of concern. "I have heard that some of our units in Nanjing have big problems keeping up the discipline. This is extremely regrettable," Colonel Uemura Toshimichi, the army of occupation's deputy chief of staff, wrote in his diary on December 16.[27] Sasaki Toichi, the commander of the 30th Brigade, described similar conditions. "Many soldiers are dressed in crazy ways. If the officers do not move decisively to maintain discipline now that the fighting is over, we will see worrying incidents again and again," he wrote in his diary in the middle of December.[28]

Yamada Senji, the commander of the 103rd Brigade, was also extremely dissatisfied with his men's behavior. This was especially true of the reserve, which had been mobilized just a few months earlier and still had not put the habits of civilian life behind them. "There are major problems with the discipline of the soldiers who have been called up. They do not salute. Their uniforms are not according to regulations, and they wear rings on their fingers. They do not properly care for their weapons, letting them rust, and they allow their tarpaulins to become dirty," he wrote in his diary on December 24.[29] The man at the top of the hierarchy, General Matsui Iwane, was out of the loop, incapacitated due to malaria for several days around the time of the conquest of Nanjing. "Lately, there have been a small number of cases involving looting and rape among my men. That phenomenon is more or less inevitable in view of the situation," he wrote in his diary in the middle of December.[30]

General Matsui Iwane, the commander of Japanese forces in the Yangtze area, makes his entry into Nanjing on December 17, 1937. (Japanese press photo)

Japanese soldier during a moment of leisure. (Photograph by Malcolm Rosholt. Image courtesy of Me-fei Elrick, Tess Johnston and Historical Photographs of China, University of Bristol)

Even if Matsui and the officers around him had wanted to proceed more decisively against the transgressions committed by their soldiers, they would have had severe problems implementing a tougher line. "The real military police numbered 17 at the time that over 50,000 soldiers were turned loose on Nanjing," the university professor Bates wrote in a report.[31] Some Japanese soldiers were actually punished by their army for crimes such as murder and rape. The 10th Army court-martialed around 100 soldiers during the weeks after the fall of Nanjing, but given the extent of the abuse, this affected only a fraction of the perpetrators and probably had little preemptive effect.[32] Besides, the attempts at maintaining discipline were offset by the instances when the officers were active participants in the violence. Bates describes a night when a column of Japanese vehicles arrived at Nanjing University: it was "actually conducted by officers themselves, who pinned our watchman to the wall and raped three women refugees before carrying off one of them."[33]

Revenge was also a motivation for many. They had just been through the bloodiest combat the Japanese army had seen since the war with Russia at the start of the century. They had seen their comrades die in a conflict which their propaganda had told them was entirely the fault of the Chinese. Now they had the opportunity to pay back, and many jumped at the chance. Sasaki Toichi of the 30th Brigade wrote in his diary about the vicious mood among his soldiers and expressed some understanding that they would react in this way: "The enemy surrendered by the thousands. Our soldiers went berserk and killed them one by one. They completely ignored the officers' attempts to stop them. When you consider how many comrades have spilt their blood, and how terrible the past days have been, I almost feel like yelling, 'Kill them all,' soldiers or no soldiers."[34]

CHAPTER 12

Christmas in Hell

December 20–27, 1937

John Rabe made a new acquaintance on Monday December 20. A young Dane, Bernhard Arp Sindberg, who had stayed at Jiangnan Cement near Qixia since the Japanese conquest a week earlier, had arrived in Nanjing and showed up at the safety committee's office inside the zone. "Sindberg had had the intention of transporting some injured Chinese to Nanjing," Rabe wrote in his diary. "When he had got halfway, he had been forced to move the injured back to Qixia because the Japanese did not want to let them pass." Sindberg himself however was determined to reach Nanjing, and after he had returned the injured to the cement factory area, he had started walking in the direction of the capital. He had been picked up by a Japanese truck along the way and had been given a ride all the way to the city.[1]

Sindberg had heard on the radio that there was peace and quiet in Nanjing, and that the power and water supply as well as the telephone network were fully functioning. He was, therefore, extremely surprised to learn how bad the situation in the city actually was. Besides, he was now faced with the challenge of finding a way to get back to the cement factory. Later the same day, Sindberg visited Rabe in his home in order to borrow a car, of the brand Ford, from the German businessman's assistant, Han Xianglin. "Unfortunately, Han Xianglin agrees," Rabe wrote. "I am not completely fine with that, since the car will probably be lost during the journey—and if not the whole car, then at least all the tires."[2]

Sindberg kept the car for a while. He needed it as he was becoming a frequent visitor to Nanjing in the following days. "Sindberg drives back and forth between Jiangnan Cement, which is roughly one and a half hours away, and Nanjing, without being stopped," Rabe wrote three days later, when Sindberg was on his second expedition to the city. He no longer traveled with any hope of being able to move the injured to the city's hospitals, but in order to buy as many provisions as could be had.[3] At the same time he befriended Nanjing's

Sindberg had at his disposal a modern carpool at Jiangnan Cement, which he used for his frequent trips to downtown Nanjing. On some occasions he also borrowed automobiles from the remaining Westerners. This is a car belonging to the German embassy. Standing next to it is A. Hürter, one of very few diplomats who had not left the Chinese capital. Note the swastika on the pennant in front. (Bernhard Arp Sindberg Papers and Photography Collection, Harry Ransom Center, University of Texas at Austin)

foreign community at a time when its members, virtually all Christians of various hues, were preparing for the most sinister Christmas ever.

"Christmas in Hell," was the headline that the university professor Miner Searle Bates had chosen for an article he planned to write in late December about the conditions in Nanjing.[4] It was no exaggeration, despite Japanese promises that the situation would soon improve. For example, the American missionary John Magee had been informed that new and more disciplined Japanese troops would be deployed in the city ahead of the holiday. "I hope so for it would be nice to have a peaceful Christmas," he noted in a letter to his wife. He was soon disabused of any illusions. December 22 was a day like any other: "Today the soldiers have been leading away men again. I have heard the machine guns and slow regular rifle fire again a number of times which means more slaughter."[5]

Rabe spent the hours before Christmas Eve paying a horrifying visit to a hospital managed by the doctor Robert O. Wilson. Initially, Wilson showed him a number of patients whom he had tried to save after being maltreated by the Japanese. One of them was a woman who had had a miscarriage, with bayonet injuries all over her face. Then Wilson led the German to the hospital's morgue where he showed him corpses brought in over the past 24 hours, most of them with terrible wounds. Among them was a Chinese civilian whose head was nearly charred, with the eyes missing completely, after the Japanese had doused him with gasoline and lit a match. Rabe also saw the body of a boy of about seven years of age who had lost his life after being stabbed with a bayonet four times.

"During the past week I have seen so many bodies that even at the sight of these terrifying cases I have been able to keep my composure," Rabe wrote later the same day in his diary. "You are not in any Christmas spirit after an experience such as this. But I want to persuade myself about these shameful acts by seeing them with my own eyes, so that later I can speak about them as an eyewitness. This kind of atrocities should not be ignored!"[6] Minnie Vautrin was just as dejected. "This will be a year without Christmas," she wrote in her diary. "Did not even have time to think of my friends."[7]

Nanjing was completely sealed off from the outside world, and apart from a few diplomats, Sindberg was the only foreigner who was able to move about in and around the city in a fairly unrestrained manner. Besides, as the only person with access to a radio he was the sole source of news for the isolated foreigners in Nanjing. During his visit on December 23 he was able to report some promising developments: "Britain and France have allegedly reached an agreement whereby the French take over control of the Mediterranean, permitting Britain to send its fleet to the Far East. According to the reports, the United States has also dispatched a number of ships to an unknown destination," Rabe wrote in his diary and continued: "Unfortunately, what Sindberg cannot tell is what Germany and Italy have to say about these events."[8]

***

If the news which Sindberg had heard on the radio triggered any hopes among the Westerners in Nanjing about an imminent foreign intervention in China, this had no basis in reality. The transfer of the British fleet to the Far East, which had been mentioned in the news reports, probably referred to a broader strategy decided in London which had nothing to do with events in Nanjing. The naval base in Singapore was undergoing rapid expansion in the 1930s as part of Britain's plans to protect its global empire. No Western power wanted to be dragged into the war in China. Even the Japanese attack on the gunboat *Panay* was settled discreetly and peacefully. The U.S. government accepted Japanese compensation and an apology in return for sweeping the entire potentially explosive incident under the carpet.

Very little information had reached the outside world about conditions in Nanjing in the days immediately after the Japanese entry. However, more complete reports were now gradually emerging in the foreign media. Archibald Steele, the correspondent of the *Chicago Daily News*, broke the news of the horrific situation in Nanjing to the world public. As early as on December 15, the newspaper carried his detailed account of what he had seen before escaping the city on board an American vessel. "'Four days in hell' would be the most fitting way to describe the siege and capture of Nanjing," he wrote. "It was like killing sheep. How many troops were trapped and killed it is difficult to estimate, but it may be anywhere between 5,000 and 20,000."[9] In a follow-up report, he made it clear that captured soldiers were not the only ones to be targeted by Japanese brutality: "I saw the Japanese beating and jabbing helpless civilians, and in the hospitals I saw many civilians suffering from bayonet wounds. I saw the dead scattered along every street, including some old men who could not possibly have harmed anyone."[10]

During the next few days, *The New York Times* also carried detailed descriptions of the horrors in Nanjing, and in a report published at Christmas, the newspaper told its readers about an "almost complete collapse of the discipline of Japanese soldiers." The result, according to the paper's correspondent Hallett Abend, included "wholesale massacre of civilians, executions of disarmed Chinese soldiers, the violation of and murder of Chinese women and the systematic destruction and looting of property." The paper quoted letters that had made it out of Nanjing, describing how few survived being taken prisoner for very long: "Thus far there is no trace of Chinese prisoners in Japanese hands other than squads actually or apparently on the way to be executed."[11]

The article in *The New York Times* prompted the Swedish envoy to China, Johann Beck-Friis, to prepare a report for his foreign minister, Rickard Sandler, carrying the headline "The Japanese Army Loots Nanjing" and providing a comprehensive account of the situation. Beck-Friis referred to the *Times* report, adding that it was in accordance with what he himself had learned from other sources. Specifically, he cited a conversation he had had the day before with an unnamed Italian journalist who had left Nanjing just before the arrival of the Japanese but remained informed about conditions in the city through his contacts.

"He confirmed that atrocities are taking place. As for the cause of the mass killings, he referred to the Japanese fear of ambush. This was the reason why the Japanese, as far as he knew, murdered every man who was physically

Chinese captives under Japanese guard at Nanjing. (Wikimedia Commons)

capable of holding a rifle. When I asked him if there was any truth in certain rumors that 50,000 people had been killed during the days after the conquest of the city, he replied that probably 'only' 15,000 to 20,000 people has been put to death," wrote Beck-Friis, adding that "my source is an eager Fascist and enthusiastically pro-Japanese," so as to indicate that he was unlikely to exaggerate the extent of the bloodshed.[12]

Beck-Friis went on to outline conditions in the large area between Shanghai and Nanjing, where an estimated 10 million people had lived before the war. Of these, eight million were believed to have fled, he wrote. To illustrate the huge impact of this migration away from the war zone, he pointed out the city of Suzhou, which had previously been home to 200,000 people, but had a population of just 500 when the Japanese arrived. "The entire space between Shanghai and Nanjing appears to have been turned into a wasteland, with most of the buildings damaged," he wrote.

He noted that the Japanese had officially encouraged the residents to return to Nanjing and probably other occupied areas as well, but added: "The Chinese civilians, aware of the monstrous acts that have been carried out, probably will show no major inclination to heed the call." Japan had shot itself in the foot, according to the Swedish diplomat: "It seems to me that following the occupation of Nanjing, Japan has missed a chance to reestablish order and create some goodwill for itself. It also seems to me that the unbelievable atrocities in Nanjing have undermined the constant Japanese reassurances that the Japanese troops only fight the Chinese government and are the friend of the Chinese people."[13]

***

On one of his expeditions to Nanjing during Christmas, Sindberg was carrying a petition. It was written by representatives of the inhabitants in a refugee camp located a few miles from Jiangnan Cement, in and around the famous Buddhist temple at Qixia. The site was nearly as old as Buddhism itself in China, with a history of 1,500 years. It had been through the ups and downs of China's turbulent history, and it had been entirely rebuilt after having been destroyed during the all-consuming Taiping rebellion of the mid-19th century. Now a possibly even more violent showdown was raging around the temple, and people had sought protection behind its thick walls, often walking long distances to reach their destination.

One of them was Liao Yaoxiang, a 31-year-old officer in the Chinese army's Standard Division. Liao was born in the south Chinese Hunan province, and

Chinese refugees gathered inside the Qixia temple compound. (Bernhard Arp Sindberg Papers and Photography Collection, Harry Ransom Center, University of Texas at Austin)

after having attended the prestigious Whampoa Military Academy near Hong Kong, he had received advanced training at the French military academy Saint-Cyr near Paris, steeped in proud martial history. He had taken part in the prolonged battle for Shanghai, being injured twice, and during the defense of Nanjing, he had participated in heavy fighting in the hills east of the city. During the chaotic last hours before the Japanese entry, he had escaped by changing into civilian clothes. He had, however, kept a pistol in case the Japanese were to find out about his real identity.[14]

He had walked along the southern bank of the Yangtze and had seen how dead bodies clogged its water. The Japanese had traveled up and down the river in boats, shooting at everything that moved in an attempt to prevent Chinese soldiers from crossing to the other side and fight another day. Initially, he had sought refuge with a grain merchant, who quickly realized that his thick Hunanese accent would immediately give him away as not belonging there. As a precaution, he remained silent during his stay, pretending to be the merchant's mute son. A few days later, he moved on to Qixia Temple, hiding in the crowd. Among the thousands of others, he chanced upon a soldier whom he knew from his time in France. Like he himself, he pretended to be a civilian. The two soldiers agreed to stay at the temple and bide their time.[15]

As early as mid-December, the temple was home to close to 17,000 people.[16] Many had probably sought out this particular place as they reasoned that the Japanese, most of them Buddhists, would restrain themselves near a site that they also considered holy. They were soon disabused of that illusion. "The Japanese were there every day, several times a day," said Guo Shimei, then 25, who had fled her home along with her husband, their six-year-old daughter and two-year-old son. "They also chopped off the head of a Buddha statue inside the temple."[17] It was in this situation that the petition was penned, and Sindberg, who had already befriended several monks from the temple, was chosen as the messenger.[18] "These people beg for mercy and protection from the abuse of the Japanese soldiers, who are on a rampage similar to here in Nanjing," Rabe wrote, when he received the petition from Sindberg.[19]

The petition had no palpable effect, but a few days later, Christian Kröger, a member of the zone committee and an engineer with the German trading firm Carlowitz & Co., drove from Nanjing to visit both the temple and Jiangnan Cement. As only members of the diplomatic corps enjoyed a certain limited freedom of movement, he probably traveled under cover of being a representative of the German embassy. It was testimony to the extreme material want in the region that just as Sindberg traveled to Nanjing in a desperate hope of finding new supplies, Kröger now traveled in the opposite direction with the same objective. What he saw along the way reminded him of accounts from the Thirty Years' War, and he described it as a "shock" to realize how much the once fertile landscape had been transformed. "If until then I had believed that the Japanese army's sinister justice only targeted Nanjing as the capital and center of anti-Japanese feelings, I now was forced to realize that their rampage had extended to this area in a similar if not even more unbridled manner," he later wrote in a report.[20]

Everywhere there were burnt-out ruins as silent testimony of not just the Chinese army's scorched-earth tactics, but also the additional ravages that the Japanese troops had inflicted subsequently. "The Japanese have also randomly shot farmers along with their wives and children in the fields, all in accordance with the motto of 'looking for hostile Chinese soldiers'. Many dead water buffaloes, horses and mules are scattered in the fields and along the road and have already been half devoured by dogs, crows and magpies," Kröger wrote. "During the daytime, the farmers flee with their possessions into the mountains, and only old men and woman are left behind, but they, too, are threatened. During my drive, which lasted an hour, I did not see a

The German engineer Christian Kröger visited the refugee camp at Jiangnan Cement, praising what Sindberg and Günther had achieved. Here, he said, the terror stopped. (Bernhard Arp Sindberg Papers and Photography Collection, Harry Ransom Center, University of Texas at Austin)

single human being, not even in the big villages. Everything is charred and dead, and everyone runs away the moment they see a vehicle approaching."

Kröger described what he heard from the refugees at Qixia Temple:

> Here, too, the Japanese soldiers are completely uninhibited. Here, too, young men are randomly pulled from the crowd and shot, while the girls are raped, and the drunken Japanese soldiers derive much fun from stabbing anything they don't like and also maltreating people in other manners with their bayonets. All of this happens in a place where no medical aid is possible. Temple art is stolen or destroyed, and the monks are also not in any way protected from maltreatment.

By contrast, conditions at the cement factory nearby were completely different, Kröger remarked: "In that place, the terror is halted in a way, all because of two Europeans, one German—Herr Günther—and the other one a Dane."[21]

CHAPTER 13

The Man with the Flag

December 28, 1937–January 13, 1938

Twenty-five-year-old Guo Shimei, who had arrived at Qixia Temple with her husband and two children and witnessed the Japanese rampaging and vandalizing Buddhist art, decided after a few days that the temple was no longer a safe place to be. As a matter of fact, nowhere seemed a safe place to be at the time. Her own brother, two years her senior, had been apprehended for no reason by the Japanese in their home village a few miles from the temple, and together with two other young men, he had been sent off to Nanjing. She never saw him again. The uncertainty and the terror reigned everywhere, with one single exception: Jiangnan Cement. Rumors about the factory, where the Japanese did not dare to enter, spread among the scared refugees, and like many others, Guo Shimei and her family decided to settle down there.

They followed the example of the others who had arrived before them and built a shelter from straw and bamboo sticks. They fetched the building materials from their home village, stealing back at times of the day when the Japanese would not be near. "The shelter was so low that we had to bend down to crawl inside," Guo recalled later. "When it snowed, it was terribly cold, and when it rained, the water seeped through all the holes in the roof." Initially they ate rice which they had brought from their village. "When we went home for more rice, it was important to take off early. If we departed too late in the morning, we risked being seized by the Japanese," she said. When the rice had been depleted, they walked into the hills searching for edible wild plants.

The conditions were harsh, but even so, they were far better than any of the alternatives. This was because of the strange foreigner with the blond, wavy locks who knew how to keep the Japanese at bay. It was pure magic, and Guo Shimei watched it again and again. "When the Japanese arrived, the foreigner walked out to talk to them, and after some time, they departed again. If the Japanese wanted to grab some women, the foreigner produced a flag, and after they had exchanged a few words, the Japanese retired," she explained when she was interviewed as an old woman.[1] She was not alone in noticing the peculiar respect which the Japanese apparently felt for the foreigner's flag: "When he hoisted the Danish flag, the Japanese did not dare enter," one of them said many years later.[2]

The Chinese refugees often arrived at Jiangnan Cement after much hardship, and they were surprised by the order maintained at the factory. "It was a refugee camp managed by a Dane. There were guards posted around its perimeter, and there were patrols of the area," said Zhou Zhongbing, then a boy of just 15. "When the Japanese arrived in order to make trouble, the Dane walked out and stopped them." Many also noticed what to them was the Dane's exotic appearance. They were struck by his light skin, and since they had never seen blond people before, they thought his hair was white.[3]

Some refugees ended up at Jiangnan Cement by coincidence. This was the case with Luo Zuowei, a veterinarian from the Beijing area, who had been drafted into the Chinese cavalry. With another former soldier he had been on the run from the Japanese army after the defeat at Nanjing, and initially their plan had been to seek refuge at Qixia Temple. Luo later explained in his memoirs why it turned out differently: "When we passed by Jiangnan Cement, we heard that there was also a refugee camp there, and we decided to try to gain entry to the cement factory first. We saw that the iron fence at the gate was closed, and that a worker was performing guard duty. We asked if we could stay there, and when he heard our Beijing accent, he immediately retorted, 'We are from the same place. You are most welcome!'"

The worker led the two new arrivals to a sort of waiting room, and shortly afterwards they were introduced to a blond foreigner. They were told that he was a supervisor who had been sent by the owner of the factory. The two were allowed to stay at Jiangnan Cement, but in return they were to help the foreigner with a grisly job. Every morning on the following days they walked down to the banks of the Yangtze looking for corpses which had drifted ashore, burying them on a slope nearby. Most of the dead were victims of mass executions, perpetrated by the Japanese army in Nanjing. "I collected altogether eight bodies. They were all charred, and it was not possible to make out any individual features at all," Luo Zuowei wrote in his memoirs.

Luo Zuowei and his companion remained at Jiangnan Cement for a week. Then suddenly one evening they were visited by the worker whom they had met on the first day. He carried a warning. "The Japanese would inspect the factory on the following day, and he advised us to disappear as soon as possible," Luo Zuowei wrote in his memoirs. "He gave us a cotton blanket and a pair

Bernhard Sindberg left an indelible mark in the memories of countless refugees because of the courage he showed at Jiangnan Cement, often confronting the Japanese armed with no more than a flag. (Anita Günther)

of fabric shoes each. In return he took my military jacket and threw it into a ditch." The worker had found a boat which could be used to cross the Yangtze. He accompanied the two to the boat, and under the cover of darkness they succeeded in making their way to the opposite, unoccupied shore.[4]

***

By early 1938, the new rulers of Nanjing did their best to signal that the period of chaos was over, and that order had been reinstated. In the afternoon of December 31, the various districts in the safety zone received instructions to send representatives to an official ceremony to be performed in a park in the center of the city. A new government was paraded in front of the public, surrounded by both Japanese flags and flags of the newly established puppet regime. "One of our representatives felt sick at heart about it and would eat no supper," Minnie Vautrin wrote in her diary.[5] At the same time, the Japanese army employed the crass methods of its propaganda apparatus, seeking to portray itself as a benefactor of the people it had just been busy slaughtering. "Japanese news squads went around staging pictures of Japanese soldiers giving candy to a child or an Army doctor examining 20 children," wrote the sociologist Lewis S.C. Smythe, who was a member of the safety committee. "But these acts were not repeated when no camera was around!"[6]

The real conditions in occupied Nanjing were very different from the official image that Japan tried to project. The Chinese soldiers who still had been able to hide among the civilian population were hunted down mercilessly. The Japanese administrators now decided to proceed systematically and register every single person inside the city walls. "We are now entering a new epoch—the period of registration," Vautrin wrote on December 28. It began at eight in the morning inside the area of the safety zone. Initially, the male population was targeted for registration, Vautrin wrote, describing the procedure in more detail: "We got our men together, they were first lectured through an interpreter, then told if there were any ex-soldiers in the group, they should confess; they would not be hurt but would be put into a labor corps."[7]

In fact they were doomed, and the methods of killing them were often barbaric. John Rabe described how Japanese soldiers turned up at a school which served as a temporary shelter for refugees, ordering all former soldiers to take one step forward:

> They were promised protection. They just had to be detailed to various work teams. After that, some of the refugees stepped forward. In one case, about 50 persons. They were taken away immediately. According to what we are now being told by survivors, they were led into an empty building, where they were robbed of all valuables and were stripped completely, after which they were tied together in groups of five. Then the Japanese lit a large bonfire in the courtyard of the building, pulled the groups up one by one, stabbed the people with bayonets and threw them, still living, onto the fire. Ten of them were able to extricate themselves from their chains, jumping over the wall surrounding the courtyard and dispersing among the crowd, who readily provided them with new clothes.[8]

The same day, there was a dramatic worsening of the weather. It began as an icy drizzle but, in the afternoon, it developed into regular snow. "The poor refugees living in huts, many no longer than a pup tent, will have a miserable time of it, for most of these huts are not rain proof. And then there is the sticky mud," the missionary Fitch wrote in his diary. He completed a tour of the camps in the zone and concluded that they were filled to capacity and beyond, and that it was impossible to maintain essential hygiene. The camp administrators, both foreigners and Chinese, made an enormous effort, but Fitch was getting frustrated: "How long must we maintain these camps? When are the people going to be permitted to return to their homes—those who have any homes left?"[9]

He was right to ask that question, for as it continued its assaults on the people of Nanjing, the Japanese army was also in the process of carrying out the physical destruction of the former capital. The systematic plunder which had kicked off immediately after the conquest of the city was kept up until the end of December.[10] A steady stream of stolen goods flowed in the direction of the port and the train station. Some of the loot ended up with the Japanese army's quartermaster service, but in addition a large number of luxury items were taken by individual soldiers and sent home to family in Japan. Mørch-Hansen's personal car, a Studebaker, was removed by unknown perpetrators, probably Japanese soldiers who needed a vehicle to transport all the other booty they had acquired.[11]

As an added humiliation, many Chinese were forced to assist the Japanese in emptying their own homes. "If no means of transportation was available, the servants of the households, or refugees who had sought shelter there, were forced to help carry the loot away," Christian Kröger wrote. "Often you would see a soldier with a weapon and four coolies in front of him, weighed down by his loot. Prams were also used, along with wheelbarrows, donkeys, mules—in short, everything that could be found."[12] Vautrin described how she spent days worrying about a bicycle messenger who was employed by Ginling College and had gone missing. It turned out that during an errand in Nanjing, he had been stopped by two Japanese soldiers, who had poked him menacingly with their bayonets and stolen his bicycle. "He was forced to go to Xiaguan, where for ten days he did nothing but carry loot for them, and load it on trucks," Vautrin wrote.[13]

Foreign property was not exempt. Texaco's warehouse was also ransacked by Japanese soldiers. On December 30, a group of Japanese visited the facility, wielding pistols to force the building's supervisor, a Chinese man by the name of Wang Jingyong, to open the gate. They stole two trucks and two cars, 400 liters of gasoline and 40 boxes containing the personal possessions of Texaco's employees. They also tore down the American flag, trampled on it in a show of disdain, and burned it. Fitch described the incident in a protest note to the Japanese embassy: "They then tried to force Wang to sign a receipt for one thousand dollars. This he refused to do, so he was bound and taken away until the following day, when he finally consented to sign, and then was permitted to return. He was told that if he reported this matter his entire family would be killed."[14] On the very same day that Fitch handed in his protest, the Japanese once again attacked Texaco's warehouse. This time, four Japanese soldiers drove up in two separate trucks carrying about 100 forced Chinese laborers and removed everything that was left of the gas and oil, Fitch said in a follow-up note.[15]

For the Japanese, it was no longer a question of securing essential supplies at a time when their own logistical services had proven unable to keep up with the advancing troops. Now it was all about personal enrichment, as had been the wont of soldiers for millennia, and in the tradition of Genghis Khan, the Japanese increasingly set fire to buildings that they had just searched for valuable items. A carpet of smoke covered the city as entire districts gradually were engulfed by the flames. It seemed that few of the perpetrators ever considered that Nanjing would at one point have to reemerge as a functioning big city, even if under a changed regime. As Nakajima Kesago, the commander of the 16th Division, put it in conversations with his commander-in-chief, Matsui Iwane: "We have occupied their country and killed many of them. What's wrong with our soldiers wanting to bring some of their possessions home? Who would benefit if we just left the things here?"[16]

***

During the period around New Year, Sindberg continued his expeditions into Nanjing. His ability to move at liberty through areas where armed Japanese soldiers kept an eye on everything was so remarkable that he ended up in a report prepared by U.S. Naval intelligence which, however, mistakenly identified him as a German:

> Severe restrictions are placed upon every foreigner in the city; practically none has been allowed to pass out of the city gates, except the diplomatic representatives. It is told, however, that one German, representative of a German firm, has maintained his home outside the city and when he wishes to enter the city he travels in a fearfully-dilapidated old car carrying two live ducks from his place, and he presents the gate sentry with a duck. This usually gains him admittance, and on the way out he presents another duck, which serves to pass him out.[17]

In a letter to a friend in Denmark, Sindberg described the technical hassles he had to tackle in order to maintain the constant round trips between Jiangnan Cement and the capital:

> I have terrible trouble with my cars… The roads are completely damaged by tanks and potholed by bombs and grenades, and in many places, soldiers have even dug trenches across them. You can probably understand that you need sturdy vehicles to negotiate that kind of surface. It's no wonder that each trip costs me a broken coil and several flat tires. Sometimes I even need a dozen soldiers to help me across the ditches and the holes in the road, or out of them.[18]

In the same letter, Sindberg described the sight that met him during his expeditions to Nanjing:

> On a trip like that all you see is devastation everywhere. All villages have been burned down. All cattle and all poultry have been stolen. Wherever you look there are corpses of farmers or Chinese soldiers which now serve to feed stray dogs and wild animals. Only occasionally you come across an old Chinese, who has been spared and now walks around in a lonely search for a bit of food.

On his trips to Nanjing, Sindberg encountered a nightmarish, deserted landscape. He took this photo, adding the following note: "Chinese farmer deliberately shot and killed by Japs." (Bernhard Arp Sindberg Papers and Photography Collection, Harry Ransom Center, University of Texas at Austin)

He also mentioned with a clear note of sadness an area outside Nanjing's city wall where there had previously been swimming pools, schools, and other prestige projects completed under Chiang Kai-shek: "Now it is an assembly of ruins, and completely deserted. Oddly enough, the only thing that has been spared is a large national monument for the father of the Chinese revolution, Dr. Sun Yat-sen."[19]

Sindberg was always a welcome visitor in Nanjing, and for good reason. Jiangnan Cement was an essential source of food, as the German diplomat Paul Scharffenberg explained in his reports to his embassy, which after the fall of Nanjing had moved up the Yangtze to the large city of Wuhan:

The streets outside the zone are empty. The ruins offer a desolate, frozen spectacle. There are no hotels, movie theaters, pharmacies, shops, markets. Nothing. Food supplies have dropped to a dangerously low level, and in the safety zone they have started consuming horses and dogs[20]… The supplies that we receive from the Japanese are completely insufficient. If we had to rely only on them, we would have starved to death by now. Yesterday the Dane Sindberg from the cement plant once again brought food and gave us a small pig, eggs and two ducks. He had been arrested along the way, but he managed to get past the sentry with a case of beer, for which he even received the escort of an officer and three soldiers.[21]

For the Westerners inside Nanjing's walls, Sindberg was also one of the only sources of information about what happened in the rural districts outside the city. This emerges from a letter which John Magee wrote to his wife on January 4: "Yesterday morning I had a talk with two Chinese from the Texas Oil Co. warehouse… They said there were a great many dead bodies of men, women, and children. Mr. Sindbery [sic], a Dane, said that the same was true outside the Zhongshan gate [at the eastern end of the city wall]."[22] Almost nine years later, Magee still remembered Sindberg's detailed descriptions of the conditions in the area around Nanjing. At the war crimes tribunal for the Far East after the end of World War II, Magee had been summoned to deliver testimony about the Nanjing massacre, and during a lengthy interrogation he brought up his acquaintance: "A Dane, living fifteen miles outside the city, told me he had seen a soldier giving himself up. When he went back to Nanjing he saw the body of a soldier, apparently beaten to death."[23]

***

On Sunday January 9, 1938, the Danish daily *Politiken* carried a short item on page two, written by the newspaper's China correspondent Vagn Meisling:

Shanghai, Saturday. The Japanese consul in Shanghai has informed the Danish Consul General Scheel that the new cement plant which F. L. Smidth has built in Nanjing is undamaged and has been guarded by Bernhard Sindberg during the fighting. Sindberg is still in Nanjing and is doing well. As the readers will remember, Sindberg was in the company of British journalist Pembroke Stephens when the latter was killed by Japanese machine gun bullets.[24]

It was the first time in over a month that anyone outside had heard from Sindberg, and it was repeated the following day in other Danish media.[25]

Two days later, on January 11, Sindberg sent a letter to Niels Jensen, F. L. Smidth's representative in Shanghai:

A couple of words, jotted down in all haste, to let you know that everything is fine here, and nothing has been damaged. There are approximately 100 people in the factory, including workers and their families. Outside the factory, there are about 3,000 to 4,000 refugees who have sought the protection offered by our flag. Food is scarce. We have sufficient supplies until the middle of February, but after that God knows how we and the refugees are going to get our food.

Sindberg mentioned that two diplomats from the German embassy in Nanjing had visited the factory the day before and had handed over 1,000 dollars to Günther, probably in response to the request by the Danish mission the month before that 1,000 British pounds be paid to Jiangnan Cement.[26]

Sindberg explained in his letter to Niels Jensen that the Japanese soldiers in the area generally behaved in a correct manner towards the plant and its staff. However, there was also disconcerting news: "Yesterday we were visited by a Japanese gentleman who identified himself as the secretary of Mr. S. Iwasaki, vice president of the Tokyo Chamber of Commerce and Industry, Japan. He was accompanied by Japanese officers, inspecting the entire factory and taking several photos. The name of the secretary is Mr. J. Saito." To F. L. Smidth in Shanghai, this was the first sure indication that the Japanese perceived an economic interest in Jiangnan Cement. The factory had escaped damage during the Japanese attack on Nanjing, and abuse of its staff had largely been avoided. What was emerging now was a new and likely much more complicated battle to protect the plant against expropriation. In this battle, F. L. Smidth was represented by a man who had shown his courage but had still to demonstrate that he also possessed the necessary diplomatic skill to keep the Japanese at bay.

CHAPTER 14

Friendships

January 14–February 3, 1938

On Friday, January 14, an old Chinese man dragged himself through the gates of Jiangnan Cement. Early on the same day, a group of Japanese soldiers had visited him at his farm. They had been looking for women. The old man had given the soldiers rice wine and cigarettes, which they had accepted, but he had been unable to provide any women. The soldiers persisted in their demand and started threatening him, and when the old man fell onto his knees and begged them to be spared, they lost patience and fired two shots at him. One projectile penetrated the lung, and the other hit the groin.[1]

It was a medical case like many others that Sindberg was faced with in his sparsely equipped clinic without any medical training beyond the most basic. "The people who have sought shelter here are mostly peasants from the area within a radius of 20 miles. Many of them are ill or injured, from bombs, hand grenades and bullets, and since the nearest doctor is in Nanjing, where no one can go, I have become a kind of doctor to them. Up till now I have treated about 50 patients, and currently around 30 remain in treatment," he wrote in a letter to Niels Jensen.[2]

Even so, only one of his patients had died. It was a young Chinese man who had chanced upon a Japanese patrol three miles from the cement factory and had been left behind with a deep gash to the back of his neck caused by a sword. "He lived for twenty days and was on his way to recovery, but suddenly he was hit by fever, and nothing helped. After severe pains, he passed away here among us," Sindberg wrote. "This is just a couple of examples of what happens here. Rape, looting and burning of farms are the order of the day."

A month had passed since the fall of Nanjing, but nothing suggested that conditions in the vicinity of Jiangnan Cement would become any more peaceful soon, Sindberg explained in his letter:

We, our flag, the factory and the surrounding compound are the only ones who have so far escaped damage, but how long this will last is anyone's guess, since the cases of abuse are increasing rather than decreasing. In other words, things are getting worse all the time. Every day more soldiers arrive in the area, and we can hardly turn in any direction without bumping into a patrol or a sentry. They all have to live off the land, and the peasants' grain and cattle have been seized long ago.[3]

When Japanese patrols passed through villages near Jiangnan Cement in search of food, violence was in the air. The same day that the old man was carried into Sindberg's clinic, he received another two patients, a man and his five-year-old son. Japanese soldiers had marched into their farm and had tried to catch the family's poultry. When they failed, they tried to kill them with hand grenades. "One hand grenade exploded near the little boy, seriously wounding him all over the body, tearing out one eye, etc.," Sindberg wrote in a report. The boy's father had been hit by a splinter, causing an injury that could be dressed at the clinic, but the boy's condition was so serious that Sindberg decided to take him to Nanjing in a car from the factory's automobile pool.

After a month, the German and Danish flags retained the power to keep the Japanese at bay. Still, Sindberg had begun to worry that he might not be able to hold off the Japanese military in the long run. (Bernhard Arp Sindberg Papers and Photography Collection, Harry Ransom Center, University of Texas at Austin)

He arrived with his young patient at one of Nanjing's city gates at the eastern end of the wall but was stopped by the sentry. He attempted to persuade the soldier to allow the injured boy to be passed on to one of the hospitals inside the city, but that, too, was turned down. Sindberg did not give up but drove along the wall until he reached the next gate, which was further north. "At high speed [I] went past the sentry and no attempt was made to stop me," he wrote in his report. He drove on to a hospital managed by the American doctor Robert O. Wilson, where he left his patient in the care of professionals.[4]

Two days later, Sindberg returned to Nanjing to visit the injured boy and complete a number of small errands. In particular, he hoped to get hold of some coffee, which had not been available anywhere for several weeks. For the first time he was able to use the brand-new Dodge, which had been sitting unused for a month, because the driver had left. Now he was back, and he had brought the keys. Sindberg loaded the automobile with 12 ducks, four chickens, 36 eggs, and vegetables. Following the experience of two days earlier, he avoided the eastern city gate and instead tried to enter Nanjing via the northern gate. "I was stopped at the gate and was nearly not allowed to pass. I only succeeded after I gave them a duck and allowed a soldier to accompany me, promising to be back within two hours. I managed to attend to all my errands," Sindberg wrote in a letter.[5]

When Sindberg turned up at the city two hours later, he had bought bandages and medicine for his clinic as well as 125 bullets for his hunting rifle. He had even managed to find a bottle of Haig whisky, a pack of Camel cigarettes, and two cigars, but the coveted coffee had proven impossible to find anywhere. Hardly had he exited the city gate when he realized that something was wrong with the car's steering. He stopped and discovered that the front left wheel was losing air, and just as he was pumping up the tire, three Japanese soldiers passed by. "They wanted a ride, which I always allow when it's impossible to avoid. One of them wanted to take over as the driver, and as they started to be threatening, I had no choice but to let him do it," Sindberg wrote. "The thing is, this piece of road is a regular battlefield, full of craters etc., and very narrow, with the city wall on one side and deep slopes on the other. He had only driven for about 100 yards when he lost control of the car, veering off the road and down the deep slope."

> Luckily the slope was overgrowing with small fir trees, which slowed down the car, but only after having felled 15 or 20 of them and flying over a large bomb crater did the vehicle come to a halt. No one was hurt, and the soldiers disappeared, leaving me to my own devices, 20 miles from Jiangnan. Hauling the car back up by myself was impossible, and it was loaded with more parcels than I could carry myself, so I hid everything in the forest, and started

walking. I only reached home late at night after much trouble, carrying the whiskey and the cigars. The next day, I reached out to two local [Japanese] soldiers that we count as friends and explained the situation to them. They drove with me in the Ford, and with the help of 12 soldiers, we managed to edge the car down the slope to a road further down. After some minor repairs carried out on the spot—among other things, the steering arm had been torn off, probably causing the accident, but could be immediately reattached—the car could be used again. Apart from the front bumper, which had broken off but could be welded back on, nothing had been damaged, not a scratch, and everyone is happy now.[6]

***

Sindberg's many trips to Nanjing brought him into frequent contact with the Japanese army, and if he not had an open-minded approach to individual Japanese people, he would have got nowhere. At the same time that he was faced with the enormity of the Japanese army's behavior in the form of the steady stream of horrific injuries turning up at his clinic, he also had to actively socialize with members of the occupying power. "We entertain soldiers at the club [at Jiangnan Cement], and on several occasions, we have arranged major dinner parties. We have to stay on good terms, and therefore we are open all day long," he explained in a letter to Niels Jensen.[7] Sindberg also went on hunting trips in the area, most likely accompanied by Japanese officers. "There is a lot of game. So far, I have only been able to get two wood pigeons and a pheasant. It's harder to get within range of deer," he wrote in a letter.[8]

Spending time with members of the Japanese military also meant that Sindberg occasionally was privy to important information, which he made sure was passed on to people who could make use of it. For instance, he appears in a confidential report prepared by John M. Allison, a diplomat with the U.S. Embassy, about the Japanese army's attempts to create a new stream of revenue through the sale of drugs:

> Some two weeks ago I was informed by a Danish subject who lives several miles outside Nanjing that on the occasion of a recent visit of his in company of some Japanese officers, to a restaurant which caters to the Japanese military, he had discovered young women smoking opium in one of the rooms and that he had been informed by the women that the soldiers had furnished the supply.[9]

The foreigners inside Nanjing were in the same unpleasant situation as Sindberg where on the one hand they had to witness on a daily basis multiple crimes, one worse than the other, while on the other hand they had to maintain a correct or even friendly demeanor towards the men who were ultimately responsible for the atrocities. Only in this way was it possible to stay in contact with the Japanese authorities. Even so, it was with decidedly mixed feelings that John Rabe, Minnie Vautrin, and seven other representatives of the zone committee took part in a dinner party at the Japanese embassy on January 15. "Am I to go and eat with the murderers?" asked a missionary who had just seen a close Chinese colleague be pulled out into the street and shot.[10] The food turned out to be excellent, forming a sharp contrast to the famine in the streets outside, and the conversation flowed in an easy manner.[11] "We had a pleasant evening," Vautrin wrote in her diary, "and our lips uttered jokes, though often our hearts were heavy. I think it was worthwhile to come to know each other better."[12]

During the dinner, Rabe rose and asked for everybody's attention, cleared his throat, and delivered a carefully prepared message:

> We appeal to the noble feeling of the Japanese, to the spirit of the samurai, of whom we foreigners have heard and read so much—those samurai who have fought so gallantly for their country in countless battles and at the same time did not deny mercy to an enemy who could no longer defend himself. You, gentlemen of the Japanese embassy, have listened patiently to our entreaties and our complaints, of which there have been many. And as far as possible, you have done everything in your power to help us. For this help, which we appreciate beyond measure, we want to thank you!

Rabe later confided to his diary that he had felt terrible about praising the Japanese at a time when the abuse was continuing unabatedly, but he needed

Sindberg and his colleagues were forced to maintain correct and sometimes even friendly relations with members of the Japanese army. This was necessary in order to obtain permission to drive to Nanjing, and besides, the Japanese were often important sources of vital information. The photo shows Sindberg's translator Li Yulin with Japanese soldiers at the Qixia railway station. (Bernhard Arp Sindberg Papers and Photography Collection, Harry Ransom Center, University of Texas at Austin)

the connections in the Japanese camp. As Rabe remarked: "The end justifies the means."[13]

Just as Sindberg and the other Westerners had an ambivalent relationship with the Japanese, their views of the Chinese were also mixed. There is no doubt that they felt intense sympathy for the civilian population, which was exposed to the worst horrors of modern war. Many also felt they had a direct stake in the future of China, often having spent decades in the country. "As most members of the safety committee have been active as missionaries here, they have considered it their Christian duty to stay with their Chinese friends in times of war," Rabe said in his remarks at the Japanese embassy. "Being a merchant myself, I have joined them after spending 30 years in this country. After having enjoyed the hospitality of its inhabitants for so long, I think it is fit not to leave the Chinese to their own devices in the middle of their misfortune."[14]

Sindberg had also developed great sympathy for the Chinese after having witnessed a long series of Japanese atrocities, beginning with the executions in the Shanghai docks. At the same time, however, there were invisible but impenetrable barriers between the Europeans and the Chinese, brought about by a century of imperialism in the Middle Kingdom. The Westerners usually did not mix with the locals, and vice versa. The conditions at Jiangnan Cement were an example, as described in a letter from Sindberg to Niels Jensen on January 20:

> It is Thursday evening, and Dr. Günther and I are sitting, warm and cozy, in the living room. There is a fire in stove, music from the radio, electrical lighting, etc. Outside there is a blizzard. It has been snowing or raining for two days straight. Everything outside is cold and miserable. All roads have been turned into mud. Over five thousand Chinese war refugees are outside the factory's bamboo fence, where they live in holes in the ground, grass huts, or, if they have been lucky enough to get to the plant's supply sheds before the others, homes built from bamboo and straw mats.[15]

Another invisible barrier between Sindberg and the Chinese was the language. It was all the more obvious because Karl Günther, who was born in China, spoke it fluently. In his correspondence with Niels Jensen, Sindberg did not try to conceal the difficult position this put him in: "I am handicapped by not speaking Chinese, which Dr. Günther speaks very well, and naturally everyone turns to him about everything, and since he is older than me, it is actually okay. Besides he knows everyone, receives letters and money from Shanghai, so I have allowed him to take charge in order to avoid friction. After all, there can be no more than one captain on a ship."[16] Still, Sindberg had acquired just enough of the exotic language to be able to communicate with the inhabitants of the refugee camp, exposing a wicked sense of humor. "He stayed in a house in the factory," said Cao Chengying, then an 11-year-old girl. "When he emerged, he would sometimes prank us. Occasionally, he scared us by yelling, 'The Japanese devils are here!' and then he would burst out laughing. But when the Japanese really did arrive, it was a completely different matter. Then he would intervene."[17]

***

The Shanghai-based Swedish envoy Johann Beck-Friis was convinced that a massacre with few parallels in modern history was taking place in Nanjing. After his first report on conditions in Nanjing written during Christmas 1937, he wrote a new and even more alarming report on January 31, 1938. Although Shanghai was only separated from Nanjing by a day-long train journey, it was virtually impossible for anyone except members of the Japanese military to travel between the two cities, and there might as well have been an entire continent between them. The Chinese capital remained sealed off from the outside world, and only a tiny trickle of news escaped about the situation there. "Apart from some foreign warships and representatives of certain embassies, all foreigners, including journalists, have been prevented from visiting or leaving Nanjing," Beck-Friis wrote, warning that his information was necessarily scarce and incomplete.

"However," he continued, "it should be safe at this stage to conclude that the Japanese troops have made themselves guilty of excesses of an extent and of such a brutal character that they completely overshadow the worst behavior of Chinese bandit armies of the previous decades and that, was it not for the fact that we have the fully credible testimony of neutral observers, one would have refused to associate this with the previously well-disciplined Japanese army." He emphasized that this was not a case of individual incidents of violence committed during the first few days of victory fever, and they seemed to be continuing as of late January, albeit on a smaller scale. Among diplomats, it was held that General Matsui and the other senior commanders sincerely regretted what had happened but had been incapable of reinstating discipline. In any case, their efforts were undermined by the fact that junior officers behaved no better than their men, the Swedish diplomat wrote.

"According to witness testimony, the soldiers have murdered, burnt, looted and raped women without worrying about the presence of witnesses. Rape of even small girls has thus to some extent taken placed even on the compounds of American missionary stations," Beck-Friis wrote, adding that according to some estimates, between 10,000 and 20,000 women had

Refugees inside the Qixia temple compound. Many had hoped that the Japanese, who themselves were mainly Buddhist, would be less aggressive in a sacred place like this, but this was often not the case. (Bernhard Arp Sindberg Papers and Photography Collection, Harry Ransom Center, University of Texas at Austin)

been raped in Nanjing since the fall of the city. Estimates of the number of people killed were highly uncertain and ranged anywhere between 10,000 and 50,000, according to Beck-Friis. As for the large area between Shanghai and Nanjing which the Japanese forces had invaded in late 1937, it was even harder to arrive at a reliable casualty figure. The Swedish envoy quoted the *Manchester Guardian*'s correspondent as saying that about 300,000 had lost their lives there. "It's likely that his estimate is on the low side. Many believe the number of innocent people who have been killed to exceed one million," he added.

"Apart from the humanitarian aspect, it seems that the Japanese have committed a serious political blunder with their excesses, since many Chinese, who otherwise might have been willing to collaborate with the Japanese now are reluctant to have anything to do with them, especially after the events in Nanjing," Beck-Friis wrote. "Previously, most Chinese, regardless of their personal opinions about the Japanese, associated them with order and organization, but this has now received a considerable blow. Those who might still have believed in the official Japanese reassurances about the Japanese army's friendly objectives towards the Chinese people have now been alerted to a harsh reality."[18]

***

On February 2, Sindberg was visited at the cement plant by a Japanese soldier. He had been sent by his lieutenant, who needed to go to Nanjing the following day, and he wished to inquire if Sindberg could give him a ride. Sindberg immediately agreed since a Japanese officer in the passenger seat would make it significantly easier to get past the various checkpoints. Besides, Sindberg had urgent business in Nanjing. The fuel pump of the company's Dodge had to be repaired, but more importantly, he was carrying yet another petition from Qixia Temple, written by one of its main clerics and signed by 20 representatives of the refugees. It was similar to the one Sindberg had handed over to Rabe during Christmas, and it showed that the Japanese crimes in and around the temple had continued and were as bad as ever.[19]

"To whom it may concern, in the name of humanity!" read the introduction of the Chinese-language letter.

> What follows is a short summary of conditions and our problems at this temple. Since the fall of Nanjing, the refugees have come here in hopes of shelter and help, arriving by the hundreds every day. As of this writing, 20,400 people have already been assembled here, mostly women and children. The men have either been shot or have been captured by the Japanese soldiers to carry out hard work for them.[20]

It went on to outline the basic conditions that the thousands of inhabitants lived under:

> Eighty percent of the refugees who seek protection here have lost everything they owned. Their homes have been destroyed, their livestock killed, their valuables stolen. Many women have lost their husbands, and children their fathers, because most young men have been put to death by the Japanese soldiers. Many are injured and sick, and they have no way to see a doctor, since no one dares traveling for fear of being shot. Very little rice is left. How are the farmers supposed to work in the field once spring arrives, since they have neither water buffalo to plow the field, nor seeds to sow? We beg you to help our people.[21]

The petition then described a number of episodes from the previous month. On January 4, a group of Japanese soldiers drove up on a truck. They picked nine cows and forced a number of refugees to slaughter them for ease of transport. While the work was ongoing, some of the soldiers took off into the vicinity and burned down buildings. Two days later, the Japanese appeared once more, this time dragging away a donkey. From now on, the Japanese visits became more frequent, and also more terrifying. On January 7, they raped a woman and a 14-year-old girl, in a prelude to what would happen over the next two days. At bayonet point, women and girls were forced to let the soldiers have their way. Once again on January 11, the Japanese returned. Some were drunk and fired their weapons aimlessly. Several Chinese were injured. Two days on, they reappeared. They looted, and they raped a mother and her daughter.[22]

On January 15, a large group of Japanese soldiers broke into the temple area and detained all young women they came across. Among them, they selected the ten they liked the most, led them to a room in the temple area, and raped them. Later the same day, a lone Japanese soldier, blind-drunk, blundered into the temple, demanding women and more wine. He received wine, but no women. Infuriated, he started shooting wildly, killing two young boys. Then he disappeared. On the way back to his camp he broke into a random house, killed a 70-year-old woman and stole her donkey, before setting fire to the property.[23]

The list of atrocities was long, and it was in sharp contrast to the order reigning at Jiangnan Cement. To be sure, the last couple of weeks, the situation in and around the temple had changed somewhat. A new Japanese unit had been given responsibility for the area around the nearby village of Qixia. The lieutenant commanding the newly arrived soldiers was "a good man," the refugees at the temple thought. "Since his arrival, conditions have improved a great deal," they wrote in the petition. "He has placed a sentry here, which has proved to be of great benefit, as he stops Japanese soldiers from elsewhere turning up looking for women or things to plunder."[24] Still, no one knew when the Japanese lieutenant would be transferred elsewhere and replaced with a less friendly newcomer. Therefore, the petition was necessary.

When Sindberg turned up with his Dodge at the agreed spot to pick up the Japanese lieutenant on February 3, he was nowhere to be seen. Instead he met two Buddhist priests from Qixia Temple, who knew him from before and had heard that he planned to go to Nanjing. "The thing is, if you don't have Japanese soldiers among your passengers, it is almost impossible to get past Nanjing's city gates," Sindberg wrote to a friend, explaining the difficult situation. "Therefore, I drove to a train station in the neighborhood, where I have befriended a lieutenant, and asked him to provide me with a soldier to accompany me on the trip. Then we took off—with him, the two priests and me myself—in the new Dodge."

Sindberg continued his detailed account of the trip to Nanjing:

> I managed to get through the city gate in one piece, past the sentry who was standing in a corner seeking protection from the storm. Today I saw the first signs that they have started burying the dead in Nanjing. They have been lying out in the open since the middle of December. Apart from my passengers, I carried 20 live ducks, a butchered pig, 100 eggs and

some vegetables in the car. They were destined for the foreigners' headquarters, where the produce was received with the usual cheers. The two priests were to visit some charities and also the office of the new Chinese government, and they could not make it for my return trip. I will have to come back and pick them up the day after tomorrow.

In Nanjing several new Japanese shops had opened up for business, which made it easier than before to purchase the necessary products: "Fresh food is still not available, but there is beer and alcohol, and I acquired both. Coffee can also not be had, and I haven't had coffee since New Year. The same goes for potatoes. But there is still ample amounts of rice." It turned out that the damage to the fuel pump on the Dodge was more complicated than expected, and he had to leave it at the workshop. Instead, he borrowed a Buick, which he could drive back to the cement factory. "After a nice dinner at the American ambassador's home, I drove home in the middle of a mighty blizzard," he wrote.[25] All told, it had been a successful trip. Sindberg was satisfied, and for good reason. However, back home at Jiangnan Cement, new major problems were waiting for him.

CHAPTER 15

The New Order

February 4–20, 1938

When Sindberg returned to Jiangnan Cement from Nanjing in the borrowed Buick, Günther told him that there had been unannounced visitors. A major group of people had arrived from Shanghai, led by Masuda Kanichi, an engineer and local representative of Onoda, Japan's second-largest cement maker. In addition, the group had consisted of another Japanese cement engineer as well as two Japanese military people. Finally, here had been two Chinese representatives of Longtan Cement, which was located in the vicinity and had already been taken over by the Japanese, as well as a third Chinese, sent by an engineering company in Shanghai. "This group asked many odd questions, inspected the entire factory, took many photos and said something to the effect that we could expect a visit by two Japanese cement engineers in the near future," Sindberg wrote later in a letter.[1]

Günther had shown the visitors around and subsequently hosted a dinner party in their honor, before they had driven off for Longtan Cement, where they would stay until their return trip to Shanghai the day after. At Jiangnan, the unexpected event caused a crisis atmosphere, and Sindberg and Günther held an emergency meeting with the factory's Chinese managers.[2] The Japanese visit had been the first of its kind since January 10, when a group of civilians and military officers had also inspected Jiangnan Cement and taken photos of the facilities. The difference was that this time the Japanese had been accompanied by a group of Chinese. All military resistance had been eradicated in the Nanjing region, and the Japanese army of occupation was in the process of establishing a new order, aided by local collaborators. The inauguration of the new government in Nanjing had been an initial step in the political sphere, and now the economy, too, was to be placed under Japanese control.

The participants in the meeting agreed that the first priority was to send a message to F. L. Smidth in Shanghai about the growing Japanese interest in

F. L. Smidth's equipment at Jiangnan Cement was world-class, and several leading Japanese cement makers wished to take over the plant, while the Japanese army also vied for access to the strategic product manufactured here. (FLSmidth Archives, Valby)

Jiangnan Cement. Sindberg sat down to put together a letter to Niels Jensen about the new situation, arguing that it was now essential that he had a better understanding of the machinery.

> In a way it was fortunate that I was not present yesterday, as people often ask lots of questions that I am not able to answer, especially about the machinery, which I know absolutely nothing about. People find it odd that as an F. L. Smidth employee I have no expertise when it comes to the machines, as everybody thinks I am an engineer. Therefore, it is essential that we receive information as soon as possible about the current situation, in order that we can provide satisfactory answers to the questions. I would also appreciate written explanations about the machinery and the making of cement, the power needed for the production, and the value of the various equipment, so that I no longer have to make a stupid impression on the Japs.[3]

***

Sindberg had no way of knowing this, but at this time complaints were starting to emerge about his behavior at Jiangnan Cement. For six weeks, he had openly defied the Japanese army and persistently barred individual Japanese soldiers from entering into the refugee camp. Some of the complaints had now reached Jiangnan's main shareholder Chee Hsin Cement. His direct style probably annoyed more than just the Japanese, and it is possible that some of the complaints originated from inside Jiangnan Cement, where frictions had begun to develop between Sindberg and Günther. Both of them were uncompromising characters who left their mark on the factory, each in his own way. Günther wielded greater formal authority due to his engineering skills and his knowledge of the Chinese language. Still, he was overshadowed by Sindberg, who was saving lives in the factory clinic and was also popular with the refugees, and he may also have felt a certain nagging envy at the attention that Sindberg received from the Westerners in Nanjing.

In other words, Sindberg and Jiangnan Cement were already on Chee Hsin Cement's radar when the company's Shanghai office was visited on February 6 or 7 by Masuda Kanichi, the Onoda representative, fresh from his inspection tour of Nanjing. Masuda was welcomed by Thomas K. Yu, Chee Hsin Cement's representative in Nanjing, and was just as inquisitive as he had been at Jiangnan Cement. Masuda wanted to know the price of the machinery and its capacity, whether it could become operational immediately and would function as planned, and who paid for Sindberg. He also wished to see the employment contract, but was told by Thomas K. Yu that it was kept at Chee Hsin Cement's headquarters in Tianjin in northern China. Apart from the most basic questions, Yu and his staff pretended that they did not know the answer, referring the Japanese to the Tianjin office, which, they said, was in possession of all the facts.[4]

Until the end of November, Thomas K. Yu had been preoccupied with the construction of Jiangnan Cement, and consequently he knew much more about the cement business than he let on in front of Masuda.[5] For example, he was very well aware that Longtan Cement operated far below capacity, because the foremen and engineers had fled prior to the Japanese occupation. This posed a major headache for the Japanese authorities who were in desperate need of cement both for civilian and military purposes, and they were eager to start using the brand-new machinery at Jiangnan Cement. It seemed as if a Japanese takeover of Jiangnan Cement was imminent, and following Masuda's appearance, Thomas K. Yu visited the F. L. Smidth office on February 7. Niels Jensen was away on a business trip to Hong Kong and the Philippines, and in his absence the business was managed by his resourceful secretary, the American-born Margaret Stang-Lund, who had received Sindberg's letter about Masuda's visit that morning and was in fact reading it just as Thomas K. Yu entered. He was accompanied by G. Schultz, Günther's cousin with the close relationship to Chee Hsin Cement.

In the complicated situation that had evolved, Sindberg's role had suddenly become crucial, which made it all the more inconvenient that complaints about his behavior were to be received at this very moment. "Mr. Yu said that they had heard that Mr. Sindberg was inclined to be somewhat quarrelsome, and they wished for that reason that he would stay as close in to the works as possible," Stang-Lund wrote in a letter to Niels Jensen, summarizing the conversation. She had to be vague in her choice of words, given the likelihood of Japanese censors reading her letter, but the sentence seemed to be an expression of Chee Hsin Cement's hope that Sindberg would keep a distance from the refugee camp, which was outside the factory fence, thus avoiding clashes with the Japanese military. Therefore, Stang-Lund and Yu quickly agreed on one thing: "[Sindberg] must on no account get into any quarrels with the Japanese."[6] Stang-Lund also noted that Sindberg had asked in his letter for technical data of the various machinery, and she had got the impression that he wanted to pose as an engineer, risking problems both for himself and for F. L. Smidth. "It is very important that none of us tells any lies, as if the Japanese check up and find out they have been told lies the whole arrangement is promptly quite discredited," she wrote in her summary. "Under these circumstances it is all to the good that Sindberg is genuinely unable to answer questions."[7]

After Thomas K. Yu had left F. L. Smidth's office, Stang-Lund went straight to the Danish consulate. Consul Poul Scheel's animosity towards Sindberg, built up in the course of a series of incidents beginning with the violence on board the *Falstria*, was undiminished and was now further reinforced by news that the hard-hitting Dane allegedly was the cause of tension with the Japanese in the Nanjing area. "He was very 'het up' about it, and said he didn't at all like Sindberg," Stang-Lund wrote in her summary. "[He] thought he would be certain to talk too much and too boastfully, pretending to be more important than he actually was. He advised me to write Mr. Sindberg quite frankly that he was nothing but a watchman and should comport himself as such. Consul Scheel advised me to put Sindberg back in his place with no uncertain words."[8]

Stang-Lund left the Danish consulate and immediately wrote a sharply worded letter to Sindberg but decided to sleep on it. The following day she revised the letter, scaling down the acidity in several passages. "After all I am in only a subordinate position myself, and have no right to 'tick off' Mr. Sindberg—and anyway, there is no object in getting his back up if it can be avoided," as she explained in her report. Even so, the letter that she ended up sending to Sindberg was stern enough, with underlining of sentences which she felt required special attention. In the new situation, she wrote, Sindberg's primary responsibility was to ensure that the machinery was not put into operation until F. L. Smidth's own engineers had arrived and been allowed to perform a final test of the equipment. Still, it was essential that Sindberg displayed diplomatic finesse in performing his job. Stang-Lund wrote:[9]

> At the same time that you do not give your sanction or permission for any interference with the machinery whatsoever, it is, however, important to bear in mind that any protests which you make must be <u>verbal only</u>. On no account, <u>nor under any provocation whatsoever</u>, must you resort to any kind of violence, but must rather be quietly courteous to and friendly with the Japanese visiting the works. It is not necessary for you to know anything about the machinery, either as regards its price or how to run it. You are not an engineer, nor are you supposed to be one, and it will be a great mistake for you to pretend that you are one... <u>It is not necessary for you to be able to answer any questions whatsoever; anyone wanting any information, whether technical or otherwise, can apply for it at our office</u>, and get it from our managing engineer, who is the only authorized and reliable source of such information.

Stang-Lund repeated her instructions on the last page of the letter, especially emphasizing the need to avoid confronting the Japanese:

> Above all, you must not resort to violence of any kind, no matter what the provocation might be. You must exert yourself to be unfailingly courteous and friendly, and any protest you may have to make must be made in a courteous and tactful manner. This is most important. I have discussed this matter fully with the Consul here, and he agrees with me that the attitude you must adopt is as outlined above.[10]

***

Sindberg was still not aware that his popularity in Shanghai was declining, and that his wisest choice in this situation was to keep a low profile. Rather, he was more entrepreneurial than ever and made sure to inform his bosses about everything he achieved. While Günther remained the dominant figure inside the factory compound, Sindberg was the plant's face to the outside world with his nearly daily trips to Nanjing, where he maintained the continued contact with both the Japanese authorities and the remaining Westerners. His untiring activity was known to everyone in the occupied capital, and when the German diplomat Georg Rosen met with leading Japanese officers, the Dane's unhindered travel was even used as an argument in favor of lifting some of the strict limits that were still imposed on most other foreigners' travel in the vicinity of the city.[11]

While he was waiting for instruction from Shanghai about how to react to the intensified Japanese interest in the cement plant, Sindberg adopted countermeasures on his own accord, inviting a Russian visitor, Nikolai Podshivalov, to stay at the factory. Podshivalov, who had the nickname "Cola," was known and appreciated throughout the foreign community in Nanjing for his language talent, which was also the main reason why Sindberg wanted him to be present: "As Cola had nothing to do in Nanjing, he is now staying here for a couple of days. It's in order for us to have some company, but also because he speaks fluent Chinese and Japanese, which is the real reason why I want him around. In case we are once again visited by shady figures, he may be able to pick up interesting details."[12]

In addition to his work safeguarding the factory and maintaining order and safety in the refugee camp, Sindberg remained key to the continued operation of the factory clinic and arranged for two educated Chinese nurses to stay permanently at the plant.[13] He also saw it as his responsibility to document the horrors taking place around him. He did so, partly by keeping a detailed journal of all patients who were treated at the clinic, partly by journeying through the devastated countryside, taking photos of the victims of the Japanese. The photos were later accompanied by Sindberg's own notes, which tersely described the contents: "Farmer killed in his field," "This child was deliberately shot, its mother was wounded," or "This farmer boy was killed with the butt of a rifle because he did not take off his hat."[14]

The result was a series of terrifying photos which showed more clearly than anything else the brutal conduct of the army of occupation, and the consequences for Sindberg could have been fatal, had the Japanese found out what he was doing. Therefore, he was extra careful when the photos were to be developed, which could only be done in Shanghai. On February 10, he attended a dinner in Nanjing hosted by Georg Rosen from the Germany embassy and was introduced to the Dutch diplomat Hendrik Bos, who was briefly visiting Nanjing. Bos was to return to Shanghai the same day on board the British gunboat *Cricket* and agreed to carry a film roll against receiving a copy of the photos.[15] "The photos are mostly of a personal nature, but there are some showing the factory, which might interest them, as well as some gruesome shots of corpses, which speak for themselves," Sindberg wrote in a cover letter to F. L. Smidth. "Please be careful how you handle the photos, since there might easily be one or two among them that could fetch a tidy sum. Unfortunately, I don't have my own camera here, and it is possible that none of the photos has worked out, but if you have the time and the inclination, you are free to try to commercialize the photos as best you can."[16]

Stang-Lund received the film roll, which the Dutch diplomat had secretly brought to Shanghai, had it developed and was shocked by what it showed. "Some of them are pretty horrible, so don't look at them just before a meal," she wrote when she mailed the photos on to Niels Jensen.[17] It is unclear exactly how Sindberg thought the photos could be used commercially, but he possibly hoped to sell them to the press or release them directly to the public in the form of short photo series, often with sensational contents, that were popular at the time. However, nothing indicates that Stang-Lund ever considered a sale, realizing the negative consequences for F. L. Smidth if the

One of many pictures of murdered Chinese which Sindberg sent to Shanghai for development. (Bernhard Arp Sindberg Papers and Photography Collection, Harry Ransom Center, University of Texas at Austin)

Japanese were to be alerted to the existence of the photos and their origin. "I do not think it is advisable for me to try to send copies up to you, but shall keep them in the office here for you," she wrote in a reply to Sindberg on February 19, reminding him once more about the need to stay on friendly terms with the occupying power: "Mr. Jensen is most anxious that you should avoid any actions which the Japanese might resent."[18]

She enclosed a letter addressed to Sindberg which had arrived from Niels Jensen in Hong Kong. Jensen started off with turning down Sindberg's request to have detailed information on the machinery at Jiangnan Cement sent to him:

When you traveled to the plant, I was happy that you had the necessary courage, as it was a rather dangerous job at the time—and you are being paid handsomely because of the danger that was associated with staying at the factory as a watchman—not in order that you should pose as an engineer, for which of course you do not have the qualifications. I hope that this will now be completely clear to you, and besides, I think it should not be a concern to you if people see you simply as a watchman. As far as you are concerned, I think the most important thing must be the fact that you earn a significant amount of money performing the job you have taken as watchman at the factory.

Niels Jensen thanked Sindberg for his letters which had warned about the sudden Japanese interest in the plant but encouraged him to be discreet and not let his emotions show in future correspondence.

I still would like to hear from you if there are additional visits. However, I would also like to ask you to refrain from writing to me or any other person about your personal feelings, positive or negative, towards people you meet. Do not forget that you are in a country at war where one must keep one's sympathies and antipathies to oneself. When you return from your job at the factory, you can always make an oral report, but you are not to write anything in letters either to me or to anyone else. For the same reason I must also ask you to stop keeping a diary. That kind of thing can easily fall into the wrong hands. The job you currently have requires diplomatic skill, and even though it can sometimes be hard to be a diplomat, I trust that you will keep your promise to me from when you traveled to the factory. Do not get into any fights with anyone, avoid going to Nanjing more often than strictly necessary and stay at the factory—while keeping your personal opinions to yourself without writing any of them down in letters or in any other way.[19]

Niels Jensen concluded the letter with a wish that Sindberg "remain in good health and get along with all people that cross your path." In fact, it turned out the exact opposite way. The same day that the letter was sent off from Shanghai to Nanjing, February 19, Sindberg ended up in a fierce argument with Günther. It took place during a visit which a group of Japanese officers paid to Jiangnan Cement, and while the exact cause is unclear, it was obvious that it resulted in mutual animosity of such intensity that it was difficult to see how the two would ever become reconciled.

Today only Günther's version of the row is preserved, reproduced in a letter written by Stang-Lund, and the details must therefore be treated with caution. "Sindberg," Stang-Lund wrote, "had made trouble in front of Japanese officers who were guests in their house, accusing Dr. Günther and some of his Chinese assistants of being communists [...] Dr. Günther had had to show his papers and swear he was a good German Nazi and not a communist, and [...] Dr. Günther had been forced to move out of the house after that, as Sindberg when angry became violent and dangerous and threatened Dr. Günther and his Chinese assistants with the revolver which he carried always with him."[20]

CHAPTER 16

Troublemaker

February 21–March 15, 1938

When the Japanese were approaching in late 1937, the 37-year-old chief accountant Xu Shennong had fled across the Yangtze, along with most other managers at Jiangnan Cement. After the situation had settled somewhat, he returned to assume his old position with the company. Apart from looking after the finances, he was also an avid observer, and during the first months of 1938, he sent a number of letters to Jiangnan's senior management in Shanghai about conditions at the cement plant. In early spring there was news of a somewhat disturbing kind: "The daughter of one of the refugees was smuggled into the factory under the cover of darkness by Mr. Sindberg. After having spent the night, she reemerged. She had received 20 dollars, a bag of candy and a pack of cigarettes. Now her father is approaching and wants him to marry her."[1]

Xu Shennong did not mention the case again in his future correspondence with Jiangnan, and in all likelihood, it was discreetly solved. However, it was typical of a number of complaints which the management in Shanghai and Tianjin received about Sindberg's behavior during the months after the establishment of the camp. Sindberg was inclined to mix too much with the refugees, according to his Chinese colleagues, who also thought that he could be something of a troublemaker.[2] The exact nature of this trouble is not entirely clear from the extant sources, but the many requests directed at Sindberg not to confront the Japanese suggest that he was in a constant state of tension with the army of occupation.

Sindberg's past as a driver and assistant for Philip Pembroke Stephens only made him more suspect in the eyes of the Japanese military, and some believed that he still worked as a journalist. It is also possible that his stint as a member of the team selling Madsen machine guns to the Chinese army contributed to his notoriety with the Japanese, Margaret Stang-Lund thought. "All the military people with whom we have been [in] touch, including the common soldiers out at the North Station [in Shanghai]... seem to know about Mr. Sindberg, who is definitely on the Japanese blacklist," she wrote in a letter to Niels Jensen. "I don't know how much of this is Sindberg's fault, and hesitate to hold it against him, but rather I consider it as just being unfortunate. It is, however, true that Sindberg has an unfortunate flair for publicity."[3]

At the same time, the mood at the factory worsened, as Sindberg was involved in a dispute with his Chinese driver, whom he accused of unsatisfactory job performance.[4] This was, however, nothing compared with the tension with Günther, which had exploded on February 19. "Mr. Günther and Mr. Sindberg are unable to see eye to eye on anything, and their disagreement worsens with each passing day," Xu Shennong wrote.[5] It seems that a regular power struggle had erupted between the two, and that Günther was actively conspiring to have Sindberg removed. Sindberg's formal role was limited to guarding F. L. Smidth's machinery, but the fact that the extraordinary circumstances had motivated him to take the lead both in the refugee camp and in the clinic apparently was a source of intense irritation for Günther, since it challenged his position as the undisputed leader at the factory.[6]

As if this was not enough, the two men's personalities were also a match from hell. In one corner was Sindberg, who was not the easiest person to work with and had a rebellious streak: Stang-Lund cited a confidential assessment by the Danish consulate in Shanghai, stating that "every job Mr. Sindberg got he seemed to have trouble with his superiors, in some cases possibly justified, but in other cases not justified, and that he had the reputation of being hot-tempered and inclined to violence when aroused by some fancied or real injustices. However, there is no reason to suppose that Mr. Sindberg is not perfectly well intentioned and honest."[7]

In the other corner, to cope with his radically anti-authoritarian Dane and nominally in a superior position, was Günther, described by people who knew him as "overbearing and ambitious and [preferring] to run things himself."[8] Among the Chinese, both the factory staff and the refugees' opinions on Günther were mixed. One refugee remembered him as "a good man."[9] Others said that he occasionally would threaten them with letting the Japanese soldiers have a free rein if they did not obey him. Sindberg's translator Li Yulin was also not in Günther's good graces. When the enmity with Sindberg had just been brought out into the open, Günther wanted Li to sign a formal complaint about the Dane, addressed to Jiangnan Cement and F. L Smidth. Li refused, as he did not wish to be involved in a private row. "After that," Stang-Lund wrote, "Dr. Günther was very angry with Mr. Li."[10]

**

Karl Günther, in the center with his back to the photographer, during an inspection tour of the refugee camp. The German engineer's relationship with Sindberg was increasingly tense, and in the end the contradictions blew up. (Bernhard Arp Sindberg Papers and Photography Collection, Harry Ransom Center, University of Texas at Austin)

In addition to the exhausting tensions, the refugee camp placed ever greater demands on Sindberg, and by February it had grown to between 6,000 and 10,000 inhabitants.[11] The American missionary John Magee, who visited the camp at the end of the month, later explained in a report that at this time the population in the camp was growing rapidly because more and more refugees resettled from the crowded conditions at Qixia Temple. Liao Yaoxiang, the Chinese officer from the French military academy Saint-Cyr, was among the many newcomers in this group, and he later moved on, succeeding in reaching the other bank of the Yangtze.[12]

"New huts were being built as I walked through the camp. Most of the huts are built of rice straw while there were a few larger mat sheds," Magee wrote.[13] He described in his report a meeting he had with 25 leading representatives of the refugees in Sindberg's camp. They told him that within an area of less than 6 miles the Japanese had killed between 700 and 800 farmers since the beginning of the occupation in December. The outrages continued. In a village roughly 5 miles away, soldiers had killed seven people and injured one. "These villagers had recently been vaccinated and the soldiers avowed that the marks were bullet wounds and that therefore they were soldiers," Magee wrote. He was also told that the number of women aged 30 to 40 who had been raped was too large for any reasonable estimate to be made, while there were also report of girls as young as ten being raped.

Later, Magee was given a tour of Sindberg's clinic, recording what he saw with a camera he had brought. "A child was brought to the dispensary while I was there who had been horribly burnt when Japanese soldiers set fire to the house in which it was living. As the father had fled at their approach the soldiers asked this child of three where its 'ma-ma' was and when he made no satisfactory answer they set fire to the house. A neighbor rescued him. The mother was already living in the camp," he wrote in his report. "I also talked to a young farmer in the dispensary who had been badly burnt in the upper part of his body when soldiers threw kerosene oil on him and set him afire. They had demanded money from him but he had told them that he was a poor farmer and had no money."

The clinic primarily kept operating with medicine and bandages donated from established hospitals in Nanjing. The staff was taking care of six in-patients, while Magee counted 24 dispensary cases during the morning that he visited. The clinic had played an important role despite the complete lack of educated doctors, but the arrival of trained nurses had improved the situation. "Cases were there needing an operation and it is unquestionably true that more lives would be saved if they had a more adequate staff," Magee wrote.

> If a doctor could attend, even once a week, a great deal of suffering could be relieved and many lives would be saved. In the substantial buildings belonging to the Cement Works an operating room could be easily set up. Once there were proper facilities for medical and surgical work the news would spread over the countryside and the numbers of patients would greatly increase.

During his visit to Jiangnan Cement, Magee was driven through the surrounding area by Sindberg. It was a desolate sight. Along the main road to Nanjing, 80 percent of the houses had been burned down, and along smaller roads, 40 to 50 percent of the houses had been destroyed. The big unsolved issue was food. The wealthy families had enough for the next four months, but the vast majority just had sufficient provisions for the coming month. The main problem was the lack of draft animals, which had either been slaughtered or taken by the Japanese. "In reply to my question as to what crop they might be able to produce without oxen and with human labor alone they said they would only be able to produce 1/3 of a normal yield," Magee wrote.

"They reported very little seed on hand and went on to say that even if they had seed the farmers would not dare to go back to their farms in any large numbers in present circumstances," the missionary wrote. Still, there were actually scattered signs that life was gradually returning to rural areas:

> In my drives with Mr. Sindberg over the countryside as well as on the road between Qixia and Nanjing I saw a few people on the roads apparently going back to their farms. They seemed to be particularly noticeable near to the Qixia camp at night. One woman casting manure on her fields as though nothing had happened stands out in my memory as women were so rare. In one village I saw three men, two women and some children starting to rebuild their home, the substantial stone walls of which were still standing.

***

February 21 was General Matsui Iwane's last day in China. The entire top brass had assembled in Shanghai's docks to bid farewell, when his steamer, the *Mizuho*, sailed off headed for Japan. The old officer was moved by the devotion his subordinates signaled in this way, and the bright sunshine combined with the still sea made the day almost perfect. However, he was not alone on board the ship. In addition, there were 200 injured soldiers on their way to hospitals at home. Some had such severe wounds that they would need all the surgical expertise that Japan could mobilize. Accompanying them were 60 nurses who did their best to make the passage as tolerable as possible for their patients. Matsui asked the young women how many they had helped bring home since the beginning of the campaign. More than 4,000 on this vessel alone, they answered.[14]

Casualties were not the only cost that the war had imposed on Japan. It was increasingly obvious that the behavior of the Japanese forces, especially in the Nanjing area, had blemished the reputation of the Japanese army all over the world. Matsui's return was to some extent forced and reflected disappointment among his superiors that he had been unable to control his own soldiers. To be sure, Matsui had been bedridden with malaria during the days when Nanjing was taken, but in the weeks since then he had had ample opportunity to strengthen the discipline among his troops, but it had only happened slowly and with insufficient results.

Only in early February had Matsui used a ceremony commemorating the battle as a chance to criticize his soldiers for their conduct in Nanjing, albeit in cautious terms. The Japanese news agency Domei described the incident in a characteristically watered-down way, but the report was nonetheless remarkable for the simple reason that it reflected official recognition that the Japanese military had been anything but exemplary in its conduct: "Matsui called the attention of his subordinates to the necessity of putting an end to various reports affecting the prestige of the Japanese troops. This action, said to be unprecedented in the annals of the Japanese army, was taken in the face of recurring adverse comment on reported breaches of discipline by Japanese troops."[15]

At this time, the first assessments of the number of killed in Nanjing had begun circulating. The American journalist Tillman Durdin estimated in early 1938 that 33,000 Chinese soldiers had lost their lives in Nanjing, including 20,000 who had been put to death after the fighting was over.[16] From then on, the numbers started rising. In early 1942 Chiang Kai-shek reported that 200,000 had been killed,[17] and by the time of a war crimes trial in Nanjing after the war, the official figure was 300,000.[18] This is also the number that the Chinese government insists on using today. A Japanese-Canadian historian has analyzed the existing literature and pronounces that the "academically valid" number of victims usually is in the range between 40,000 and 200,000.[19]

In 1938, it was still far too early to arrive at even an approximate estimate. On March 8, Oscar O'Neill Oxholm from the Danish consulate after much delay finally filed a report to Copenhagen about Japanese crimes against Chinese civilians, but only after having mentioned recent "international incidents," including the sinking of the American gunboat *Panay*. This was typical of the foreign priorities when commenting on the Nanjing battle, primarily focusing on the Western victims. Still, Oxholm also paid attention to Chinese suffering:

> Shortly afterwards, the first intelligence emerged about the Japanese troops' outrages primarily in Nanjing but also in many other occupied areas. The whole truth will probably never be revealed, but what was reported was bad enough and sufficient to demonstrate the complete lack of discipline among junior officers and privates. The accounts of the atrocities in Nanjing scared Chinese whose support the Japanese could possibly have counted on, and it also affected Japanese troops on other fronts. Even in northern China, where complaints of this sort had not been encountered before, the soldiers started looting, also there making it more difficult for the Japanese to establish an autonomous regime with people of any significance.[20]

***

Meanwhile, the Japanese interest in Jiangnan Cement continued in unabated fashion. Mitsui Bussan, a vast Japanese trading firm which acted as an agent for Onoda Cement and others, decided in March to send a representative by the name of Yonezawa to Shanghai. On Saturday, March 5, at 9.30 a.m. he visited F. L. Smidth, immediately leaving a pleasant impression on Stang-Lund: young, intelligent and polite. Still, a tense conversation played out between the two, as Stang-Lund pretended to know nothing about the cement factory, while Yonezawa tried in a friendly but firm manner to squeeze information out of her.[21]

"I have been sent over by the Mitsui company to investigate the cement industry in China, and I would much appreciate some information from you," the Japanese said. "I would be only too glad to help you," Stang-Lund replied, assuming the coat of ignorance that she had decided beforehand would be her best defense. "But I am afraid that my knowledge of the cement industry is very sketchy, as I am only the stenographer in the office. It would be better if you could wait and talk to Niels Jensen, as he would be much better qualified to assist you."

The problem was that Niels Jensen would be away on his business trip at least until the end of March, and Yonezawa could not wait that long. For instance, the Japanese wanted to know when Jiangnan Cement would be able to commence production. "This is dependent on conditions becoming peaceful enough for us to send our engineers back up," Stang-Lund said. "We never sanction the starting up of our machinery for which we have given guarantees and so on without the presence of one of our men to supervise it." Yonezawa retorted that as far as he was informed F. L. Smidth already had a man at the factory. "That is so," Stang-Lund replied, "but the man that we have up there at present is not a qualified engineer or a highly educated man, but only a kind of super-watchman."

Yonezawa suddenly changed the subject: "How much money is outstanding on the machinery you have put up at the works?" Stang-Lund said this was confidential information which she did not handle: "I don't know much about the terms or amount of the contract, but I do know that we have received the first installment of our money." Stang-Lund immediately realized she had said too much, but it was too late. Yonezawa sensed that she was withholding information, and pushed her: "If you don't know the details and amount of the contract, how do you know that only one installment has been paid?" Stang-Lund replied: "I know this because it has come out in the ordinary correspondence, and furthermore, I keep the books and accounts."

Once again, Stang-Lund wished she had kept her mouth shut. She immediately was worried that Yonezawa would now ask detailed questions about the accounts, and that she would be forced to either lie or refuse to provide information. She was only saved by the sound of someone knocking on the door to the office. A new visitor had arrived, but it was the exact kind of visitor she did not need at this point. It was a delivery boy from Mactavish Photo Shop carrying an envelope with developed and enlarged photos. What if, Stang-Lund thought with sudden panic, Sindberg's gruesome photos of war crimes were among them?

"So you are interested in photography," Yonezawa said. "What kind of camera do you have?" With bated breath, Stang-Lund opened the envelope. She imagined that the photos would be of horribly mutilated Chinese corpses. However, her fears were unfounded: the photos were of her dogs and other private motifs. Yonezawa's visit ended on a friendly note. Stang-Lund apologized profusely for not being of any more help. Yonezawa on his part apologized for having taken so much of her time, and then walked away.

Forty-five minutes later Thomas K. Yu from Chee Hsin Cement turned up at F. L. Smidth's office. He had spoken to Yonezawa and expressed his hope that Mitsui Bussan, which the Japanese represented, could enter into an agreement to act as a sales agent for Jiangnan Cement. The benefit would be substantial, as Jiangnan Cement would be able to take advantage of Mitsui Bussan's support and protection in a Japanese-dominated market where Chinese companies might have a hard time surviving on their own.

The prospect of closer cooperation with Mitsui Bussan could also have positive consequences for Sindberg. Yonezawa had told Thomas K. Yu that it would actually be preferable to be represented locally by one of the company's own men "to keep out the soldiers, who might otherwise take it into their heads to overrun the plant." According to Yonezawa, it was also important that Sindberg prevented all attempts at looting the machinery. He did not specify who he thought was most likely to plunder the factory, but he probably was referring to roving bands of former Chinese soldiers. Coming from a Japanese, this was a surprising change of mind, and it meant that Thomas K. Yu's view of Sindberg abruptly improved. He no longer called for his removal, but rather referred to him as "such a brave man."[22] It seemed that Sindberg's position was suddenly no longer in danger. However, that was not the case. For there was still the matter of Sindberg's nemesis, Karl Günther.

CHAPTER 17

Günther's Letter

March 16–April 25, 1938

On March 16, Margaret Stang-Lund sent an urgent telegram to Niels Jensen, who had now reached Manila, the capital of the Philippines: "Jiangnan report Sindberg often bad-tempered and violent threatening Dr. Günther with firearms etc. so that Dr. Günther absolutely refuses to remain unless Sindberg is recalled. Stop. Reinforcement of another Dane to replace Sindberg can be arranged on the same terms and conditions. Danish consulate also considers Sindberg dangerous and says can get another reliable Dane, suggesting Sindberg be recalled at once."

During the period until the next Danish watchman was installed in Jiangnan, Günther would temporarily take over responsibility for F. L. Smith's interests, and the Danish flag would still fly over the compound, Stang-Lund explained.

> If you are agreeable, I can arrange everything same as last with the assistance of the Danish Consulate. Stop. The Consul General says the Danish Consulate can through the Japanese Consulate order Sindberg to return to Shanghai, but we consider it preferable to arrange it amicably if possible and suggest telegraphing Sindberg at once as follows: "Please return immediately to Shanghai for conference." Jiangnan is willing to pay Sindberg's fare to Denmark, but the Consul General considers this unnecessary as the Consulate in any case will order him to go.[1]

Earlier on the same day, Stang-Lund had received a visit by Thomas K. Yu, who just a few days earlier had called Sindberg brave, but now once again wanted him removed. He brought a letter from Karl Günther, in which the German engineer said it was impossible to work with Sindberg, referring among other things to the incident on January 19, when Sindberg had accused him of being a communist. The letter was phrased as an ultimatum as Günther threatened to resign unless Sindberg was let go. "Dr. Günther said in his letter that he was so afraid, by now, of Mr. Sindberg, that if Sindberg were recalled he would ask us not to let Sindberg know until he had left the works that it was at Dr. Günther's instigation, as Sindberg might then become violent and do Dr. Günther harm."[2]

Thomas K. Yu at this point wished to get rid of Sindberg at almost any cost and was willing to pay large amounts of money to encourage him to not just leave the factory but depart from China altogether. Chee Hsin Cement wished to pay a generous bonus in addition to the 400 British pounds that he was owed for his work during the months from December to March, and in addition the company offered to pay for his trip back to Denmark. "Mr. Yu was afraid that if Sindberg remained in Shanghai he might make some kind of trouble which would involve Jiangnan in unpleasantness, and they were extremely anxious to avoid this," Stang-Lund wrote in a report.[3]

Stang-Lund promised Yu that she would see to the matter but pointed out that first of all she needed to discuss it with the Danish consulate. Consul Poul Scheel reacted by openly voicing his dislike of Sindberg. "Mr. Scheel said he was not at all surprised, and was only astonished that there had not been trouble before, as he knew Sindberg from before, and he was a really bad fellow," Stang-Lund wrote, then going on to cite the consul as making a remarkable offer: "Mr. Scheel suggested that the Consulate should take the matter up, and get Sindberg back through the Japanese authorities, under arrest." Stang-Lund declined the offer, pointing out that Chee Hsin Cement wished to solve the problem as discreetly as possible and was adamant to avoid any kind of negative publicity. Still, Scheel maintained that he was "fed up with" Sindberg and would insist on his departure from Shanghai.[4]

Stang-Lund then asked if the consulate would be able to help in finding a replacement for Sindberg, to which Scheel replied he had "just the man in mind." Everything was now set, and Stang-Lund was able to contact Niels Jensen by telegram, asking for permission to have Sindberg removed. Niels Jensen telegraphed his answer the following day, on March 17, giving the green light for implementing the plan.[5] Equipped with this authorization to act, Stang-Lund now wrote a telegram for Jiangnan Cement, asking the Danish consulate in Shanghai to have it sent to Nanjing as soon as possible, which at the time meant via the U.S. Navy's radio. The message to Sindberg was brief and to the point: "Mr. Niels Jensen requires you to return to Shanghai immediately and call at our office."[6]

***

Margaret Stang-Lund had never met Sindberg before, and she was worried about how their first encounter would play out. Sindberg telephoned her immediately after arriving in Shanghai on March 20 together with his Chinese translator Li Yulin but was told to be at the office the following day. She was afraid of how Sindberg might react to the news about his removal, and during the hours prior to the meeting she was contemplating asking Scheel to be present. However, she thought that the consul would only agree to attend the meeting if she, in return, was willing to file an official complaint about Sindberg's behavior, and in her opinion, that would be going too far. Thomas K. Yu was not much help either, since he downright refused to meet the troublesome watchman face-to-face.[7]

Her premonitions turned out to be groundless once Sindberg turned up, accompanied by Li Yulin. "I was agreeably surprised to find that Mr. Sindberg didn't wave a gun at me or anything like that," she wrote. "Mr. Sindberg was in fact so quiet and well-behaved that I felt quite silly remembering how worried I was about it." Sindberg still had no idea why he had been summoned to Shanghai, and Stang-Lund now provided a detailed account of the complaints that had been leveled against him as well as the decision to have him removed. "Mr. Sindberg (and also Mr. Li) seemed very much surprised at this, and said that they were not aware that there had been so much friction," Stang-Lund wrote. Still, she explained to Sindberg that the decision was final, but that Jiangnan was grateful for his effort, and that he could expect some form of bonus on top of the salary that had been agreed on.[8]

Thomas K. Yu was very keen to give Sindberg an offer he could not refuse, whereas Stang-Lund, thinking more strategically, did not want to leave Sindberg with the impression that people were scared of him—a situation which, she thought, he might want to exploit to his advantage. They did, however, reach an agreement on a bonus of 100 British pounds, so that Sindberg's total severance package amounted to 500 pounds. Now that the affair had been resolved with less drama than originally feared, Thomas K. Yu's initial reluctance to even meet with Sindberg dissipated, and he suggested a farewell dinner for the Dane, as was the local custom.[9]

Later the same day, the consulate introduced Stang-Lund to the Dane who was to take over Sindberg's job. It was 30-year-old Einar Nielsen, who had been a volunteer ambulance driver during the battle of Shanghai and had almost been killed in the attempt to save an American family caught in the crossfire between Chinese and Japanese forces. He struck Stang-Lund as "a quiet, reasonable chap," but remembering only too well Sindberg's behavior, she did her utmost to make him understand the job and its possible pitfalls. "I explained carefully and emphatically to Mr. Nielsen that under no circumstances may he indulge in any violence, either towards Chinese or towards Japanese," she wrote. "I particularly emphasized that he must not write anything or say anything,

H. W. Yuan, right, was the son of the former Chinese President Yuan Shikai and among the top managers of Chee Hsin Cement. In this capacity he was very dissatisfied with Sindberg's behavior at Jiangnan Cement and demanded that he be removed. However, this had already happened. (FLSmidth Archives, Valby)

or take any pictures, etc., that could be construed either by the Japanese or the Chinese as any kind of propaganda." In addition, she stressed that part of the job consisted in staying on good terms with Günther.[10]

After F. L. Smidth had already decided to get rid of Sindberg, an official request arrived from Chee Hsin Cement with a somewhat belated demand to dismiss the controversial Danish watchman. H. W. Yuan, the son of China's former President Yuan Shikai and a board member at Chee Hsin Cement, sent a letter on March 22 addressed to F. L. Smidth in Shanghai, calling for Sindberg to be removed from his position from Jiangnan Cement with effect from April 1. As motivation, Yuan wrote that Sindberg's services were no longer needed, as conditions around the factory were now more stable.[11] In a private letter to Niels Jensen accompanying the official request he was franker. "Besides the reasons given in our official letter, there is another which [leaves us with no alternatives]. The conduct of Mr. Sindberg at the works is, as you perhaps already heard from our Mr. Yu, far from respectable, and we can not afford to have the name of this Company thus affected," the Chinese businessman wrote.[12]

***

The more Stang-Lund got to know Sindberg, the more surprised she was that he had managed to get such a bad reputation. It was gradually clear to her that Sindberg had in fact done his best to look after F. L. Smidth's interests to the greatest extent possible. After the farewell dinner which Thomas K. Yu had proposed, a small group of private guests were invited to watch a film from the Nanjing area in an event organized by the well-known Australian correspondent Harold John Timperley. The footage of Chinese victims shocked the viewers. "Horrible, but perfectly marvelous how they were able to get them," Stang-Lund remarked.[13]

The film also contained footage from Jiangnan Cement, recorded by John Magee during his visit the month before. While Jiangnan's Chinese staff had not found it problematic that the American missionary had walked around in the factory compound with his camera, Sindberg had been alert to the fact that some of the buildings were easily recognizable, and in order not to get into trouble with the Japanese authorities, he had requested that these parts of the footage not be included in the final film. "He is of course uneducated (which he admits himself, and which he wishes to improve), and rough," Stang-Lund wrote. "But he seems quite straightforward and very careful of our interests in the way he talks, for instance with Mr. Timperley."[14]

From the F. L. Smidth correspondence during the days after Sindberg's removal, it emerges that no one really understood the massive animosity expressed by the consulate against him. "Although it is true that he has a somewhat violent temper, we do not consider him as dangerous as the Danish Consul General apparently does, and we believe altogether that the Consul General for various reasons is somewhat prejudiced against Sindberg," Niels Jensen, still in Manila, wrote in a letter to F. L. Smidth in Copenhagen on March 28.[15] The letters of the time even revealed a discreet note of regret that Sindberg apparently had had to be sacrificed in the interest of a cause that no one seemed to understand fully.

The question is, what cause was it? It could, for example, be a struggle over the control of Jiangnan Cement. Stang-Lund suspected that Günther, after orchestrating the removal of Sindberg, actually had no desire to find a replacement and now conspired with contacts in the Japanese camp to make it difficult for F. L. Smidth to dispatch Einar Nielsen to the plant.[16] The number of refugees outside the fence had fallen drastically,[17] and from Günther's point of view, the need for assistance was almost non-existent. It is impossible to determine with any certainty if this was the case, but the fact is that the Japanese dragged out work on providing a travel permit for Nielsen that would enable him to go from Shanghai to Nanjing, and after a few weeks had passed, the Japanese authorities informed F. L. Smidth that no document would be issued until Sindberg had left China. "There is no doubt that Mr. Sindberg is very much in the Japanese black books, and they are taking it out on us," Stang-Lund wrote.[18]

Meanwhile, intricate negotiations were taking place behind the scenes about the future of Jiangnan Cement. Not only Onoda Cement, but also Asano Cement, another Japanese heavyweight, had expressed an interest. For both the Danes and the Chinese, it was paramount to carry out a delicate diplomatic balancing act, even as Japanese censorship of all letters made it extra complicated for F. L. Smidth and its local allies to coordinate. "Of course, it is impossible for the Jiangnan people here to write fully to their Head Office about anything," Stang-Lund explained. "Even if they send their letters by messenger, the person carrying them may be searched, so they are obliged to send any important messages by word of mouth, which makes everything a little difficult."[19]

Among the possible alternative scenarios for Jiangnan Cement, one was now rumored to involve a huge, but unnamed cement company in Japan that wished to take over the plant and in return proposed to pay the money F. L. Smidth had still not received for its work on the factory. This was, however, associated with all kinds of complexities, as F. L. Smidth's headquarters in Copenhagen explained to staff at its branch in Tokyo:

> It would, of course, be very tempting for us to get our money for the machinery supplied from one of the said Japanese firms now, but we may then run the risk of spoiling our good relationship with the Chee Hsin Cement Co. On the other hand, we fully realize that care must be taken not to jeopardize the good relation to the Onoda Cement Company and the Asano Cement Company, but we hope that these firms will understand that we also have to pay regards to our Chinese clients.[20]

First, however, Sindberg had to be taken out of the equation. He briefly toyed with the idea of staying in China for yet another few months, as he was under the impression that Erik Nyholm, the agent for the Madsen machine gun, might have work for him in Wuhan.[21] Nyholm could, however, inform Sindberg almost immediately that this was not the case and, possibly encouraged to do so by F. L. Smidth's people in Shanghai, he advised him to leave China as soon as possible.[22] Now that all options in China had been exhausted, Sindberg returned to his long-term plan, which was to get an education in the United States. "He said he was aware that his schooling was very deficient, and was anxious to get some more schooling," Stang-Lund wrote.[23]

Sindberg had originally planned to sail straight for the United States on board the passenger ship *Grete Mærsk*, which departed on May 2.[24] It seems, however, that he changed his mind at the last moment, probably since the vessel passed through three Japanese harbors, Kobe, Nagoya, and Yokohama, prior to crossing the Pacific.[25] Sindberg explained his concern in an interview with the Danish newspaper *Demokraten* after returning home: "Many of the ships from Chinese ports also stop over in Japanese ports, and in Japan they simply detain everyone who has shown Chinese sympathies and put him in jail."[26] Instead he left Shanghai as early as April 25 on board the steamship *D'Artagnan* owned by the French shipping company Messageries Maritime, bound for Europe.[27] As he explained: "Luckily I managed to steer clear of any Japanese harbors."[28]

CHAPTER 18

After Nanjing

April 1938–March 1983

D'Artagnan sailed via Hong Kong to Saigon and on to Singapore, Colombo, Djibouti, and Port Said.[1] After a brief stop at the port city of Brindisi in southern Italy, Sindberg continued across the Adriatic Sea to Trieste in the country's northeast. Here he met on May 31 with his father, Johannes Sindberg, who had been informed via telegram only five days earlier that his son was on his way home, and had departed immediately by train from Aarhus, Denmark.[2] Father and son spent some days sightseeing in Trieste and Venice and then traveled on by train to Switzerland, arriving in Geneva in the evening of June 2. Bernhard Sindberg had received an invitation to visit the League of Nations, extended by the Chinese delegation, which wished to thank him for his service in Nanjing.[3]

Johannes Sindberg later wrote a series of articles about the journey with his son for his own newspaper *Uge-Avisen for Odder og Omegn*, describing how the day after their arrival they were invited to a dinner with the Chinese delegation and were introduced to an exotic menu consisting of pork belly and hardboiled duck eggs. "We were supposed to use chopsticks, but as the Chinese soon realized that I did not master this skill, they very kindly produced a knife, a fork and a spoon for me," Johannes Sindberg wrote, adding with more than a touch of fatherly pride: "Bernhard, on the other hand, was able to use the chopsticks with the same dexterity as the Chinese." In the afternoon they went on a ride by light rail into the mountains, briefly crossing into French territory, to the surprise of the two Danes. They had to pass through both passport control and a customs check, but Sindberg, who was still a wanted man in France after escaping from the Foreign Legion several years earlier, avoided unwanted attention.[4]

The official program kicked off the following day and began in the morning in an expensive villa on the outskirts of Geneva belonging to

China's chief representative at the League. The Chinese diplomat told Sindberg that his government had decided to thank him for his bravery by giving him an expensive tea set which had to be taken from an official Chinese art collection in the Swiss city. Discreetly, Johannes Sindberg advised his son to politely decline the gift as the Danish customs bill would be considerable. "I admit," he wrote in his paper, "that I was quietly hoping that the Chinese might decide instead to give Bernhard the corresponding value in cash, which he needed more, but they did not. Rather, they presented him with a genuine Chinese wall carpet, also fetched from a Chinese art collection."[5]

In the evening Sindberg was invited to an event with about 100 guests, mainly members of Geneva's Chinese community, who were shown a film about the dreadful conditions in Nanjing, in all likelihood the same film that Sindberg had watched in Shanghai about two months earlier. The head of the Chinese delegation started off the evening by introducing Sindberg to the audience. "Among other things, he informed them that Bernhard had saved thousands of their compatriots from mutilations or a horrible death," his father wrote. "Due to his gallant actions, which had often placed himself in mortal danger, the delegation head said, he had now been forced by the Japanese to leave the Far East."[6]

Women and children were discouraged from watching the actual film due to the horrifying contents, but no one left the room. While the film was being shown, Bernhard Sindberg supplied explanations when needed, and some of the particularly unpleasant footage sent minor shock waves through the rows of spectators. Still, once the film was over, those present seemed completely unaffected by what they had seen. Johannes Sindberg was puzzled, and a British journalist, who was proficient in Swedish and was the only person he could communicate with, provided an explanation: "He told me that the Chinese are not like Europeans. They never show strong emotion in front of strangers. The Chinese, he said, have two faces, and their inherent politeness and strong discipline force them to always show a happy face to their guests, especially when they have a different nationality."[7]

Bernhard Sindberg now returned home, stopping over briefly in Berlin. He spent about a month in Denmark before on July 4, he departed from the port of Aarhus on board the Polish steamship *Pilsudski* bound for New York.[8] It was his intention to study at a university in California and make up for his educational deficiencies, which evidently bothered him. "I very much like to visit Aarhus," he told the newspaper *Demokraten* just before his departure, "and it's no more than 20 months since I was home last.

Sindberg as lieutenant commander in the U.S. Merchant Marine during World War II. (Mariann Arp Stenvig)

Still, I can't stay. Denmark is far too peaceful for me. I must travel, just as I have traveled my entire life."[9]

In his luggage he brought a recommendation written by Margaret Stang-Lund for use in his application to emigrate to the United States:

> Mr. B. A. Sindberg first became known to me the beginning of December last year, when he took on the job of going into the interior of China on a rather dangerous mission for the firm for whom I am also working. Mr. Sindberg showed himself, in this connection, a man of considerable courage and resource, both in reaching his destination under particularly dangerous and difficult circumstances, and in his actions during the months he remained at his post.[10]

***

The refugee camp at Jiangnan Cement had almost been abolished in late spring, as most of the Japanese forces had pulled out, and the murders and rapes in the surrounding area became less frequent, allowing the farmers to return to their fields. After weeks of waiting, Einar Nielsen was finally able to obtain his travel permit to Nanjing, and in early June he reached the cement plant.[11] As far as F. L. Smidth in Shanghai was concerned, this was not a moment too early. In a letter to the company headquarters in Copenhagen, Niels Jensen described his suspicion that Günther was hoping for a permanent job at Qixia, arguing that F. L. Smidth should pull all the stops to prevent this from happening:

> Dr. Günther is undoubtedly an extremely difficult man to deal with and as, furthermore, he is very pro-German we would have endless troubles with him if he should ever enter into the services of the Jiangnan organization. We are therefore anxious to get a man who is quiet, steady and reliable as Mr. Nielsen is reported to be, up to Jiangnan so that Dr. Günther feels that he cannot act exactly as it pleases him.[12]

Einar Nielsen initially found Günther to be friendly, but clearly showing signs of strain after half a year in the war zone: "After having been at the works for seven days, I am sure that Dr. Günther needs to be relieved and get away from the works for at least a few days to prevent him from going insane or crazy. He is very nice but there are troubling signs that he sometimes gets a wild look and starts saying silly things," he wrote in a letter to F. L. Smidth in Shanghai. The Japanese army did not cause any major problems, he added: "The only Japanese who have been here are the usual patrol who come in for a cup of tea, and we always give them cigarettes."[13]

By contrast, the threat from local Chinese bandits became a growing issue during the spring and summer of 1938, as the Japanese military reduced its presence in the area. At 7 a.m. on June 19, Einar Nielsen was called to a village just outside the factory's south gate, where farmers had been attacked in their homes during the night. The assailants had beaten a peasant to death in an attempt to extort money from him. Another peasant had been horribly tortured and was covered in burn marks from head to knees. He died while Nielsen was trying to save him. From then on Nielsen, Günther, and three of their Chinese colleagues introduced a new routine, spending the nights in the factory clubhouse and taking turns keeping watch.[14]

Over the following weeks, local bands carried out new attacks. During the night between July 14 and 15 a three-hour-long firefight erupted at the factory, and when Einar Nielsen later inspected the surrounding fence, he discovered that it had been cut up in three different places.[15] The continued armed attacks also contributed to worsening the relationship between Nielsen and Günther. Nielsen wrote in a letter to F. L. Smidth in Shanghai that Günther had arrested a Chinese in late July, possibly with suspected ties to the gangs, threatening to execute him if there was any further shooting during the night. "He let the man go in the morning, but this only serves to worsen the feeling among people outside," Einar Nielsen wrote.[16]

In her reply to Einar Nielsen, Stang-Lund expressed understanding of his difficult situation but warned against getting involved in any kind of conflict with Günther, as she thought F. L. Smidth would be powerless to do anything to help. The German engineer seemed to enjoy undiminished backing from the Chinese owners, she explained. "I spoke with the Jiangnan people this morning about the matter, and although they agreed that perhaps Dr. Günther's actions are often not well-considered, they did not appear to take a very serious view of the matter, although they already had reports about his doings from other sources," she wrote.[17]

Einar Nielsen's accusations against Günther nevertheless continued throughout the summer, while Günther for his part complained that the Dane had begun keeping pigs, geese, and chickens in the factory area. In the end, Stang-Lund sent a letter in August urging Einar Nielsen to refrain from escalating the situation to an extent where Jiangnan Cement would find it necessary to remove either one of them. "I am not at all sure that our Chinese friends could be prevailed upon to recall Dr. Günther, and it might therefore mean that you would be the one to be recalled, in spite of anything I might advise to the contrary," she wrote.[18] The tensions seemed to decrease somewhat from then on, and a kind of truce evolved between the two men.

Meanwhile, Japanese businessmen continued to display an intense interest in Jiangnan Cement, as especially Onoda Cement had progressed far with plans for future cooperation. However, Onoda had forgotten to ask the Chinese counterparts, and neither Jiangnan Cement, nor its main shareholder Chee Hsin Cement had any desire whatsoever for partnership and tried to evade concrete discussions by stating that the time was not yet ripe. "They consider it certain that the cement to be produced would be utilized by the Japanese army, and if Jiangnan willingly enters into a cooperation with the Japanese this can by the Chinese Government only be considered as treason," Niels Jensen wrote in a report to Copenhagen. "Chee Hsin and Jiangnan would therefore spoil their future in China entirely if they agreed to come to some understanding with the Japanese."[19]

***

Germany invaded Denmark in April 1940, making it impossible for Sindberg to be directly in touch with his family from his new American home, but there were ways. In February 1941, a shopkeeper by the name of Christensen in the town of Ranum in northern Denmark received a shipment of dried apples from California. Since the United States was not yet a belligerent, it was still possible for American goods to reach certain European markets, even in the occupied parts of the continent. Yet, when the shopkeeper opened one of the boxes, he was in for a surprise. Inside the lid, someone had written, with blue chalk:

> Oakland, California, October 24
> Please say to Otto Nielsen, Vejgaard Dairy: Merry Christmas and a Happy New Year.
> Bernhard. Thank you very much.

Bernhard Sindberg had befriended Otto Nielsen while they had both trained to become dairy workers. The message must have been written in a playful moment since the chances of it ever reaching the addressee were minuscule. It was, therefore, an almost incredible coincidence that the box of dried apples were to reach shopkeeper Christensen of all people since he had gone to school with Otto Nielsen and still kept in touch with him. He wrote to him immediately.[20]

News of the greeting from the free world slipped past the censors and was printed in the Aarhus newspaper *Demokraten*, where it caught Johannes Sindberg's attention. He immediately understood that it was about his Bernhard, since he knew that he was friends with dairy worker Nielsen. "Bernhard Sindberg's greeting from California was all the more welcome since the family has not had news from him for an entire year," Johannes Sindberg told the same paper.[21]

Only scattered information about Bernhard Sindberg had reached his family since he left Denmark in July 1938. In August of that year he had, according to reports in the Danish media, been awarded a medal from the Shanghai municipal government for his role in protecting the city one year earlier, most likely in recognition of his time in the Shanghai Volunteer Corps.[22] In January 1939, his family in the city of Odder south of Aarhus received a piece of silk cloth from the refugees at Qixia, passed on by the Danish consulate in China. A quote by Confucius was woven into the cloth, praising "the one who understands a noble cause and fights for it."[23]

Sindberg took part in the battle for the Japanese-occupied Pacific atoll of Kwajalein in January and February 1944, as a member of the crew on board a transport ship taking Marines to the invasion area. (National Archives)

Sindberg's activity after arriving in the United States is only sporadically reflected in the extant sources. His plans to receive an education in California seem to have been quickly abandoned, and in the period from November 1938 until October 1939, he worked on board the steamships *Vitus Bering* and *Knud Rasmussen*, which plied the American West Coast for the Danish shipping company Dampskibsselskab Gloria.[24] In 1940 he settled down in the San Francisco area and made a living as a shipyard worker at Bethlehem Steel Co.[25] In 1941 and 1942 he worked at Richmond Shipyard Number One, also near San Francisco, and he took part in the building of the transport ship *Ocean Vanguard*, which was part of the rapidly growing U.S. assistance to the British war effort.[26] Shortly after he left the Richmond shipyard, in late 1942 he made the pledge of allegiance and became a naturalized citizen of the United States.[27]

Even while still applying for American citizenship, Sindberg had expressed a wish to serve his new country as a member of the U.S. Merchant Marine,[28] and during the last years of World War II, he was once again a sailor, now aboard ships in Pacific war zones. He served on board the transport ship *Perida*, which played a role in the battle for the atoll Kwajalein in early 1944.[29] "[The ship] had a bow like that of an icebreaker. It could run right up on the beach and land the marines," Sindberg wrote in his short autobiography.[30]

After Japan's capitulation in 1945, Sindberg continued his life at sea. He later took on a job as an instructor attached to a fleet of fishing trawlers donated by the United States to China in an attempt to contribute to rebuilding the war-ravaged Chinese economy. When a new conflict broke out in Korea in 1950, he once again was in the middle of events on board the American freighter *Edward Luckenbach*, which transported cargo to the busy Korean port of Busan.[31] This gave him the opportunity to visit the Danish hospital ship *Jutlandia* in order to "enjoy Danish bread, Danish drink and Danish conversation," as he told a journalist in a later interview.[32]

Johannes Sindberg had suddenly died at the age of 64 on June 30, 1947, in Odder.[33] Bernhard Sindberg himself was married in 1949 and divorced three years later.[34] He was a sailor until well into the 1960s, occasionally returning to Denmark for brief visits, but California had become his permanent home. The last years of his life were spent in Harbor Tower, a housing community for senior citizens in the district of San Pedro, Los Angeles, only a few hundred yards from the Pacific Ocean.

"He has dropped anchor in one of our retirement residences," Sindberg wrote in his autobiography, referring to himself in the third person. "For how long, who knows? The long blue vistas of sea, the swaying palms and the beauties of the Orient may call again in voices he can't resist. Once again he may sail out of San Pedro."[35] It remained a dream. He died alone on March 25, 1983, aged 72. When an employee at the mortuary released his remains, he handed over a pre-printed form with a brief description of the deceased. The form also had a box to list the valuables he had on him when he died. It was empty.[36]

Sindberg's 104 Days

Bernhard Sindberg arrived at Jiangnan Cement on December 5, 1937, and left on March 19, 1938, after a total of 104 days. On history's large canvas, his stay at the factory was just a detail. It was a tiny footnote in the Second Sino-Japanese War, which lasted eight long years and cost up to 20 million lives. Even within the narrower context of Jiangnan Cement's history, Sindberg's three-month presence does not count for much. By comparison, Sindberg's successor Einar Nielsen remained at the plant until the mid-1940s, while his old rival Karl Günther did not return home to Germany until 1950. Similarly, the shadowy Japanese–Chinese struggle for control over the factory continued behind the scenes throughout the war years.

In history, however, duration is not equivalent to importance, and Sindberg's 104 short days represented something entirely unique. At a time when almost all foreigners had prioritized their own safety and left Nanjing, leaving behind only a small handful of Westerners consisting mostly of Christian missionaries, he put his life at risk, facing a powerful army that was known for its ferocity and could easily have made him disappear during one of his many forays into the man-made wasteland that surrounded Nanjing during the weeks following the conquest of the city. Instead of listening to the most basic human instinct for personal survival, he staked everything on protecting the Chinese people of his refugee camp.

It is hard to give an exact figure for the number of people he saved, mainly because the size of the refugee camp he defended and helped manage is not known with any degree of precision. It seems to have reached about 4,000 inhabitants in just a matter of days immediately after the Japanese army occupied the Jiangnan Cement area. Two months later, it had grown to about 10,000, according to several independent sources. At that time, its size peaked, and subsequently the number began to decline, as conditions became gradually less violent, and it was safer for people to return to their homes and fields.

Statue of Sindberg erected inside the compound of Jiangnan Cement. (Peter Harmsen)

Ten thousand people is a large number. By contrast, in one of the most celebrated episodes of World War II in Denmark, approximately 7,000 Danish Jews were rescued from the Nazis in October 1943, when the entire Jewish community in the small Scandinavian nation was poised to be sent to concentration camps in Germany, but hundreds of mainly anonymous Danes conspired to transport them secretly to unoccupied Sweden instead. The key difference was that Sindberg often acted alone, and when he acted in cooperation with others, he was always at the center and the main driving force. The bloody chaos that unfolded at the nearby Qixia Temple shows what conditions would have been like at Jiangnan Cement without Sindberg. This makes him one of the great unrecognized humanitarians of modern history.

***

It makes sense to compare Sindberg with one of the 20th century's most iconic figures, the ethnic German businessman Oskar Schindler, who saved hundreds of Jews employed at his factory during the bloody Nazi occupation of Poland. The comparison is somewhat wanting, since most of the 10,000 Chinese in Sindberg's camp would probably have survived anyway, albeit with emotional scars, whereas virtually all the Schindler Jews would have been killed in the gas chambers. Yet there are striking similarities between Sindberg and Schindler. Both men were fearless in situations where there could be no doubt that their behavior might cost them their lives, and both knew how to navigate the inhuman system that surrounded them. They were prepared to associate with the German and Japanese executioners and use all their natural charm because the situation required it.

First and foremost, both Sindberg's and Schindler's biographies show that we cannot predict in advance who will stand out in extreme situations. Neither of them was a saint. Schindler's love of women has often been pointed out as it goes to show that he was a human who often let his passions dictate his behavior. We know enough about Sindberg's history before his arrival in Nanjing to conclude that he, too, was a highly emotional individual prompted to action by his feelings, sometimes with greatly negative consequences for himself. It is important to note this common trait, since faced with an abyss of cruelty, both Sindberg and Schindler chose to abandon cold rationality and follow their instincts, regardless of the costs.

Prior to the war, both were average human beings, with all the blemishes that we often encounter in people in our daily lives. Schindler was a businessman with a fondness of liquor and with only limited success to boast of, while Sindberg was a tough and often violent sailor who did not easily accept authority, especially when wielded randomly and unfairly. They stayed average until history suddenly placed them in situations where they had to make decisive choices, opting for either action or inaction. Both made the difficult but right choice. Their abrupt appearance on the stage of history was a striking and improbable event, and it was just as striking that once they had played their historic role to the end, they returned to the gray, faceless mass of humanity from which they had emerged. Schindler was almost forgotten after the war. Sindberg was entirely forgotten.

Important questions remain, most crucially this one: what made Schindler and Sindberg exhibit aspects of their personalities that no one knew about beforehand, least of all themselves? Were they transformed overnight into different people, by some unknown, yet-to-be-discovered magic? The answer is, of course, no. Many modern psychologists tell us that an individual's personality is formed in childhood, and that he is forced to live with it, and all its inherent deficiencies and flaws, until the very end. The dramatic character changes that sometimes occur in works of fiction are just that, fictitious. Still, extreme situations do something to people. Some characteristics are weakened to the point of vanishing, while others become more pronounced and often take command of the person. War is the most extreme of all situations, and it is often the most unlikely people who end up as villains and heroes, executioners and saviors.

Historians and others who engage with the past may try to identify the specific factors that caused certain individuals to break with their habits and act in uncharacteristic ways. In Steven Spielberg's film *Schindler's List* from 1993, the decisive moment was the cloudy day in 1943 when Schindler was sitting on horseback on a hill outside Krakow's Jewish ghetto, watching the SS soldiers' brutal cleansing of the district. The scene, which is loosely based on a similar passage in Thomas Keneally's eponymous book,[1] makes sense dramaturgically speaking, but according to American historian David Crowe, who has studied Schindler's life story in detail, it is not backed up by historical fact: "I think his transformation took place slowly over a long period... In the end, there was no one, dramatic, transforming moment when Oskar Schindler decided to do everything he could to save his Jewish workers."[2]

What about Sindberg? Was he placed in the role as protector of the defenseless on the shores of the Yangtze by a single crucial moment, or was it the accumulated results of a long series of events? It is tempting to point to individual episodes that undoubtedly shocked Sindberg and awakened him to the danger posed by Japanese imperialism. The cruel execution of the nine convicted Chinese men in the Shanghai docks in August 1937 was one such episode. Sindberg's own detailed account of that particular episode is testimony to the deep impression that the bloody spectacle left on him. But perhaps the explanation for Sindberg's bravery must be sought in his childhood, when his father taught him and his siblings the importance of helping others. The early lesson may have been almost forgotten later on, during a youth of reckless adventure and drunken brawls, but it was brought back to life by Sindberg's encounter with the bloody face of Japanese colonial power, and it came to full fruition at Jiangnan Cement, where he initially looked the other way when Chinese refugees settled down outside the factory fence, only to quickly turn to an active stance as their protector and guardian.

***

Sindberg's efforts on behalf of thousands of Chinese refugees were forgotten for over six decades. One of the most important Danish feats of the entire world war was absent from the public consciousness, in Denmark and elsewhere. After a very short period in the late 1930s, when Sindberg's association with the war correspondent Philip Pembroke Stephens turned him into a minor celebrity in Denmark, everything fell quiet and he largely disappeared from public view. He only merited a brief story in a local Danish newspaper in 1951 when he passed by as the first mate of an American coal boat, but the report did not mention his humanitarian role in Nanjing with a single word.[3]

During that time, the Cold War spread across the globe, and old friendships disappeared behind new enmities. Most people in the West forgot that just a few years in the past, China had been an important ally in the effort to bring Japanese imperialism to a halt. There was almost no awareness of Japanese war crimes in China, and no focus at all on the resistance offered by an unknown Dane in the Chinese interior. Towards the turn of the century, the situation slowly changed, and the Western public was gradually alerted to the enormity of the Nanjing massacre. The publication in 1997 of German businessman John Rabe's diaries brought Sindberg to the fore for the first time. He is mentioned countless times by Rabe, and he is identified as a Dane.

It was not until the year 2000, however, that Sindberg's role became widely known. Chinese historians had encountered his name over and over again in their research into the Nanjing massacre, and through the Chinese Embassy in Copenhagen, they tried to find out more about who he really was. All they had to go by was his last name, but the quest paid off. Sindberg's younger sister, who was still alive, responded to public Chinese pleas for information, and all the pieces suddenly fell into place. The Chinese were given the full name and personal details of the mysterious Dane.

Why did it have to take so long? Part of the explanation is almost certainly that Sindberg did not live in Denmark after the war and thus was isolated from the kind of social networks that in a Danish environment would sooner or later have alerted a journalist or a historian to his story. More surprisingly, Sindberg did not himself attempt to write about his time in Nanjing, not even privately. This may be partly due to the ban imposed on him by F. L. Smidth against keeping a diary. The lack of a reference in the form of diary entries may have prevented Sindberg from completing a regular memoir about the period at Jiangnan Cement, especially as his memory weakened due to old age.

Instead, in order to learn about Sindberg's almost incredible achievement, we must resort to various historical sources located in archives in China, the United States, and Europe—as well as a large body of oral history records collected by Chinese researchers. Recognition comes late for some people. For Sindberg it never came. But some kind of posthumous justice is found in the fact that, more than 80 years on, there are still people in China who remember the tall, blond man with the strange red-and-white flag.

Notes

Introduction: The Dane

1 The description of Wang Liyong and his family is based on *Nanjing datusha shiliaoji [Collection of Historical Sources for the Nanjing Massacre]* (hereafter *NDS*), Nanjing: Jiangsu renmin chubanshe, 2005–2010, vol. 26: 706–707.

2 The average height for young Danish men in 1940 was exactly 5 feet 8 inches. See *65 år i tal. Danmark siden 2. verdenskrig [65 Years in Numbers: Denmark Since World War Two]* (Copenhagen: Danmarks Statistik, 2014), 7.

3 See for example Iris Chang, *The Rape of Nanking: The Forgotten Holocaust of World War II* (New York NY: Basic Books, 2012).

Chapter 1: Heir of the Vikings

1 Sankt Paul's parish, parish list 1910–1913, 60.

2 "Aarhusianer Jorden rundt 2½ Gang paa 20 Mdr." ["Aarhus Resident Travels Around the World 2.5 Times in 20 Months"], *Demokraten (Aarhus)*, July 4, 1938, 3.

3 Line Holm Nielsen, "Kinesernes danske helt" ["A Danish Hero in China"], *Berlingske Tidende*, February 13, 2008, 13.

4 Odder parish, parish list 1946–1955, 22.

5 Farmers in the village of Vinten built their first dairy in 1888, see *Trap Danmark* (5th edition), vol. 8 (Copenhagen: G.E.C. Gad, 1964), 722.

6 Branderslev parish, parish list 1892–1914, 180.

7 Sandby parish, parish list 1901–1918, 28.

8 Aarhus cathedral parish, parish list 1906–1912, 148.

9 Klaus Christian Arp (ca. 1819–1890) was related to the couple through Johannes Sindberg's father. Tamdrup parish, parish list 1892–1907, 335; "Avertissementer" ["Announcements"], *Kongelig allernaadigst privilegeret Horsens Avis eller Skanderbog Amtstidende*, June 23, 1890, 3.

10 Aarhus cathedral parish, parish list 1906–1912, 148.

11 *Demokraten (Aarhus)*, November 17, 1912, 1.

12 "Aarhus Mælkehandlerforening" ["Aarhus Milk Merchants' Association"], *Aarhus Stiftstidende*, June 26, 1913, 2; *Aarhus Stiftstidende*, August 8, 1913, 5.

13 J.C. Christensen, "Til 'Aarhus Mælkehandlerforening" ["Letter for Aarhus Milk Merchants' Association"], *Aarhus Stiftstidende*, June 30, 1913, 4.

14 Johannes N. Sindberg, "Svar til J.C. Christensen" ["Reply to J. C. Christensen"], *Aarhus Stiftstidende*, July 2, 1913, 5.

15 *Aarhus Stiftstidende*, April 7, 1914.

16 "Beskæftigelse søges" ["Employment Wanted"], *Demokraten (Aarhus)*, October 9, 1915, 4.

17 Johannes N. Sindberg, "Mejeri-Trustens Prisforhøjelse" ["The Price Hike by the Dairy Trust"], *Demokraten*, December 15, 1914, 2.

18 Johannes N. Sindberg, "De høje Priser paa Landbrugsprodukter" ["The High Prices of Agricultural Produce"], *Demokraten*, December 22, 1914, 1.

19 Johannes N. Sindberg, "Meddelelse fra Mælkehandler Johs. N. Sindberg" ["Announcement by Milk Merchant Johs. N. Sindberg"], *Demokraten*, April 18, 1915, 1.

20 "Beskæftigelse søges" ["Employment Wanted"], *Demokraten (Aarhus)*, October 9, 1915, 4.

21 Johs. N. Sindberg, "Dyrtiden" ["Rising Prices"], *Fredericia Social-Demokrat*, October 24, 1916, 1.

22 *Demokraten (Aarhus)*, July 2, 1918, 3.

23 *Aarhus Stiftstidende*, September 2, 1919, 7.

24 Aarhus Municipal Archives, tax payer register for Frederiksgade 1918 and 1919.

25 Aarhus Municipal Archives, Aarhus municipal schools. Ingerslevs Boulevard School. IV. Students. 1904–31: Exam results for boys, 1st and 2nd form; Students 1904–21: Exam results for boys, 3rd to 6th form; IV. Students. 1921: Exam results for boys, 3rd to 7th form.

26 Aarhus Municipal Archives, Aarhus municipal schools. Ingerslevs Boulevard School. Students. 1902–23: Enrolment of boys.

27 *Aarhus Stiftstidende*, April 5, 1920.

28 Interview with Mariann Arp Stenvig, April 24, 2019.

29 "Spejderne i Havn" ["Scouts Arriving"], *Politiken*, August 2, 1924, 8.

30 Line Holm Nielsen, "Kinesernes danske helt" ["A Danish Hero in China], *Berlingske Tidende*, February 13, 2008, 13.

31 Erik Korr Johansen (ed.), *Fra kysthavn til storhavn—Århus havns historie 1915–1995 [From Coastal Harbor to Major Harbor: The History of the Port of Aarhus, 1915–1995]* (Aarhus: Århus Byhistoriske Udvalg, 1994), 21.

32 National Archives and Record Administration (NARA), Washington DC, Passenger and Crew Lists of Vessels Arriving at New York, New York, 1897–1957. Microfilm Publication T715, Microfilm Roll: 4229; Line: 4; Page Number: 107 og Line: 7; Page Number: 109. NAI: 300346.

33 Ove Kjeldsen, "Jorden rundt i 60 år" ["Around the World in 60 Years"], in *Årbog 1995* (Kronborg: Handels- og Søfartsmuseet, 1995), 82.

34 Hans Bendix, *Med Ryggen til Europa [Putting Europe Behind You]* (Copenhagen: Atheneum, 1939), 9.

35 NARA, Passenger and Crew Lists of Vessels Arriving at New York, New York, 1897–1957. Microfilm Publication T715, Microfilm Roll: 4252; Line: 15; Page Number: 269. NAI: 300346.

36 Ibid, Microfilm Roll: 4295; Line: 3; Page Number: 188. NAI: 300346.

37 Ibid, Microfilm Roll: 4585; Line: 28; Page Number: 178. NAI: 300346.

38 Bjerager parish, census, 1930.

39 "Marlene Dietrich i 'Marokko'" ["Marlene Dietrich in *Morocco*"], *Politiken*, March 10, 1931, 2.

40 Prince Aage, *Legionær. Skæbner i Fremmedlegionen [Legionnaire: Lives in the Foreign Legion]* (Copenhagen: Berlingske Forlag, 1936), 6.

41 Bennett J. Doty, *The Legion of the Damned: The Adventures of Bennett J. Doty in the French Foreign Legion as Told By Himself* (London: Jonathan Cape, 1928).

42 Erwin Rosen, *In the Foreign Legion* (London: Duckworth, 1910), 87–89.

43 *Politiken*, April 8, 1930, 11.

44 Prince Aage, *Tre Aars Kampe i Fremmedlegionen [Three Years of War in the Foreign Legion]* (Copenhagen: Gyldendalske Boghandel, 1927), 18–19.

45 Doty, *The Legion of the Damned*.

46 Interview with Mariann Arp Stenvig, April 24, 2019.

47 Douglas Porch, *The French Foreign Legion* (London: Macmillan, 1991), 328.

48 Royal Danish Navy, Office for Compulsory Service, "Certificate of Behavior" (copy), November 25, 1942, Harry Ransom Center, University of Texas at Austin.

49 Danish National Archives, Ministry of the Interior, 2nd Bureau. Conscription Registry 1861–1932, 4th conscription region, no. 0003, conscription no. 230, 1929; Danish National Archives, Ministry of Defense, Ship Journals 1650–1977, no. 0028: "Mågen Inspektionsskib Skibsjournal 1932 m.m."

50 See for example the entry for June 20 in "Mågen Inspektionsskib Skibsjournal 1932 m.m."

51 Bernhard Sindberg, *Sketch of a Lifetime*, Harry Ransom Center, University of Texas at Austin. This extremely brief autobiography seems to have been written in the 1970s or 1980s. The episode involving the German trawler during the mission to Greenland is the only incident dealt with in some detail. The autobiography does not mention the time in Nanjing at all.

52 Royal Danish Navy, Office for Compulsory Service, "Certificate of Behavior" (copy), November 25, 1942, Harry Ransom Center, University of Texas at Austin.

Chapter 2: The Prisoner of the *Falstria*

1 "Saarbruecken Arrives From Europe Today; Falstria Docks From U.S. Today, President Jefferson On Monday," *The China Press*, April 14, 1934, A1 og 4.

2 Excerpts from *Falstria*'s logbook in Danish National Archives, Ministry of Foreign Affairs, consular arcives. Shanghai. No. 02-2035, 27.P.a.50: "Sømand Bernhard Arp Sindberg on board m/s 'Falstria'. Assault."

3 Letter from Melchior to Lunn, April 14, 1934 in Danish National Archives, No. 02-2035, 27.P.a.50.

4 What follows is my summary and interpretation of testimony made during two sessions of the Danish consular court on April 14 and 19, 1934, described in two detailed reports in the Danish National Archives No. 02-2035, 27.P.a.50. In addition, the case was spectacular enough to also be mentioned in the local English-language press. See "MS Falstria Seaman Charged With Assault In Danish Court Here," *The China Press*, April 17, 1934: A1; "Danish Consular Court: Seaman Charged With Assault," *The North-China Herald and Supreme Court & Consular Gazette*, April 18, 1934: 83. Sindberg is erroneously spelled "Sinberg" in both reports. See also Hans J. Hinrup, "Sindberg. The Good Dane in Nanjing 1937," paper presented at conference organized by the Nordic Association for China Studies, Stockholm, June 11–13, 2007.

5 "Ex-13 Spends A Month In The Amoy Road Gaol," *The China Press*, November 4, 1933, 9; "Ex-13 Serves Time In Amoy Road Gaol," *The China Press*, November 5, 1933, 11.

6 Frank Dikötter, *Crime, Punishment and the Prison in Modern China* (London: C. Hurst & Co., 2002), 321–322.

7 "Ex-13 Spends A Month In The Amoy Road Gaol," *The China Press*, November 4, 1933, 9.

8 The consular court was able to pass judgment in the case, as Denmark, similarly to a number of other foreign powers, enjoyed special privileges in Shanghai and other Chinese cities, meaning that Danish citizens did not have to appear in front of a Chinese judge for crimes committed in these special areas.

9 Summary of meeting in the consular court on April 25, 1934, in Danish National Archives. No. 02-2035, 27.P.a.50.

10 Ibid. The comparison with a "slave ship" appears in a letter from Melchior to Lunn, April 14, 1934.

11 Sindberg, *Sketch of a Lifetime*.

12   NARA, *Passenger and Crew Lists of Vessels Arriving at Seattle, Washington.* Record Group Number: *85*; Series Number: *M1383*; Roll Number: *197.* NAI: *4449160*; Certificate of Seaman's Service, Seattle, January 9, 1943, Harry Ransom Center, University of Texas at Austin.

13   NARA, New York, Passenger and Crew Lists (including Castle Garden and Ellis Island), 1820–1957; Microfilm Publication T715, Microfilm Roll: 5608; Line: 25; Page Number: 42; om *Peter Mærsk*, se Ove Horny, *"Ved rettidig Omhu": Skibsreder A. P. Møller 1876–1965 ["By Due Diligence": Shipping Magnate A. P. Møller 1876–1965]* (Copenhagen: Schultz, 1988), 111–112.

14   "Population Of Greater City Jumps In '35," *The China Press*, March 7, 1936, 9.

15   J. V. Davidson-Houston, *Yellow Creek: The Story of Shanghai* (Philadelphia PA: Dufour Editions, 1964), 142.

16   Steen Eiler Rasmussen, *Rejse i Kina [China Travel]* (Copenhagen: Carit Andersens Forlag, 1958), 60–61.

17   "Shanghai—the World's Fifth Metropolis," *The China Press*, October 10, 1936, C134.

18   On the 1932 battle, see Donald A. Jordan, *China's Trial by Fire* (Ann Arbor MI: The University of Michigan Press, 2001).

19   "Shanghai—the World's Fifth Metropolis," *The China Press*, October 10, 1936, C134.

20   Rasmussen, *Rejse*, 60–61.

21   Erling Bache, *Hvide under Tropesol [White People under the Tropical Sun]* (Copenhagen: H. Hirschsprungs Forlag, 1939), 206.

22   Olaf Linck, *En Dansker i Østen. Laurits Andersens Livs Eventyr [A Dane in the East: The Life and Adventures of Laurits Andersen]* (Copenhagen: Gyldendalske Boghandel, 1927), 48–49.

23   Bache, *Tropesol*, 204.

24   Peter Abildgaard, "Den danske helt i Kina-massakren er fundet" ["The Danish Hero in the Massacre Has Breen Found"], *Aarhus Stiftstidende*, July 14, 2000, 14; Chaplin visited Shanghai in March and May 1936, see "Chaplin Likes China; 'Girls Are So Lovely,' He Declares," *The China Press*, March 10, 1936, 1 and "Charlie Chaplin Here Again," *The North-China Herald and Supreme Court & Consular Gazette*, May 20, 1936, 328; Bernhard Sindberg, *Sketch of a Lifetime.* Sindberg writes in his autobiography about "an Italian princess." This must be an error, and he is most likely referring to the Spanish princess, who stayed at Cathay Hotel in January 1936, see "Here and There," *The North-China Herald and Supreme Court & Consular Gazette*, January 15, 1936: 119.

25   Letter from Mogens Melchior, May 18, 1937 in Danish National Archives. No.02-2035, 27.P.a.71: "Juncker Jensen vs. B. A. Sindberg, Assault."

26   Ibid.

27   Hinrup, "Sindberg."

28   Declaration by Bernhard Sindberg in letter to the Danish consulate in Shanghai, December 1, 1937. Copy is kept in Japan-Kina 1937–38, FLSmidth archives, Valby.

29   *Uge-Avisen for Odder og Omegn*, August 14, 1936, 1.

30   Ibid.

Chapter 3: "A Stupid Nincompoop"

1   Jørgen Juncker-Jensen, *Facts & Episodes of My Life* (Copenhagen: Self-published, 1983), 159.

2   "Ung Aarhusianer saaret i Shanghai" ["Young Aarhus Resident Injured in Shanghai"], *Aarhus Stiftstidende*, November 11, 1937, 2.

3   For background and details regarding Danish Recoil Rifle Syndicate's sale of machine guns in China, see Hinrup, "Sindberg."

4   Letter from Mogens Melchior, May 18, 1937. Danish National Archives. No. 02-2035, 27.P.a.71. "Juncker Jensen vs. B. A. Sindberg, Assault."

5   Juncker-Jensen, *Facts*, 159–160. The description of Yangtze Hotel is from "Nanking Again Becomes China Culture Center," *The China Press*, June 23, 1936, 13.

6   Juncker-Jensen, *Facts*, 161.

7   Ibid, 163.

8   Ibid, 162.

9   Ibid, 162–163.

10 Ibid, 162.

11 Letter from Mogens Melchior, May 18, 1937. Danish National Archives. No. 02-2035, 27.P.a.71.

12 Ibid.

13 Letter from Scheel to Nyholm, May 15, 1937. Danish National Archives. No. 02-2035, 27.P.a.71.

14 Ibid.

15 Letter from Nyholm to Scheel, May 23, 1937. Danish National Archives. No. 02-2035, 27.P.a.71.

16 Letter from Mogens Melchior, May 25, 1937. Danish National Archives. No. 02-2035, 27.P.a.71.

17 Letter from Scheel to Nyholm, May 25, 1937. Danish National Archives. No. 02-2035, 27.P.a.71.

18 Letter from Nyholm to the Danish consulate in Shanghai, June 6, 1937. Danish National Archives. No. 02-2035, 27.P.a.71.

19 Bernhard Sindberg, "Enroute to the Battle-zones," 1.

20 Ibid.

21 "Den rædselsfulde Uge, før Shanghai-Danskernes Børn og Kvinder naaede i Sikkerhed" ["The Terrible Week Before Women and Children of the Shanghai Danes Were Safe"], *Politiken*, September 16, 1937, 4.

22 Danish National Archives. Ministry of Foreign Affairs. Dispatches 1848–1972, Shanghai 1936–1945 etc., no. 0002, 173 D 21, dispatch from Oxholm to Munch, August 22, 1937.

23 Sindberg, "Battle-zones," 1.

24 Zhang Fakui, *Reminiscences of Fa-K'uei Chang: Oral History, 1970–1980* (Columbia University Libraries, Oral History Research Office), 457.

25 "Store Dele af Shanghai staar i Flammer" ["Large Parts of Shanghai are Ablaze"], *Politiken*, August 14, 1937, 1.

26 Vagn Meisling, "Et natligt Besøg ved den japanske Front" ["A Nightly Visit at the Japanese Front"], *Politiken*, August 23, 1937, 1.

27 "Dagligt Liv i Shanghai under Bombe-Rædslerne skildret i Brev fra Dansker" ["Daily Life in Shanghai during the Air Raid Horrors is Described in Letter from a Dane"], *Politiken*, September 7, 1937, 9–10.

28 Ibid.

29 Peter Harmsen, *Shanghai 1937: Stalingrad on the Yangtze* (Havertown PA: Casemate, 2013), 62.

30 Sindberg, "Battle-zones," 1.

31 Sindberg's family received a letter from him in late summer, "apparently sent from Japan," in which he explained that he was on his way to Shanghai. "Ung Aarhusianer saaret i Shanghai," *Aarhuus Stiftstidende*, November 11, 1937, 2.

32 Sindberg, "Battle-zones," 1–2.

33 Ibid, 2.
34 Ibid.
35 Sindberg, "Battle-zones," 3.
36 Ibid.
37 Sindberg, "Battle-zones," 4.
38 Ibid.
39 Ibid.
40 Sindberg, "Battle-zones," 4–5.

Chapter 4: Death in the Streets

1   Ibid, 5–6.
2   Haldore Hanson, *"Humane Endeavour": The Story of the China War* (New York NY: Farrar & Rinehart, 1939), 64.
3   Ernst Wickert (ed.), *John Rabe: Der gute Deutsche von Nanking [John Rabe: The Good German of Nanjing]* (Stuttgart: Deutsche Verlags-Anstalt, 1997), 261.
4   Sindberg, "Battle-zones," 7.
5   Ibid.
6   For details about the corps, its uniforms and arms, see Martin Sugarman, *"Hagedud Ha-Sini*: The Jewish Company of the Shanghai Volunteer Corps, 1932–42," *Jewish Historical Studies*, Vol. 41 (2007), 189.
7   "Shanghai's Volunteers," *The North-China Herald and Supreme Court & Consular Gazette*, August 16, 1933, 273.
8   Sindberg, "Battle-zones," 7.
9   Ibid.
10 Sindberg, "Battle-zones," 9.
11 Ibid, 10–11.
12 Sindberg, "Battle-zones," 12.
13 Ibid.
14 Vagn Meisling, "Dansker i Shanghai, der stadig undslipper Døden" ["Dane in Shanghai Who Still Evades Death"], *Politiken*, October 31, 1937, 1–2.
15 Henry Hellssen, "De danske Frivillige vender tilbage til Kontorerne, men de tager deres Rifler med" ["The Danish Volunteers Return to Their Offices, But Bring Their Rifles"], *Berlingske Aftenavis*, August 31, 1937, 8.
16 Danish National Archives. Ministry of Foreign Affairs. Dispatches 1848–1972, Shanghai 1936–1945 etc., no. 0002, 173 D 21, dispatch from Oxholm to Munch, August 22, 1937.
17 Sindberg, "Battle-zones," 13; Hallett Abend, "Planes Bomb Auto," *The New York Times*, August 27, 1937, 1.
18 Sindberg, "Battle-zones," 12.

Chapter 5: "My Friend Sindbad"

1   Pembroke Stephens, "Japan's Bid for Speedy Victory," *Belfast Telegraph*, September 8, 1937, 12.
2   "British Journalist Killed," *The Midland Daily Telegraph*, November 11, 1937, 1.
3   "Notable Career," *The Scotsman*, November 12, 1937, 14.
4   Pembroke Stephens, "Shanghai Fighting," *Belfast Telegraph*, September 9, 1937, 13.

5   Pembroke Stephens, "Jap Barrage Rocks Shanghai," *Belfast Telegraph*, September 10, 1937, 12.
6   Sindberg, "Battle-zones," 14.
7   "Ung Aarhusianer saaret i Shanghai," *Aarhus Stiftstidende*, November 11, 1937, 2.
8   "Aarhusianeren i Kina har faaet et nyt farligt Arbejde" ["The Aarhus Resident in China Now Has a New Dangerous Job"], *Aarhus Stiftstidende*, December 29, 1937, 1.
9   Sindberg, "Battle-zones," 14.
10 Danish National Archives. Ministry of Foreign Affairs. Dispatches 1848–1972, Shanghai 1936–1945 etc., no. 0002, 173 D 21, dispatch from Oxholm to Munch, August 22, 1937.
11 Pembroke Stephens, "Chinese Sentry's Costly Sleep," *Belfast Telegraph*, October 8, 1937, 15.
12 Sindberg, "Battle-zones," 16.
13 Pembroke Stephens, "Shanghai Defences Pierced," *Belfast Telegraph*, October 4, 1937, 9.
14 Ibid.
15 Pembroke Stephens, "Japs Held to Blame," *Belfast Telegraph*, October 31, 1937, 11.
16 Danish National Archives. Ministry of Foreign Affairs. Dispatches 1848–1972, Shanghai 1936–1945 etc., no. 0002, 173 D 21, dispatch from Oxholm to Munch, October 28, 1937.
17 Pembroke Stephens, "Chinese Sentry's Costly Sleep," *Belfast Telegraph*, October 8, 1937, 15.
18 Sindberg, "Battle-zones," 16.
19 Pembroke Stephens, "Japan's Big Guns in Action," *Belfast Telegraph*, October 12, 1937, 11.
20 Pembroke Stephens, "Four Ulster Rifles Buried," *Belfast Telegraph*, November 1, 1937, 11.
21 Rhodes Farmer, *Shanghai Harvest: Three Years in the China War* (London: Museum Press, 1945), 92.
22 "Tokyo 'Nichi-Nichi' Publishes Scandalous Account of Death of Mr. Stephens," *The China Weekly Review*, November 20, 1937, 282.
23 "Killed on Duty at Shanghai," *The Scotsman*, November 12, 1937, 13. According to the article, the salvo lasted for 10 minutes. It is impossible for a machine gun to fire uninterruptedly for that long, and most likely it is supposed to be 10 seconds.
24 Ibid.
25 "Yui Instructed to Stop Fighting in Chinese City," *The Japan Times and Mail*, November 13, 1937, 2.
26 "Tokyo 'Nichi-Nichi' Publishes Scandalous Account of Death of Mr. Stephens," *The China Weekly Review*, November 20, 1937, 282.

Chapter 6: A Capital at War

1   Harmsen, *Shanghai 1937*, 66–67.
2   Charles D. Musgrove, Ronald G. Knapp og Xing Ruan, *China's Contested Capital: Architecture, Ritual, and Response in Nanjing* (Honolulu HI: University of Hawaii Press, 2013), 59.
3   Julius Eigner, "The Rise and Fall of Nanjing," *National Geographic*, February 1938, 217.
4   Juncker-Jensen, *Facts*, 163.
5   "Nanking Again Becomes China Culture Center," *The China Press*, June 23, 1936, 13.
6   Musgrove et al., *Capital*, 69.
7   "Nanking Again Becomes China Culture Center," 13.
8   Ernst Wickert, *Mut und Übermut: Geschichten aus meinem Leben [Courage and Arrogance: Stories From My Life]* (Stuttgart: Deutsche Verlags-Anstalt, 1991), 210–211.
9   Ibid, 211.
10 Chr. Søndergaard, "Bombardement af op til 75 Kampflyvere om Dagen" ["Air Raid with Up to 75 Combat Planes a Day"], *Østsjællands Folkeblad*, January 8, 1938, 1–2.

11 Vagn Meisling, "Danskerne rømmer Nanking" ["Danes Leave Nanjing"], *Politiken*, September 21, 1937, 2.

12 "Rædslerne i Nanking før Byens Erobring" ["The Horrors of Nanjing Before the Conquest of the City"], *Jyllands-Posten*, December 16, 1937, 3.

13 "Brev fra Dansker i Nanking" ["Letter From Dane in Nanjing"], *Frederiksborg Amts Avis*, December 16, 1937, 3.

14 Wolf Schenke, *Reise and der gelben Front [Journey Along the Yellow Front]* (Berlin: Gerhard Stalling Verlagsbuchhandlung, 1941), 64.

15 Wickert (ed.), *Rabe*, 13.

16 Interview with James Voss, Oral History no. 0680, Oral History Program, University of North Texas, 40.

17 Wickert (ed.), *Rabe*, 15.

18 "Dramatisk Tur gennem det krigshærgede Kina" ["Dramatic Journey Through War-Ravaged China"], *Jyllands-Posten*, October 1, 1937, 2.

19 Telegram from Johnson, August 15, 1937, *Foreign Relations of the United States diplomatic papers, 1937. The Far East*, vol. III (Washington DC: U.S. Government Printing Office, 1937), 415–416.

20 Lu Suping (ed.), *Terror in Minnie Vautrin's Nanjing: Diaries and Correspondence, 1937–38* (Urbana and Chicago IL: University of Illinois Press, 2008), 7.

21 "Envoys Condemn Nanking Bombings," *The New York Times*, August 28, 1937, 4.

22 "Nanking Selling Mouth Bandages Against Gas Bomb," *The China Press*, August 24, 1937, 1.

23 Lu (ed.), *Vautrin*, 3.

24 "Nanking Safer Than Shanghai, States Benino," *The China Press*, August 26, 1937, 2.

25 "Nanking Selling Mouth Bandages Against Gas Bomb," *The China Press*, August 24, 1937, 1.

26 Chr. Søndergaard, "Bombardement af op til 75 Kampflyvere om Dagen," *Østsjællands Folkeblad*, January 8, 1938, 1–2.

27 Ibid.

28 Wickert (ed.), *Rabe*, 31.

29 Lu (ed.), *Vautrin*, 8.

30 "Krigsbrev fra Nanking" ["War Letter From Nanjing"], *Holbæk Amts Venstreblad*, October 6, 1937, 6.

31 "Japanese to Bomb Nanking, Says Admiral," *The North-China Herald and Supreme Court & Consular Gazette*, September 22, 1937, 456.

32 "Foreigners Ready to Leave Nanking," *The New York Times*, September 20, 1937, 11; "Attack Is Terrific," *The New York Times*, September 22, 1937, 1.

33 Niels Jensen to F. L. Smidth & Co. Copenhagen, November 23, 1937, 3. Japan-Kina 1937–38, FLSmidth archives, Valby.

34 "Attack Is Terrific," *The New York Times*, September 22, 1937, 1.

35 Wickert (ed.), *Rabe*, 31.

36 "Nanking bombet i Morges" ["Nanjing Bombed This Morning"], *Aalborg Amtstidende*, September 25, 1937, 1.

37 "U.S. Note to Japan," *The New York Times*, September 23, 1937, 19.

38 Lu (ed.), *Vautrin*, 28.

39 "Krigsbrev fra Nanking" ["War Letter From Nanjing"], *Holbæk Amts Venstreblad*, October 6, 1937, 6.

40 "Only Combatants Warred Upon," *North-China Herald and Supreme Court & Consular Gazette*, December 1, 1937, 334.

41 Timothy Brook, *Collaboration: Japanese Agents and Local Elites in Wartime China* (Cambridge MA: Harvard University Press, 2005), 91–93.

42 Kasahara Tokushi, "Massacres outside Nanking City." Bob Takashi Wakabayashi, *The Nanking Atrocity, 1937–38: Complicating the Picture* (New York NY: Berghahn Books, 2017), 61.

43 Schenke, *Reise*, 50–51.

44 Danish National Archives. Ministry of Foreign Affairs. Dispatches 1848–1972, Shanghai 1936–1945 etc., no. 0002, 173 D 21, dispatch from Oxholm to Munch, December 23, 1937.

45 Wickert (ed.), *Rabe*, 51.

46 Marcia R. Ristaino, *The Jacquinot Safe Zone: Wartime Refugees in Shanghai* (Stanford CA: Stanford University Press, 2008), 63.

47 Zhang Kaiyuan (ed.), *Eyewitnesses to Massacre* (Armonk NY: M. E. Sharpe, 2001), xxi.

48 "Brev fra Dansker i Nanking" ["Letter From Dane in Nanjing"], *Frederiksborg Amts Avis*, December 16, 1937, 3.

49 Schenke, *Reise*, 61–62.

50 "Report of the Nanking International Relief Committee" in Zhang Kaiyuan (ed.), *Eyewitnesses to Massacre* (Armonk NY: M. E. Sharpe, 2001), 416.

51 Peter Harmsen, *Nanjing 1937: Battle for a Doomed City* (Havertown PA: Casemate, 2015), 150–151.

52 Ernest H. Forster, "Letters to Wife," in Zhang Kaiyuan (ed.), *Eyewitnesses to Massacre* (Armonk NY: M. E. Sharpe, 2001), 116.

53 Harmsen, *Nanjing*, 150.

Chapter 7: A Very Dangerous Job

1 The dinner party is described in Niels Jensen to F. L. Smidth in Copenhagen, December 10, 1937, 10. Japan-Kina 1937–38, FLSmidth archives, Valby. Scheel's address is provided in "Consul General of Denmark Host," *The North China Herald and Supreme Court & Consular Gazette*, March 3, 1938, 330. The long history of F. L. Smidth's activities in China, including the events surrounding Jiangnan Cement, is given in detail in Morten Pedersen, *When China Awakens… Dansk multinational virksomhed i Asien før Anden Verdenskrig [When China Awakens… Danish Multinational Business in Asia before World War Two]* (Odense: Syddansk Universitetsforlag, 2018).

2 Okazaki later went on to have a long career in the Japanese foreign ministry, both before and after 1945. He was in the group of civilian officials, in top hat and tails, who attended the humiliating Japanese surrender on board the battleship *Missouri* in Tokyo Bay in September 1945.

3 Okazaki was present in Nanjing as early as on December 16, see Wickert (ed.), *Rabe*, 121.

4 Niels Jensen to F. L. Smidth in Copenhagen, December 10, 1937, 10. Japan-Kina 1937–38, FLSmidth archives, Valby.

5 *Kraks Blå Bog*, 1957; "Emperor Honors Foreign Diplomats," *The Japan Times and Mail*, November 12, 1928, 1.

6 Scheel to Okamoto, December 2, 1937, Japan-Kina 1937–38, FLSmidth archives, Valby. The original document uses the spelling "Kiang Nan" for Jiangnan; however, the latter spelling is used throughout the text to avoid any confusion.

7 Zhang Shuoren, "Kangri Zhanzheng yu Zhongguo minzu ziben de mingyun" ["The War against Japan and the Fate of Chinese Democratic Capitalism"], *Comparative Law and Culture: The Bulletin of the Surugadai University Institute of Comparative Law*, vol. 16 (2008): 101. "Capital of Jiangnan Cement Works to Be Increased," *The China Weekly Review*, May 1, 1937, 332.

8   "Power Company to Expand," *The China Press*, September 21, 1935, 7.
9   The full name of the train station was Qixiashan Train Station, or "Qixia Mountain Train Station." In this text, Qixiashan had been abbreviated as Qixia throughout to avoid confusion.
10 Description of the factory in letter from F. L. Smidth in Shanghai to the Danish consulate general in the same city, December 2, 1937, Japan-Kina 1937–38, FLSmidth archives, Valby.
11 Zhang, "Kangri," 101.
12 Erik Nyholm to Stig Nielsen, June 7, 1935. T. Stig Nielsen, Oriental 1935, FLSmidth archives, Valby.
13 Ibid.
14 Ibid.
15 Niels Jensen to Stig Nielsen, April 6, 1935, 11–12. Oriental 1935, FLSmidth archives, Valby.
16 Niels Jensen to F. L. Smidth in Copenhagen, December 10, 1937, 2. Japan-Kina 1937–38, FLSmidth archives, Valby.
17 Erik Nyholm to Stig Nielsen, June 7, 1935. Oriental 1935, FLSmidth archives, Valby.
18 Chr. Søndergaard, "Bombardement af op til 75 Kampflyvere om Dagen" ["Air Raids by up to 75 Combat Planes a Day"], Østsjællands Folkeblad, January 8, 1938, 1–2; Niels Jensen to F. L. Smidth in Copenhagen, November 23, 1937, 4. Japan-Kina 1937–38, FLSmidth archives, Valby.
19 Chr. Søndergaard, "Bombardement," Østsjællands Folkeblad, January 8, 1938, 1–2.
20 Niels Jensen to F. L. Smidth in Copenhagen, November 23, 1937, 2–3. Japan-Kina 1937–38, FLSmidth archives, Valby.
21 Ibid., 4.
22 Ibid., 6.
23 Niels Jensen to Badstue, October 31, 1937. Japan-Kina 1937–38, FLSmidth archives, Valby.
24 Badstue to Niels Jensen, October 31, 1937. Japan-Kina 1937–38, FLSmidth archives, Valby.
25 25 Niels Jensen to F. L. Smidth in Copenhagen, November 23, 1937, 13–14. Japan-Kina 1937–38, FLSmidth archives, Valby.
26 Telegram from Badstue to F. L. Smidth & Co. Shanghai, November 15, 1937. Japan-Kina 1937–38, FLSmidth archives, Valby.
27 Niels Jensen to F. L. Smidth in Copenhagen, November 23, 1937, 18. Japan-Kina 1937–38, FLSmidth archives, Valby.
28 Telegram from F. L. Smidth & Co. Shanghai to Badstue, November 17, 1937. Japan-Kina 1937–38, FLSmidth archives, Valby.
29 Telegram from Badstue to F. L. Smidth & Co. Shanghai, November 18, 1937. Japan-Kina 1937–38, FLSmidth archives, Valby.
30 Niels Jensen to F. L. Smidth in Copenhagen, November 23, 1937, 19. Japan-Kina 1937–38, FLSmidth archives, Valby.
31 Niels Jensen to F. L. Smidth in Copenhagen, December 10, 1937, 3. Japan-Kina 1937–38, FLSmidth archives, Valby.
32 Ibid., 2–3.
33 Ibid., 4–5.
34 Ibid., 6.
35 Ibid.
36 Niels Jensen, Manila, to F. L. Smidth in Copenhagen, March 18, 1938. Japan-Kina 1937–38, FLSmidth archives, Valby.
37 Niels Jensen to F. L. Smidth in Copenhagen, December 10, 1937, 7. Japan-Kina 1937–38, FLSmidth archives, Valby.

38 Ibid, 10.

39 Niels Jensen to F. L. Smidth in Copenhagen, March 28, 1938, 8–9. Japan-Kina 1937–38, FLSmidth archives, Valby.

40 On the history, including Günther's father, ses Pedersen, *Awakens*, pp. 175ff.

41 Niels Jensen to F. L. Smidth in Copenhagen, December 10, 1937, 8–9. Japan-Kina 1937–38, FLSmidth archives, Valby.

42 Contract, Japan-Kina 1937–38, FLSmidth archives, Valby.

43 The estimate is based on the National Archives' historical currency converter at https://www.nationalarchives.gov.uk/currency-converter/

44 Contract, December 1, 1937, Japan-Kina 1937–38, FLSmidth archives, Valby.

45 "F. L. Smidth Fabriker i Krigszonen" ["F. L. Smidth Factories in the War Zone"], Aalborg Stiftstidende, December 29, 1937, 1.

Chapter 8: Journey to the Heart of Darkness

1 Scheel to Okamoto, December 2, 1937, Japan-Kina 1937–38, FLSmidth archives, Valby.

2 Niels Jensen to F. L. Smidth in Copenhagen, December 10, 1937, 11. Japan-Kina 1937–38, FLSmidth archives, Valby.

3 Ibid, 10; Chen Keqian and Chen Kecheng, *Fengyu rupan yi Jiangnan: Chen Fanyou yu Jiangnan Shuinichang [Recollections of Jiangnan in a Turbulent Time: Chen Fanyou and Jiangnan Cement]* (Suzhou: Soochow University Press, 2016), 29.

4 The route is described in detail by Niels Jensen in a letter about a trip from Shanghai to Nanjing planned by Wang Tao in November. Niels Jensen to F. L. Smidth in Copenhagen. November 23, 1937, 17. Japan-Kina 1937–38, FLSmidth archives, Valby.

5 Not to be confused with the eponymous city near Beijing where Japanese civilians were massacred earlier the same year.

6 Schenke, *Reise*, 32.

7 Chen and Chen, *Fengyu*, 31.

8 Ibid.

9 Chen and Chen, *Fengyu*, 35.

10 Telegram sent December 6, 1937 from Nanjing, received on December 9 by F. L. Smidth in Shanghai, Japan-Kina 1937–38, FLSmidth archives, Valby.

11 *NDS*, vol. 58, 123.

12 "Beishan Yu riji" ["Kiratayama Atou's Diary"], *NDS*, vol. 8, 508.

13 Before and during World War II, Chinese army groups were generally smaller and had fewer soldiers than army groups in countries such as the United States and Great Britain.

14 The account of 2nd Army Group's participation in the battle of Nanjing is based on "Dier Juntuan Nanjing zhanyi zhandou xiangbao" ["Detailed Report on 2nd Army Group's Participation in the Battles of Nanjing"], Zhang Jianjun (ed.), *Nanjing Baoweizhan dangan [Documents on the Battle of Nanjing]* (Nanjing: Nanjing chubanshe, 2018), vol. 8, 334–370; Guo Jun, "Dier Juntuan chiyuan Nanjing shuyao" ["Outlines of 2 Army Group's Forced March to Relieve Nanjing"], *NDS*, vol. 2, 366–369.

15 Bernhard Sindberg to Niels Jensen, January 20, 1938. Japan-Kina 1937–38. FLSmidth archives, Valby.

16 Chen and Chen, *Fengyu*, 31.

17 F. L. Smidth Shanghai to Great Northern Shanghai, December 3, 1937, Japan-Kina 1937–38, FLSmidth archives, Valby.

18 Chen and Chen, *Fengyu*, 31.
19 "Aarhusianer i Østen: Det største Dannebrog i Kina vajer ved Nanking" ["Aarhus Native in the East: The Biggest Danish Flag in China Flies at Nanjing"], *Aarhus Stiftstidende*, 6. marts 1938, 1, 8.
20 Nyholm to Oxholm, October 14, 1938. Danish National Archives, no. 02-2035, 65.K.56: "Kompagnie Madsen A/S."
21 F. L. Smidth Shanghai to German consulate Shanghai, December 9, 1937, Japan-Kina 1937–38, FLSmidth archives, Valby.
22 Schenke, *Reise*, 60.
23 Chr. Søndergaard, "Bombardement af op til 75 Kampflyvere om Dagen" ["Air Raids by up to 75 Planes a Day"], *Østsjællands Folkeblad*, January 8, 1938, 1–2.
24 "Brev fra Dansker i Nanking" ["Letter from Dane in Nanjing"], *Frederiksborg Amts Avis*, December 16, 1937, 3.
25 Wickert (ed.), *Rabe*, 73, 87.
26 "Brev fra Dansker i Nanking" ["Letter From Dane in Nanjing"], *Frederiksborg Amts Avis*, December 16, 1937, 3.
27 Ibid.
28 Report on the fall of Nanjing prepared Lovat-Fraser, January 2, 1938, reproduced in Lu Suping (ed.), *A Dark Page in History* (University Press of America, Lanham MD: 2012), 6.
29 Wickert (ed.), *Rabe*, 54.
30 "Brev fra Dansker i Nanking," *Frederiksborg Amts Avis*, December 16, 1937, 3.

Chapter 9: The Fall of Nanjing

1   Guo, "Dier Juntuan," 367.
2   Ibid, 367–368.
3   Chen and Chen, *Fengyu*, 33.
4   Ibid.
5   F. Tillman Durdin, "300 Chinese Slain on a Peak Ringed by Fires Set by Foe," *The New York Times*, December 9, 1937, 1.
6   Lu (ed.), *Vautrin*, 75.
7   Schenke, *Reise*, 65.
8   "Brev fra Østen" ["Letter from the East"], *Østsjællands Folkeblad*, January 8, 1938, 2.
9   "Text of Reports by Naval Court and Commander of Panay on Attack," *The New York Times*, December 25, 1937, 4.
10 "Nankings sidste Dansker har mistet alt" ["The Last Dane in Nanjing Has Lost Everything"], *Nationaltidende*, January 8, 1938, 5.
11 Paul M. Edwards, *Between the Lines of World War II: Twenty-One Remarkable People and Events* (Jefferson NC: McFarland, 2010), 77.
12 Harmsen, *Nanjing*, 208–220.
13 Yang Tianshi, "Jiang Jieshi yu 1937 nian de Songhu, Nanjing zhi zhan" ["Chiang Kai-shek and the Battle of Shanghai and Nanjing in 1937"], *Zhongguo Shehuikexueyuan xu eshuweiyuanhui jikan*, Beijing: Shehuikexue wenxian chubanshe, 2005.
14 Harmsen, *Nanjing*, 221–222.
15 Chr. Søndergaard, "Bombardement af op til 75 Kampflyvere om Dagen," ["Air Raids by up to 75 Combat Planes a Day"], *Østsjællands Folkeblad*, January 8, 1938, 1–2.
16 Lu (ed.), *Vautrin*, 75.

17 Li Tsung-jen [Li Zongren] et al. *The Memoirs of Li Tsung-jen* (Boulder CO: Westview Press, 1979), 328.

18 Report by Lovat-Fraser, reproduced by Lu, *Dark Page*, 10.

19 George Ashmore Fitch's diary in Zhang (ed.), *Eyewitnesses*, 87.

20 Report by Lovat-Fraser, reproduced by Lu, *Dark Page*, 9.

21 George Ashmore Fitch's diary in Zhang (ed.), *Eyewitnesses*, 87.

22 Report by Lovat-Fraser, reproduced by Lu, *Dark Page*, 9.

23 Danish National Archives. Ministry of Foreign Affairs. Dispatches 1848–1972, Shanghai 1936–1945 etc., no. 0002, 173 D 21. Dispatch from Oxholm to Munch, December 23, 1937.

24 George Ashmore Fitchs dagbog i Zhang (red.), *Eyewitnesses*, 87.

Chapter 10: The Massacre Begins

1 B. A. Sindberg, "List of Cases," February 3, 1938, Folder 862, Box 102, Record Group 10, Special Collection, Yale Divinity School Library.

2 "Nanjing ge junshi tuwei gaishu" ["A Brief Account of Attempts by Certain Division to Escape the Siege of Nanjing"], *NDS*, vol. 2, 238.

3 Sindberg, "List of Cases."

4 Chen and Chen, *Fengyu*.

5 *NDS*, vol. 30, 269.

6 *NDS*, vol. 26, 739–740.

7 Zhang Kaiyuan (ed.), *Eyewitnesses*, 61.

8 R. O. Wilson, "Dear Folks," letter from Robert O. Wilson to several addressees, September 24 to December 14, 1937, Folder 3875, Box 229, Record Group 11, Special Collection, Yale Divinity School Library, 36.

9 *International Military Tribunal of the Far East, Transcript of Proceedings*, 4467.

10 George Ashmore Fitchs dagbog i Zhang (ed.), *Eyewitnesses*, 87.

11 Lu (ed.), *Vautrin*, 78.

12 Wickert (ed.), *Rabe*, 108.

13 Ibid.

14 "Zhongdao Jinchaowu riji" ["Nakajima Kesago's Diary"], *NDS*, vol. 8, 280.

15 "Zuozuomu Daoyi riji" ["Sasaki Toichi's Diary"], *NDS*, vol. 8, 316.

16 Lewis Smythe, letter dated December 20, 1937, in Zhang (ed.), *Eyewitnesses*, 257.

17 Lu (ed.), *Vautrin*, 78.

18 Lu Suping, *Japanese Atrocities in Nanjing: The Nanjing Massacre and Post-Massacre Social Conditions Recorded in German Diplomatic Documents* (Lincoln NE: University of Nebraska Lincoln, 2022), 113.

19 Wickert (ed.), *Rabe*, 198–199.

20 Ibid, 108.

21 *Documents of the Nanking Safety Zone*, 11.

22 R. O. Wilson, "Dear Folks," 37.

23 Confidential reports from Trautmann to the foreign ministry in Berlin, published in Zhang Xianwen and Zhang Jianjun, *Human Memory: Solid Evidence of the Nanjing Massacre*, vol. 2 (Beijing: Renmin chubanshe, 2017), 31. Trautmann had himself left Nanjing and based his account on testimony he received from German citizens who remained in the city.

24 *NDS*, vol. 26, 525–526.

25 R. O. Wilson, "Dear Folks," 37.

26 George Ashmore Fitch's diary in Zhang (ed.), *Eyewitnesses*, 87.
27 *International Military Tribunal of the Far East, Transcript of Proceedings*, 3900–3901.
28 "Zhongdao Jinchaowu riji" ["Nakajima Kesago's diary"], *NDS*, vol. 8, 280.
29 Fujiwara Akira, "The Nanking Atrocity: An Interpretive Overview." Wakabayashi, Bob Takashi (ed.), *The Nanking Atrocity, 1937–38: Complicating the Picture* (New York NY: Berghahn Books, 2017), 45–46.
30 *International Military Tribunal of the Far East, Transcript of Proceedings*, 3897.

Chapter 11: "Blood, Blood, and More Blood"

1   Sindberg, "List of Cases."
2   Ibid.
3   Ibid.
4   Ibid.
5   Ibid.
6   "Aarhusianer i Østen: Det største Dannebrog i Kina vajer ved Nanking," *Aarhus Stiftstidende*, March 6, 1938, 1, 8.
7   Michael A. Krysko, *American Radio in China: International Encounters with Technology and Communications, 1919–41* (Basingstoke: Palgrave Macmillan 2011), 158.
8   R.O. Wilson, "Dear Folks," 36.
9   Letter from John Magee in Zhang Kaiyuan (ed.), *Eyewitnesses to Massacre* (Armonk NY: M. E. Sharpe, 2001), 172.
10 Letter from Ernest H. Forster to his wife, December 19, 1937, Folder 9, Box 263, Record Group 8, Special Collection, Yale Divinity School Library.
11 International Military Tribunal of the Far East, *Transcript of Proceedings*, 4484.
12 Fujiwara, "Nanking Atrocity," 45.
13 Ibid.
14 Report from Trautmann to the foreign ministry in Berlin, in Zhang and Zhang, *Human Memory*, 33.
15 Letter from Ernest H. Forster to his wife, December 19, 1937, Folder 9, Box 263, Record Group 8, Special Collection, Yale Divinity School Library.
16 Letter from Miner Searle Bates to the Japanese embassy, Folder 863, Box 102, Record Group 10, Special Collection, Yale Divinity School Library.
17 International Military Tribunal of the Far East, *Transcript of Proceedings*, 2634.
18 Ibid, 40139.
19 Letter from John G. Magee to his wife, Folder 2, Box 263, Record Group 8, Special Collection, Yale Divinity School Library, 7.
20 International Military Tribunal of the Far East, *Transcript of Proceedings*, 40139.
21 Wickert (ed.), *Rabe*, 175.
22 Fujiwara, "Nanking Atrocity," 48.
23 Letter from Ernest H. Forster to his wife, Folder 9, Box 263, Record Group 8, Special Collection, Yale Divinity School Library, 1.
24 Ibid.
25 Ibid.
26 George Ashmore Fitch, letter to friends, January 6, 1938, Folder 2, Box 263, Record Group 8, Special Collection, Yale Divinity School Library, 2–3.
27 "Shangcun Lidao zhenzhong riji" ["Uemura Toshimichi's War Diary"], *NDS*, vol. 8, 244.

28 "Zuozuomu Daoyi riji" ["Sasaki Toichi's Diary"], *NDS*, vol. 8, 319–320.
29 "Shantian Zhaner riji" ["Yamada Senji's Diary"], *NDS*, vol. 9, 5.
30 *NDS*, vol. 8, 153.
31 Miner Searle Bates, "Nanking Outrages," Folder 719, Box 90, Record Group 10, Special Collection, Yale Divinity School Library, 3.
32 Fujiwara, "Nanking Atrocity," 47.
33 Bates, "Nanking Outrages," 3.
34 "Zuozuomu Daoyi riji" ["Sasaki Toichi's Diary"], *NDS*, vol. 8, 316.

Chapter 12: Christmas in Hell

1   Wickert (ed.), *Rabe*, 129.
2   Ibid, 129–130.
3   Ibid, 138.
4   Lu (ed.), *Vautrin*, 93.
5   Zhang (ed.), *Eyewitnesses*, 179.
6   Wickert (ed.), *Rabe*, 138–139.
7   Lu (ed.), *Vautrin*, 95.
8   Rabe's diary, December 23, 1937. This passage is not included in the published, abbreviated version of his diary edited by Wickert, but is part of a more complete excerpt carried in Zhang og Zhang, *Human Memory*, 53.
9   A.T. Steele, "Japanese Troops Kill Thousands; 'Four Days of Hell' in Captured City Told by Eyewitness; Bodies Piled Five Feet High in Streets," *The Chicago Daily News*, December 15, 1937, 1.
10 A.T. Steele, "War's Death Drama Pictured by Reporter," *The Chicago Daily News*, December 17, 1937, 1.
11 Hallett Abend, "Japanese Colonel is not Disciplined," *The New York Times*, December 24, 1937, 7.
12 Report from Beck-Friis to Sandler, December 24, 1937. Swedish National Archives. Ministry of Foreign Affairs. HP 37 A VI.
13 Ibid.
14 Zhou Bin, "Liao Ouyang Heng nushi koushu: Wo suo zhidao de Liao Yaoxiang" ["Liao Ouyang Heng's Testimony: Liao Yaoxiang As I Knew Him"], webpage of Chinese University of Hong Kong; Liu Yishi, "Liao Yaoxiang Nanjing baoen shimo," ["Liao Yaoxiang Paid His Debt of Gratitude in Nanjing"], *Jiangsu Difangzhi*, 2007, no. 6, 58–59.
15 Ibid.
16 Wickert (ed.), *Rabe*, 138.
17 *NDS*, vol. 26, 702.
18 "Aarhusianer i Østen: Det største Dannebrog i Kina vajer ved Nanking" ["Aarhus Resident in the Far East: The Biggest Danish Flag Flies at Nanjing"], *Aarhus Stiftstidende*, March 6, 1938, 1, 8.
19 Wickert (ed.), *Rabe*, 138.
20 Transcript of report delivered by anonymous German eyewitness, later identified as Christian Kröger. Passed on by Sweden's envoy to Tokyo Widar Bagge to section chief Staffan Söderblom, May 9, 1938. Swedish National Archives. Ministry of Foreign Affairs. HP 37 A VI. The report is also reproduced, albeit in an abbreviated as partly rewritten version, in Wickert (ed.), *Rabe*, 201–202.
21 Ibid.

Chapter 13: The Man with the Flag

1 *NDS*, vol. 26, 702–703.
2 Ibid, 740.
3 Ibid.
4 Luo Zuowei, "Nanjing lunxian muduji" ["Eyewitness Testimony of Nanjing's Fall"], *NDS*, vol. 3, 493.
5 Lu (ed.), *Vautrin*, 102.
6 Zhang (ed.), *Eyewitnesses*, 308.
7 Lu (ed.), *Vautrin*, 97.
8 Wickert (ed.), *Rabe*, 150–151. An almost identical account of the same incident is given by Bates, in Zhang (ed.), *Eyewitnesses*, 13.
9 Zhang (ed.), *Eyewitnesses*, 97.
10 Wickert (ed.), *Rabe*, 199.
11 "Subject: Claims Settlement for Damages and Losses Suffered on American Embassy Premises," Box 0815, RG 59, NAII. Reproduced in Lu Suping (ed.), *A Mission under Duress: The Nanjing Massacre and Post-Massacre Social Conditions Documented by American Diplomats*, 254.
12 Wickert (ed.), *Rabe*, 199.
13 Lu (ed.), *Vautrin*, 103.
14 Lu Suping (ed.), *The Nanjing Massacre Witnessed by American and British Nationals* (Hong Kong: Hong Kong University Press, 2004), 233.
15 Ibid, 234.
16 "Zhongdao Jinchaowu riji" ["Nakajima Kesago's Diary"], *NDS*, vol. 8, 301.
17 "Weekly Intelligence Summary for week ending 30 January, 1938." Prepared on board the American gunboat *Oahu* in the Yangtze off Nanjing. Folder A8-2/FS#3, Box 195, RG 38, National Archives. Reproduced in Lu (ed.), *Dark Page*, 156. Although it might be natural to assume that this passage is about Günther, it is probably not about him since he seldom or never left Jiangnan Cement during the winter of 1937 and 1938, and that according to Sindberg it was not until February 10, 1938, that the German engineer traveled from the factory to Nanjing for the first time. See Sindberg to Niels Jensen, February 11, 1938. Japan-Kina 1937–38, FLSmidths archives, Valby. Lu also identifies the "German" mentioned in the document as Sindberg, see *Dark Page*, 200 n44.
18 "Aarhusianer i Østen: Det største Dannebrog i Kina vajer ved Nanking," *Aarhus Stiftstidende*, March 6, 1938, 1 and 8.
19 Ibid.
20 Transcript of report by anonymous German witness, dated January 13, 1938. Passed on by Johann Beck-Friis to State Councilor K. G. Westman, February 7, 1938. Swedish National Archives. Ministry of Foreign Affairs. HP 37 A VI. The report is also reproduced in an abbreviated and partly rewritten version in Wickert (ed.), *Rabe*, 186–188.
21 Wickert (ed.), *Rabe*, 222.
22 John G. Magee, letter to his wife, January 4, 1938, in Zhang, *Eyewitnesses*, 185.
23 International Military Tribunal of the Far East, *Transcript of Proceedings*, 3942–3943. It is unclear if the dead Chinese soldier in Magee's statement is the one Sindberg saw surrender. It would however be logical if it was the same person. This was also the interpretation preferred by the tribunal in its summary of the witness testimony, see International Military Tribunal of the Far East, *Narrative Summary of the Record*, 543.
24 "Danske i Nanking" ["Danes in Nanjing"], *Politiken*, January 9, 1938, 2.
25 "Bernh. Sindberg i god Behold" ["Bernh. Sindbergs Is Safe"], *Aarhus Stiftstidende*, January 10, 1938, 2.

26 Bernhard Sindberg to Niels Jensen, January 11, 1938. Japan-Kina 1937–38. FLSmidth archives, Valby.

Chapter 14: Friendships

1 Sindberg, "List of Cases."
2 Bernhard Sindberg to Niels Jensen, January 20, 1938. Japan-Kina 1937–38. FLSmidth archives, Valby.
3 Ibid.
4 Sindberg, "List of Cases."
5 Bernhard Sindberg to Niels Jensen, January 20, 1938. Japan-Kina 1937–38. FLSmidth archives, Valby.
6 Ibid.
7 Ibid.
8 Ibid.
9 "Subject: Sale of Narcotics in Nanking," Nanjing, March 18, 1938. Mikofilm, set LM63, Roll 88, RG 59, NAII. Reproduced in Lu (ed.), *Mission under Duress*, 251.
10 Zhang (ed.), *Eyewitnesses*, 308.
11 Wickert (ed), *Rabe*, 188.
12 Lu (ed.), *Vautrin*, 126.
13 Wickert (ed.), *Rabe*, 188.
14 Ibid, 188–189.
15 Bernhard Sindberg to Niels Jensen, January 20, 1938. Japan-Kina 1937–38. FLSmidth archives, Valby.
16 Ibid.
17 Cao Chengying's testimony in *NDS*, vol. 26, 720.
18 Rapport from Beck-Friis to State Councilor K. G. Westman, January 31, 1938. Swedish National Archives. Ministry of Foreign Affairs. HP 37 A VII.
19 "Aarhusianer i Østen: Det største Dannebrog i Kina vajer ved Nanking," *Aarhus Stiftstidende*, March 6, 1938, 1, 8; Bernhard Sindberg to Niels Jensen, February 4, 1938. Japan-Kina 1937–38. FLSmidth archives, Valby.
20 "Memorandum by Tsitsashan Temple," *Documents of the Nanking Safety Zone*, 135.
21 Ibid, 136–137.
22 Ibid, 135–136.
23 Ibid, 136.
24 Ibid.
25 "Aarhusianer i Østen: Det største Dannebrog i Kina vajer ved Nanking," *Aarhus Stiftstidende*, March 6, 1938, 1, 8; Bernhard Sindberg to Niels Jensen, February 4, 1938. Japan-Kina 1937–38. FLSmidth archives, Valby.

Chapter 15: The New Order

1 Sindberg to Niels Jensen, February 4, 1938. Japan-Kina 1937–38, FLSmidth archives, Valby.
2 Ibid.
3 Ibid.
4 M. Stang-Lund to Niels Jensen, February 8, 1938. Japan-Kina 1937–38, FLSmidth archives, Valby.

5   Thomas K. Yu had left Jiangnan Cement just before the Japanese arrived, and had reached Shanghai via Wuhan and Hong Kong, see Chen og Chen, *Fengyu*, 21.

6   M. Stang-Lund to Niels Jensen, February 8, 1938. Japan-Kina 1937–38, FLSmidth archives, Valby. See also Pedersen, *When China Awakens*, 395–396.

7   M. Stang-Lund to Niels Jensen, February 8, 1938. Japan-Kina 1937–38, FLSmidth archives, Valby.

8   Ibid.

9   M. Stang-Lund to Sindberg, February 7, 1938. Bernhard Arp Sindberg Papers and Photography Collection, Harry Ransom Center, The University of Texas at Austin. The letter is among Sindberg's paper bequeathed after his death, and therefore it must be the revised version of February 8, even though it is dated February 7.

10 Ibid.

11 Report from Georg Rosen, February 7, 1938. Ministry of Foreign Affairs, Berlin. Political Archive. RAV Peking II, vol. 104841.

12 Sindberg to Niels Jensen, February 11, 1938. Japan-Kina 1937–38, FLSmidth archives, Valby. Nikolai Podshivalov, born 1912, appears in several different connections, for instance Zhang (ed.), *Eyewitnesses*, 159. Cola is an attempt to provide an English rendering of Kolya, the normal Russian diminutive of the name Nikolai.

13 Yan Liufeng, "Zhu Qixia chang Yan Liufeng baogao" ["Yan Liufeng's Report About His Stay at the Qixia Plant"], *NDS*, vol. 30, 272.

14 Copies of the photos are now kept at the Bernhard Arp Sindberg Papers and Photography Collection, Harry Ransom Center, The University of Texas at Austin.

15 Sindberg to Niels Jensen, February 11, 1938. Japan-Kina 1937–38, FLSmidth archives, Valby; "Netherlands Legation in Nanking Intact," *The North-China Herald and Supreme Court & Consular Gazette*, February 23, 1938, 285.

16 Sindberg to Niels Jensen, February 9, 1938. Japan-Kina 1937–38, FLSmidth archives, Valby.

17 M. Stang-Lund to Niels Jensen, March 25, 1938. Japan-Kina 1937–38, FLSmidth archives, Valby.

18 M. Stang-Lund to Sindberg, February 19, 1938. Bernhard Arp Sindberg Papers and Photography Collection, Harry Ransom Center, The University of Texas at Austin.

19 Niels Jensen to Sindberg, February 13, 1938. Bernhard Arp Sindberg Papers and Photography Collection, Harry Ransom Center, The University of Texas at Austin.

20 M. Stang-Lund to Niels Jensen, March 22, 1938. Japan-Kina 1937–38, FLSmidth archives, Valby.

Chapter 16: Troublemaker

1   Letter from Xu Shennong, March 18, 1938, *DBS*, vol. 30, 279.

2   M. Stang-Lund to Niels Jensen, Manila, March 22, 1938. Japan-Kina 1937–38, FLSmidth archives, Valby.

3   M. Stang-Lund to Niels Jensen, Manila, April 12, 1938. Japan-Kina 1937–38, FLSmidth archives, Valby.

4   Letter from Xu Shennong, March 18, 1938, *DBS*, vol. 30, 279.

5   Ibid.

6   M. Stang-Lund to Niels Jensen, Manila, March 25, 1938. Japan-Kina 1937–38, FLSmidth archives, Valby.

7   Ibid.

8 Ibid.
9 Zhang Yicai's account, *NDS*, vol. 26, 758.
10 M. Stang-Lund to Niels Jensen, Manila, April 20, 1938. Japan-Kina 1937–38, FLSmidth archives, Valby.
11 James H. McCallum gives a number of 6,000 in a letter dated February 3, 1938. See Lu (ed.), *They Were in Nanjing*, 124–125. According to Sindberg himself, the number had reached 10,000 a little later that month, see Sindberg to Niels Jensen, February 11, 1938, Japan-Kina 1937–38, FLSmidth archives, Valby. The same number is provided by John Magee after the visit to the camp in February, see Zhang (ed.), *Eyewitnesses*, 195–198. Magee repeated the number during testimony at the war crime tribunal in Tokyo after World War II, see International Military Tribunal of the Far East, *Narrative Summary of the Record*, 538.
12 Zhou Bin, "Liao Ouyang Heng nushi koushu: Wo suo zhidao de Liao Yaoxiang" ["Liao Ouyang Heng's Testimony: Liao Yaoxiang As I Knew Him"], webpage of Chinese University of Hong Kong; Liu Yishi, "Liao Yaoxiang Nanjing baoen shimo," ["Liao Yaoxiang Paid His Debt of Gratitude in Nanjing"], *Jiangsu Difangzhi*, 2007, no. 6, 58–59.
13 Zhang (ed.), *Eyewitnesses*, 195–198.
14 Matsui's diary February 21 and 22, 1938, *NDS*, vol. 8, 186–187.
15 "Matsui Orders Tightening of Army Discipline," *The China Press*, February 8, 1938.
16 Tillman Durdin, "Japanese Atrocities Marked Fall of Nanking after Chinese Command Fled," *The New York Times*, January 9, 1938, 38.
17 Chiang Kai-shek, *The Collected Wartime Messages of Generalissimo Chiang Kai-shek* (New York NY: The John Day Company, 1946), vol 2, 665–668.
18 Bob Tadashi Wakabayashi, "Leftover Problems" in Bob Tadashi Wakabayashi (red.), *The Nanking Atrocity 1937–38: Complicating the Picture* (New York NY: Berghahn Books), 377.
19 Wakabayashi, "Leftover Problems," 384.
20 Danish National Archives. Ministry of Foreign Affairs. Dispatches 1848–1972, Shanghai 1936–1945 etc., no. 0002, 173 D 21. Dispatch from Oxholm to Munch, March 8, 1938.
21 M. Stang-Lund to Niels Jensen, March 7, 1938. Japan-Kina 1937–38, FLSmidth archives, Valby.
22 Ibid.

Chapter 17: Günther's Letter

1 Telegram from F. L. Smidth & Co. Shanghai to Niels Jensen, Manila, March 16, 1938. Japan-Kina 1937–38, FLSmidth archives, Valby. The telegram has been amended slightly for legibility.
2 M. Stang-Lund to Niels Jensen, Manila, March 22, 1938. Japan-Kina 1937–38, FLSmidth archives, Valby.
3 Ibid.
4 Ibid.
5 Telegram from Niels Jensen, Manila to F. L. Smidth & Co. Shanghai, March 17, 1938. Japan-Kina 1937–38, FLSmidth archives, Valby.
6 F. L. Smidth & Co. Shanghai to the Danish consulate in Shanghai, March 17, 1938. Japan-Kina 1937–38, FLSmidth archives, Valby.
7 M. Stang-Lund to Niels Jensen, Manila, March 22, 1938. Japan-Kina 1937–38, FLSmidth archives, Valby.
8 Ibid.
9 Ibid.

10 Ibid.
11 H. W. Yuan to F. L. Smidth & Co. Shanghai, March 22, 1938. Japan-Kina 1937–38, FLSmidth archives, Valby.
12 Ibid.
13 M. Stang-Lund to Niels Jensen, Manila, March 25, 1938. Japan-Kina 1937–38, FLSmidth archives, Valby.
14 Ibid.
15 Niels Jensen to F. L. Smidth & Co. Copenhagen, March 28, 1938. Japan-Kina 1937–38, FLSmidth archives, Valby.
16 M. Stang-Lund to Niels Jensen, Manila, April 20, 1938. Japan-Kina 1937–38, FLSmidth archives, Valby.
17 Letters from Xu Shennong, March 13 and 18, 1938, *NDS*, vol. 30, 277, 279.
18 M. Stang-Lund to Niels Jensen, Manila, April 20, 1938. Japan-Kina 1937–38, FLSmidth archives, Valby.
19 Ibid.
20 F. L. Smidth & Co. Copenhagen to F. L. Smidth & Co. Tokyo, March 26, 1938. Japan-Kina 1937–38, FLSmidth archives, Valby.
21 M. Stang-Lund to Nyholm, April 19, 1938. Japan-Kina 1937–38, FLSmidth archives, Valby.
22 M. Stang-Lund to Nyholm, April 20, 1938. Japan-Kina 1937–38, FLSmidth archives, Valby.
23 M. Stang-Lund to Nyholm, March 22, 1938. Japan-Kina 1937–38, FLSmidth archives, Valby.
24 M. Stang-Lund to Nyholm, April 20, 1938. Japan-Kina 1937–38, FLSmidth archives, Valby.
25 "Canada Brings Sir Archibald In Tomorrow," *The China Press*, April 30, 1938, 7.
26 "Aarhusianer Jorden rundt 2½ Gang paa 20 Mdr." ["Aarhus Resident Travels Around the World 2.5 Times in 20 Months"], *Demokraten (Aarhus)*, July 4, 1938, 3.
27 F. L. Smidth & Co. Shanghai to the Danish consulate in Shanghai, April 26, 1938. Japan-Kina 1937–38, FLSmidth archives, Valby. "Rawalpindi To Tie Up Today From Nippon," *The China Press*, April 24, 1938, 9.
28 "Aarhusianer Jorden rundt 2½ Gang paa 20 Mdr.," *Demokraten (Aarhus)*, July 4, 1938, 3.

Chapter 18: After Nanjing

1 "Rawalpindi To Tie Up Today From Nippon," *The China Press*, April 24, 1938, 9.
2 Johannes Sindberg, "Indtryk fra en 10-Dages Rejse gennem Central-Europa" ["Impressions from a Ten-Day Journey Through Central Europe"], *Uge-Avisen for Odder og Omegn*, July 29, 1938, 1 og 4, and August 12, 1938, 1 og 4.
3 Sindberg, "Indtryk," *Uge-Avisen*, September 16, 1938, 4.
4 Ibid.
5 Sindberg, "Indtryk," *Uge-Avisen*, September 23, 1938, 4.
6 Sindberg, "Indtryk," *Uge-Avisen*, September 23, 1938, 4, and September 30, 1938, 4.
7 Sindberg, "Indtryk," *Uge-Avisen*, September 30, 1938, 4.
8 NARA, Passenger and Crew Lists of Vessels Arriving at New York, New York, 1897–1957. Microfilm Publication T715, Microfilm Roll 6181; Line: 2; Page Number: 156. NAI: 300346.
9 "Aarhusianer Jorden rundt 2½ Gang paa 20 Mdr.," *Demokraten (Aarhus)*, July 4, 1938, 3.
10 Letter from M. Stang-Lund, March 28, 1938. Bernhard Arp Sindberg Papers and Photography Collection, Harry Ransom Center, The University of Texas at Austin.
11 Niels Jensen to F. L. Smidth & Co. Copenhagen, June 16, 1938. Japan-Kina 1937–38, FLSmidth archives, Valby.

12 Niels Jensen, Manila, to F. L. Smidth & Co. Copenhagen, May 3, 1938. Japan-Kina 1937–38, FLSmidth archives, Valby.

13 Einar Nielsen to F. L. Smidth & Co. Shanghai. No date but received on June 27, 1938. Japan-Kina 1937–38, FLSmidth archives, Valby. The letter has been amended slightly for legibility.

14 Einar Nielsen to F. L. Smidth & Co. Shanghai. June 23, 1938. Japan-Kina 1937–38, FLSmidth archives, Valby.

15 Einar Nielsen to F. L. Smidth & Co. Shanghai. July 15, 1938. Japan-Kina 1937–38, FLSmidth archives, Valby.

16 Einar Nielsen to F. L. Smidth & Co. Shanghai, July 28, 1938. Japan-Kina 1937–38, FLSmidth archives, Valby. The letter has been amended slightly for legibility.

17 M. Stang-Lund to Einar Nielsen, August 2, 1938. Japan-Kina 1937–38, FLSmidth archives, Valby.

18 M. Stang-Lund to Einar Nielsen, August 17, 1938. Japan-Kina 1937–38, FLSmidth archives, Valby.

19 Niels Jensen to F. L. Smidth & Co. Copenhagen, June 29, 1938. Japan-Kina 1937–38, FLSmidth archives, Valby.

20 *Demokraten* (Aarhus), February 18, 1941, 4.

21 *Demokraten* (Aarhus), February 20, 1941, 5.

22 *Demokraten* (Aarhus), August 13, 1938, 6.

23 *Demokraten* (Aarhus), January 25, 1939, 8.

24 Letter from Dampskibsselskabet Gloria, San Francisco, October 18, 1939. Harry Ransom Center, University of Texas at Austin.

25 Draft record, October 16, 1940, The National Archives in St. Louis, Missouri; St. Louis, Missouri; Record Group: Records of the Selective Service System, 147; Box: 1669.

26 Letter from Richmond Shipyard Number One, November 20, 1942. Harry Ransom Center, University of Texas at Austin.

27 "Oath of Allegiance," National Archives at San Francisco; San Bruno, California; NAI: 605504; Record Group 21; Record Group Number: Records of District Courts of the United States, 1685–2009.

28 Letter from Sindberg to Charles Day, Richmond Shipyard Number One, July 7, 1942. Harry Ransom Center, University of Texas at Austin.

29 Sindberg left behind a list of 16 vessels where he served from August 1943 until February 1954. According to this list, he served on board the *Perida* from January 25 to April 6, 1944. Harry Ransom Center, University of Texas at Austin.

30 Sindberg, *Sketch of a Lifetime*.

31 NARA, Passenger and Crew Lists of Vessels Arriving at Seattle, Washington; NAI: 4449160, Record Group Number: 85; Series Number: M1383; Roll Number: 329.

32 "26 Aars Eventyr—og hjem ved et Tilfælde" ["Returning Home by Accident after 26 Years of Adventure"], *Aarhus Stiftstidende*, November 13, 1951, 1.

33 Odder parish, parish list 1946–1955, 22.

34 Letters from Sindberg to V. Franklin Sørensen, August 17, 1951, and Henning Rasmussen, January 19, 1953, Harry Ransom Center, University of Texas at Austin.

35 Sindberg, *Sketch of a Lifetime*.

36 U.S. Social Security Death Index; "Report of Valuables from Morgue and Release of Remains," County of Los Angeles, March 25, 1983, Harry Ransom Center, University of Texas at Austin.

Postscript: Sindberg's 104 Days

1   Thomas Keneally, *Schindler's List* (New York NY: Simon & Schuster, 1993).

2   David Crowe, *Oskar Schindler: The Untold Account of His Life, Wartime Activities, and the True Story Behind the List* (Basic Books, 2007), 624–625.

3   "26 Aars Eventyr—og hjem ved et Tilfælde," *Aarhus Stiftstidende*, November 13, 1951, 1.

Bibliography

Published sources

Literature

65 år i tal. Danmark siden 2. Verdenskrig [65 Years in Numbers: Denmark Since World War Two]. Copenhagen: Danmarks Statistik, 2014.

Aage, Prins. *Legionær. Skæbner i Fremmedlegionen [Legionnaire: Lives in the Foreign Legion]*. Copenhagen: Berlingske Forlag, 1936.

Aage, Prins. *Tre Aars Kampe i Fremmedlegionen [Three Years of War in the Foreign Legion]*. Copenhagen: Gyldendalske Boghandel, 1927.

Bache, Erling. *Hvide under Tropesol [White People under the Tropical Sun]*. Copenhagen: H. Hirschsprungs Forlag, 1939.

Bendix, Hans. *Med Ryggen til Europa [Putting Europe Behind You]*. Copenhagen: Atheneum, 1939.

Brook, Timothy. *Collaboration: Japanese Agents and Local Elites in Wartime China*. Cambridge MA: Harvard University Press, 2005.

Chang, Iris. *The Rape of Nanking: The Forgotten Holocaust of World War II*. New York NY: Basic Books, 2012.

Chen Keqian and Chen Kecheng. *Fengyu rupan yi Jiangnan: Chen Fanyou yu Jiangnan Shuinichang Recollections of Jiangnan in a Turbulent Time: Chen Fanyou and Jiangnan Cement]*. Suzhou: Soochow University Press, 2016.

Chiang Kai-shek. *The Collected Wartime Messages of Generalissimo Chiang Kai-shek*. New York NY: The John Day Company, 1946.

Crowe, David. *Oskar Schindler: The Untold Account of His Life, Wartime Activities, and the True Story Behind the List*. Basic Books, 2007.

Dai Yuanzhi. *1937–1938: Rendao yu baoxing de jianzheng—Jingli Nanjing xingfeng xueyu de Danmairen [1937–1938: Witnessing Humanity and Violence. The Dane Who Experienced the Nanjing Reign of Terror]*. Nanjing: Jiangsu Renmin Chubanshe, 2010.

Davidson-Houston, J. V. *Yellow Creek: The Story of Shanghai*. Philadelphia PA: Dufour Editions, 1964.

Dikötter, Frank. *Crime, Punishment and the Prison in Modern China*. London: C. Hurst & Co., 2002.

Doty, Bennett J. *The Legion of the Damned: The Adventures of Bennett J. Doty in the French Foreign Legion as Told By Himself*. London: Jonathan Cape, 1928.

Edwards, Paul M. *Between the Lines of World War II: Twenty-One Remarkable People and Events*. Jefferson NC: McFarland, 2010.

Eigner, Julius. "The Rise and Fall of Nanjing," *National Geographic*, vol. 73, nr. 2 (February 1938): 189–234.

Farmer, Rhodes. *Shanghai Harvest: Three Years in the China War*. London: Museum Press, 1945.

Fujiwara Akira. "The Nanking Atrocity: An Interpretive Overview." Wakabayashi, Bob Takashi (ed.). *The Nanking Atrocity, 1937–38: Complicating the Picture*, 29–54. New York NY: Berghahn Books, 2017.

Guo Jun. "Dier Juntuan chiyuan Nanjing shuyao" ["Outlines of 2 Army Group's Forced March to Relieve Nanjing"]. *Nanjing datusha shiliaoji [Collection of Historical Sources for the Nanjing Massacre]* (hereafter *NDS*), 366–369. Nanjing: Jiangsu renmin chubanshe, 2005–2010, vol. 2.

Hanson, Haldore. *"Humane Endeavour": The Story of the China War.* New York NY: Farrar & Rinehart, 1939.

Harmsen, Peter. *Shanghai 1937: Stalingrad on the Yangtze.* Havertown, PA: Casemate, 2013.

Harmsen, Peter. *Nanjing 1937: Battle for a Doomed City.* Havertown, PA: Casemate, 2015.

Hinrup, Hans J. "Sindberg. The Good Dane in Nanjing 1937," paper presented at conference organized by the Nordic Association for China Studies, Stockholm, June 11–13, 2007.

Horny, Ove. *"Ved rettidig Omhu": Skibsreder A. P. Møller 1876–1965 ["By Due Diligence": Shipping Magnate A. P. Møller 1876–1965].* Copenhagen: Schultz, 1988.

Johansen, Erik Korr (ed.). *Fra kysthavn til storhavn—Århus havns historie 1915–1995 [From Coastal Harbor to Major Harbor: The History of the Port of Aarhus, 1915–1995].* Aarhus: Århus Byhistoriske Udvalg, 1994.

Jordan, Donald A. *China's Trial by Fire.* Ann Arbor MI: University of Michigan Press, 2001.

Juncker-Jensen, Jørgen. *Facts & Episodes of My Life.* Copenhagen: Self-published, 1983.

Kasahara Tokushi, "Massacres outside Nanking City." Wakabayashi, Bob Takashi (ed.). *The Nanking Atrocity, 1937–38: Complicating the Picture,* 57–69. New York NY: Berghahn Books, 2017.

Keneally, Thomas. *Schindler's List.* New York NY: Simon & Schuster, 1993.

Kiratayama Atou. "Beishan Yu riji" ["Kiratayama Atou's Diary"]. *NDS*, vol. 8: 474–527.

Kjeldsen, Ove. "Jorden rundt i 60 år" ["Around the World in 60 Years"]. In *Årbog 1995*, 82–100. Kronborg: Handels- og Søfartsmuseet, 1995.

Krysko, Michael A. *American Radio in China: International Encounters with Technology and Communications, 1919–41.* Basingstoke: Palgrave Macmillan 2011.

Li Tsung-jen [Li Zongren] et al. *The Memoirs of Li Tsung-jen.* Boulder CO: Westview Press, 1979.

Liu Yishi. "Liao Yaoxiang Nanjing baoen shimo" ["Liao Yaoxiang Paid His Debt of Gratitude in Nanjing"], *Jiangsu Difangzhi*, 2007, nr. 6: 58–59.

Linck, Olaf. *En Dansker i Østen. Laurits Andersens Livs Eventyr [A Dane in the East: The Life and Adventures of Laurits Andersen].* Copenhagen: Gyldendalske Boghandel, 1927.

Lu Suping (ed.). *A Dark Page in History.* Lanham MD: University Press of America, 2012.

Lu Suping, *A Mission under Duress: The Nanjing Massacre and Post-Massacre Social Conditions Documented by American Diplomats.* Lanham MD: University Press of America, 2010.

Lu Suping, *Terror in Minnie Vautrin's Nanjing: Diaries and Correspondence, 1937–38.* Urbana and Chicago IL: University of Illinois Press, 2008.

Lu Suping, *They Were in Nanjing. The Nanjing Massacre Witnessed by American and British Nationals.* Hong Kong: Hong Kong University Press, 2004.

Luo Zuowei, "Nanjing lunxian muduji" ["En øjenvidneberetning om Nanjings fald"] ["Eyewitness Testimony of Nanjing's Fall"]. *NDS*, vol. 3: 488–494.

Musgrove, Charles D., and Ronald G. Knapp og Xing Ruan. *China's Contested Capital: Architecture, Ritual, and Response in Nanjing.* Honolulu HI: University of Hawaii Press, 2013.

Nakajima Kesago. "Zhongdao Jinchaowu riji" ["Nakajima Kesago's Diary"]. *NDS*, vol. 8: 272–305.

"Nanjing ge junshi tuwei gaishu ["En kort beretning om de enkelte divisioners forsøg på at undslippe omringningen af Nanjing"] ["A Brief Account of Attempts by Certain Division to Escape the Siege of Nanjing"]. *NDS*, vol. 2: 238–240.

Pedersen, Morten. *When China Awakens… Dansk multinational virksomhed i Asien før Anden Verdenskrig [When China Awakens… Danish Multinational Enterprise in Asia before World War Two]* Odense: Syddansk Universitetsforlag, 2018.

Porch, Douglas. *The French Foreign Legion*. London: Macmillan, 1991.

Rasmussen, Steen Eiler. *Rejse i Kina [China Travel]*. Copenhagen: Carit Andersens Forlag, 1958.

Ristaino, Marcia R. *The Jacquinot Safe Zone: Wartime Refugees in Shanghai*. Stanford CA: Stanford University Press, 2008.

Rosen, Erwin. *In the Foreign Legion*. London: Duckworth, 1910.

Sasaki Toichi. "Zuozuomu Daoyi riji" ["Sasaki Toichis dagbog"]. *NDS*, vol. 8: 306–322.

Schenke, Wolf. *Reise an der gelben Front [Journey Along the Yellow Front]*. Berlin: Gerhard Stalling Verlagsbuchhandlung, 1941.

Sugarman, Martin. "*Hagedud Ha-Sini*: The Jewish Company of the Shanghai Volunteer Corps, 1932–42," *Jewish Historical Studies*, vol. 41 (2007): 183–208.

Thøgersen, Carsten Bøyer og Hans J. Hinrup. *From a Strong Past to a Dynamic Present: Danes and Danish Companies in the Greater Shanghai Region 1846 to 2006*. Shanghai: Shanghai Bookstore Publishing House, 2008.

Uemura Toshimichi. "Shangcun Lidao zhenzhong riji" ["Uemura Toshimichi's War Diary"]. *NDS*, vol. 8: 243–271.

Wakabayashi, Bob Takashi. "Leftover Problems." Wakabayashi, Bob Takashi (ed.). *The Nanking Atrocity, 1937–38: Complicating the Picture*, 357–393. New York, NY: Berghahn Books, 2017.

Wickert, Erwin. *Mut und Übermut: Geschichten aus meinem Leben [Courage and Arrogance: Stories From My Life]*. Stuttgart: Deutsche Verlags-Anstalt, 1991.

Wickert, Erwin (ed.). *John Rabe. Der gute Deutsche von Nanking [John Rabe: The Good German of Nanjing]*. Stuttgart: Deutsche Verlags-Anstalt, 1997.

Yamada Senji. "Shantian Zhaner riji" ["Yamada Senji's Diary"]. *NDS*, vol. 9: 1–9.

Yan Liufeng, "Zhu Qixia chang Yan Liufeng baogao" ["Yan Liufeng's Report About His Stay at the Qixia Plant"]. *NDS*, vol. 30: 270–273.

Yang Tianshi. "Jiang Jieshi yu 1937 nian de Songhu, Nanjing zhi zhan" ["Chiang Kai-shek and the Battles of Shanghai and Nanjing in 1937"]. *Zhongguo Shehuikexueyuan xueshuweiyuanhui jikan*, Beijing: Shehuikexue wenxian chubanshe, 2005.

Zhang Kaiyuan (ed.). *Eyewitnesses to Massacre*. Armonk NY: M. E. Sharpe, 2001.

Zhang Shuoren. "Kangri Zhanzheng yu Zhongguo minzu ziben de mingyun" ["The War against Japan and the Fate of Chinese Democratic Capitalism"]. *Comparative Law and Culture: The Bulletin of the Surugadai University Institute of Comparative Law*, vol. 16 (2008).

Zhang Xianwen og Zhang Jianjun. *Human Memory: Solid Evidence of the Nanjing Massacre*, vol. 2. Beijing: Renmin chubanshe, 2017.

Webpages

www.nationalarchives.gov.uk
www.navalhistory.dk

Published primary sources

Foreign Relations of the United States diplomatic papers, 1937. The Far East, vol. III. Washington DC: U.S. Government Printing Office, 1937.

Hsü Shuhsi. *Documents of the Nanking Safety Zone*. Shanghai: Kelly & Walsh, 1939.

International Military Tribunal of the Far East. *Transcript of Proceedings*. Tokyo, 1946–1948.

Nanjing Baoweizhan dangan [Documents on the Battle of Nanjing]. Nanjing: Nanjing chubanshe, 2018.

Nanjing datusha shiliaoji [Collection of Historical Sources for the Nanjing Massacre]. Nanjing: Jiangsu renmin chubanshe, 2005–2010.

Newspapers

Aalborg Amtstidende
Aalborg Stiftstidende
Aarhus Stiftstidende
Belfast Telegraph
Berlingske Aftenavis
Berlingske Tidende
Chicago Daily News, The
China Press, The
China Weekly Review, The
Demokraten (Aarhus)
Fredericia Social-Demokrat
Frederiksborg Amts Avis
Holbæk Amts Venstreblad
Japan Times and Mail, The
Jyllands-Posten
Kongelig allernaadigst privilegeret. Horsens Avis eller Skanderborg Amtstidende
Midland Daily Telegraph, The
Nationaltidende
New York Times, The
North-China Herald and Supreme Court & Consular Gazette, The
Politiken
Scotsman, The
Uge-Avisen for Odder og Omegn
Østsjællands Folkeblad

Archival sources

National Danish Archives

Ministry of the Interior, 2nd Bureau. Conscription lists, 1861–1932.
3rd conscription region, list no. 52, 1908.
4th conscription region, list no. 230, 1929.
Ministry of Defense. Logbooks 1650–1977, no. 0028: Maagen Inspektionsskib Skibsjournal 1932 m.m.
Ministry of Foreign Affairs. Consular archives. Shanghai. No. 02-2035.
27.P.a.50: "Sømand Bernhard Arp Sindberg on board m/s 'Falstria'. Assault (Opsætsighed og vold mod skibsofficer)."
27.P.a.71: "Juncker Jensen vs. B. A. Sindberg, Assault."
65.K.56: "Kompagnie Madsen A/S."
Dispatches 1848–1972, Shanghai 1936–1945 etc. 173 D 21.

Aarhus Municipal Archive

Tax payer register. Information on the Sindbergs' various addresses.
Aarhus school system. Ingerslev Boulevards School.
  IV. Students.
  1903–23: Enrolment of boys.

1904–31: Exam results for boys, 1st and 2nd form.
1904–21: Exam results for boys, 3rd to 6th form.
1921: Exam results for boys, 3rd to 7th form.

FLSmidth archive, Valby

Stig Nielsen, Oriental 1935. Documents on the decision to build Jiangnan Cement.
Japan-Kina 1937–38. Large internal correspondence, mainly in English, on Jiangnan Cement.

Parish registers

Registers for the parishes of Branderslev, Odder, Sandby, Tamdrup, and Sankt Paul as well as the
    cathedral parish of Aarhus.

Mariann Arp Stenvig's private archive

Bernhard Sindberg. "Enroute to the Battle-zones." Detailed account of experiences during battle
    of Shanghai in 1937.

Harry Ransom Center, University of Texas at Austin

Bernhard Arp Sindberg Papers and Photography Collection. Various documents and photos related
    to Sindberg's life, including his very short autobiography *Sketch of a Lifetime,* which unfortunately
    has no information about his time in Nanjing.

Political archive of the German Ministry of Foreign Affairs, Berlin

RAV Peking II. Archive for the German embassy in China.
R104823-E104844: German diplomatic dispatches from China.

National Archives and Records Administration, Washington DC (NARA)

Passenger and Crew Lists of Vessels Arriving at New York, New York, 1897–1957. NAI no. 300346.
Passenger and Crew Lists of Vessels Arriving at Seattle, Washington. NAI no. 4449160.
Records of District Courts of the United States, 1685–2009. National Archives at San Francisco;
    San Bruno, California; NAI no. 605504.

Columbia Center for Oral History, Columbia University Libraries

Zhang Fakui, *Reminiscences of Fa-K'uei Chang: Oral History, 1970–1980.*

UNT Oral History Program, University of North Texas

Interview med James Voss, Oral History no. 0680.

Yale Divinity School Library, Yale University

Special collections: The Nanking Massacre Archival Project.
Record Group 8, Box 263, Folder 2: Letters from John G. Magee.
Record Group 8, Box 263, Folder 2: Letters from George Ashmore Fitch.
Record Group 8, Box 263, Folder 9: Letters from Ernest H. Forster.
Record Group 10, Box 90, Folder 719: Miner Searle Bates. "Nanking Outrages."

Record Group 10, Box 102, Folder 862: B. A. Sindberg. "List of Cases."
Record Group 10, Box 102, Folder 863: Letters from Miner Searle Bates.
Record Group 11, Box 229, Folder 3875: Letters from R. O. Wilson.

National Swedish Archives

Archive of the Swedish Ministry of Foreign Affairs, HP 37 A VI and HP 37 A VII. Various dispatches from Swedish diplomats to Stockholm, 1937 and 1938.

Index